WITHDRAWN

PAPAL ELECTIONS IN THE AGE
OF TRANSITION, 1878-1922

PAPAL ELECTIONS
IN THE AGE OF TRANSITION
1878-1922

Francis A. Burkle-Young

LEXINGTON BOOKS
Lanham • Boulder • New York • Oxford

LEXINGTON BOOKS

Published in the United States of America
by Lexington Books
4720 Boston Way, Lanham, Maryland 20706

12 Hid's Copse Road
Cumnor Hill, Oxford OX2 9JJ, England

Copyright © 2000 by Lexington Books

All rights reserved. No part of this publication may be reproduced, stored in a retrieval system, or transmitted in any form or by any means, electronic, mechanical, photocopying, recording, or otherwise, without the prior permission of the publisher.

British Library Cataloguing in Publication Information Available

Library of Congress Cataloging-in-Publication Data available from the publisher

ISBN 0-7391-0114-5

Printed in the United States of America

∞™ The paper used in this publication meets the minimum requirements of American National Standard for Information Sciences—Permanence of Paper for Printed Library Materials, ANSI/NISO Z39.48–1992.

This book is gratefully dedicated to
GEORGE ALLAN CATE
at the inauguration of his sixty-sixth year
to commemorate his forty years of
dedicated scholarship and teaching

by one who is proud to have been among those countless
students who have been inspired by his complete
commitment to the life of the mind and his
illumination of the highest principles of
the greatest Victorian sages,
Thomas Carlyle and
John Ruskin.

NON "ELUCESCEBAT" SED ELUCESCIT

CONTENTS

ACKNOWLEDGMENTS ix
PREFACE xi

I. *A Long Decline* 1
II. *The Socialist Pope* 39
III. *Veto* 71
IV. *Conclave in War* 95
V. *The "Roman Question"* 123
VI. *Epilogue* 155

APPENDIX 159
SELECT BIBLIOGRAPHY 167
INDEX 177
ABOUT THE AUTHOR 185

ACKNOWLEDGMENTS

I WISH to thank George Allan Cate, Richard E. Cullen, and Laurence S. Galvin for their varied and considerable help, especially for reading the manuscript and providing much-needed criticism.

I thank William S. Peterson for his indispensable help in designing this book and creating the camera-ready copy for it. As with two of my earlier books, *The Art of the Footnote* and *Passing the Keys*, he gave freely of his time, and his very great knowledge and expertise in the history and æsthetics of the book, to create a volume which is a pleasure to hold and a joy to read.

I also wish to thank my friends who have provided me with constant encouragement and not a little assistance during the long time that I have worked on this project: G. Jean Burkle Gregord of Pittsburgh, Pennsylvania; James Calvin and Diane Hanlon Pierce of Columbus, Ohio; Peyton Randolph and Lisa Brown, John E. Thibeau, Michael Dennis Sawyer, and R. Anthony and Laura McKinnon Norris of Baltimore, Maryland. Thank you all.

I owe a large debt to Fra Raphael Brown, O.F.M., who first introduced me to the study of the College of Cardinals. I also thank the late Professor Dr. Hermann Everard Schüssler for his half-decade of guidance and advice when I was his graduate student. Among many collections, both in the United States and Europe, I am most grateful for access to the Library of Congress and the Mullen Library at the Catholic University of America.

I also would like to thank those who gave me interviews over the years or were willing to have less formal, but extensive, private conversations with me. Custom prevents me from recognizing them by name.

Finally, I am grateful for years of tolerance for cardinals and for advice, for training in scholarly research techniques, for reading and criticising my writing, and for decades of complete support, to the late Ellen Louise Burkle Young.

PREFACE

A QUICK glance at the closing years of the reign of Pope Pius IX in the 1870's shows a papacy bereft of friends in Europe, deprived of its last secular territories, and immured within the confines of the Vatican palace and the adjacent precincts of the basilica of Saint Peter's. A sudden shift of vision to the present day reveals an institution which plays a significant part in world affairs, territorially secure in its small holdings, and occupied by a figure who commands the public respect and attention of the globe's major leaders, even when they do not like him, or wish him and his Church well—as exemplified by papal journeys to Cuba, India, and Georgia in the closing years of the twentieth century.

The present state of the papacy generally is imagined to rest on the accomplishments of Pius XII, John XXIII, Paul VI, and John Paul II—popes of recent decades who internationalized the Church's hierarchy, reformed its conduct to be more in keeping with the hopes and expectations of the modern world, and led the papacy to a more complete and open engagement with the world, including membership in world organizations and active participation in international diplomacy.

In fact, their work rests firmly on the foundation that was prepared by four popes of the period immediately following the collapse of papal temporal power and the loss of prestige caused by papal ignorance of the formidable changes which took place in the developed world in industry, economics, politics, and philosophy during the eighteenth and nineteenth centuries.

The first, and greatest, of these men was Leo XIII (1878–1903). In the second longest reign in papal history, he devoted himself to reattaching the person of the pope directly to the lives of Catholics in the modern world. The most important accomplishment of his reign was linking himself, and the papal institution, to the conditions of working men in the prevailing, and growing, industrial environment of the later nineteenth century. He did this first by the publication of the encyclical, *Rerum Novarum*, on May 15, 1891. In one stroke, Leo connected himself to the broad mass of lay

Catholics more strongly than any pope had in centuries—perhaps since Innocent III (1198–1216) did so by his support of the work of Francis and Dominic. The document's restatement of Christian principles of social justice just at the moment when labor unrest was beginning to rise to dangerous proportions proved an invaluable asset to those who were trying to establish the basis of trade unionism, since it provided religious authority to the claim to basic standards of human comfort and security—a claim which was to be enforced through the medium of collective bargaining. John A. Ryan, in his useful summary for the old *Catholic Encyclopedia*, captured the essence of *Rerum Novarum*'s significance:

> Probably no other [papal] pronouncement on the social question has had so many readers or exercised such a wide influence. It has inspired a vast Catholic social literature, while many non-Catholics have acclaimed it as one of the most definite and reasonable productions ever written on the subject. Sometimes criticized as vague, it is as specific as any document could be written for several countries in different stages of industrial development. On one point it is strikingly definite: "Let it be taken for granted that workman and employer should, as a rule, make free agreements, and in particular should agree freely as to wages; nevertheless, there is a dictate of natural justice more imperious and ancient than any bargain between man and man, that remuneration should be sufficient to maintain the wage-earner in reasonable and frugal comfort. If through necessity or fear of a worse evil the workman accept harder conditions because an employer or contractor will afford him no better, he is made the victim of force and injustice."

But Leo engaged the Church and the papacy with the modern world in many other significant ways. His enlargement of the hierarchy in the Americas, in Africa, and in Asia paved the way for the successful evangelization of Catholicism on those continents in the twentieth century. His appointment of cardinals in ordinariates that had never seen a red hat—from Ireland to Australia, from the United States and Canada to North Africa—provided a focus for leadership in the development of strong national and regional Catholicism. He also expressed vigorous support for both the highest intellectual and the highest mystical traditions of the Church, strengthening them where he could; for example, by reaching out to a plain priest of international importance, John Henry Newman, and elevating him to the cardinalate.

Leo's successor, Pius X (1903–1914), a conservative reactionary quite in keeping with the spirit of Pius IX, from whom he took his name, halted or reversed much of Leo's forward-thinking modernization. While this did some injury to the process of engaging the Catholic Church with the world as it was, Pius compensated for this by a life of genuine and unfeigned piety which moved many who contemplated a secular world already beset by frequent manifestations of excessive greed and hunger for power.

The next pope, Benedict XV (1914–1922), resumed the impetus that Leo XIII had given the papacy and the Church. A disciple of Leo's last cardinal-secretary of state, Mariano Rampolla del Tindaro, who had been the favored candidate of the progressives in the conclave in 1903, Benedict did what he could in his short reign to engage the Catholic Church more deeply with the condition of common people. His failure to make his voice widely heard was caused largely by the deafening roar of World War I, which dominated his time in Peter's Chair. He did enjoy some success, however, notably in his appointment of cardinals—led in the conclave that followed his death by his cardinal-secretary of state, Pietro Gasparri—who, in the end, ensured the election of another progressive pope, Pius XI.

The new Pius (1922–1939), who kept Gasparri in his powerful office and then groomed Gasparri's successor, Eugenio Pacelli, to reign in his stead, finally settled the nagging question of papal temporal power, which had divided the loyalties of Italian Catholics for more than half a century. He also pressed forward with Leo XIII's policy of connecting pope and papacy with the lives of individual Catholics in their homes and workplaces—in his pontifical teaching, notably in the encyclical *Quadragesimo Anno* (May 15, 1931, the fortieth anniversary of the publication of *Rerum Novarum*, hence its opening words), and in practical action, as in his founding of Vatican Radio.

The purpose of this little book is to recount the stories of how each of these four men rose to the office of supreme pontiff, which gave them the freedom and power to create the essential foundations of the contemporary Catholic Church.

I
A LONG DECLINE

A LARGE, sweeping view of the history of the papacy from the high Middle Ages to the middle of the nineteenth century presents the story of a long decline in power and prestige, punctuated by catastrophes: the importunate overreaching of papal power by Boniface VIII; the Great Schism; the Reformation; the attempt to subordinate the interests of the Church to those of Spain in the second half of the sixteenth century, and to those of France in the later seventeenth century, among others. But the downward curve of the influence of the popes became more steep during the eighteenth century, when weak pope after weak pope followed in succession, even while the Age of the Enlightenment was pushing aside centuries of conceptions about government, society, and the individual person. Only Benedict XIV (Prospero Lambertini, 1740–1758) seemed to be aware of the general condition of Europe in his time and, good man though he was, he had no power left to modernize the Church in his time in any significant way.

How unimportant the papacy had become by the end of the eighteenth century can be estimated by examining the conclave of 1774–1775. Clement XIV had died on September 22, 1774. At that time, there were fifty-five living cardinals, but only forty-four of them bothered to come to Rome for the election, in spite of the fact that the conclave, which should have opened on October 2 if canonical procedures had been followed, did not begin until November 23. Those who did participate found the whole event not one of somber deliberation to choose the next successor of Saint Peter but rather a long winter party. The doors were opened repeatedly to admit visitors, and other violations of secrecy and procedure were common. True, the ceremony of sealing the doors had happened, and the *ruota* had been installed—the latter was a revolving walled door with shelves, invented by Paris de Grassis for the second conclave of 1503, which was used to pass food and other necessities into the conclave, since there were no cooking facilities in the precincts—but their existence largely was ignored. The host of the gathering, for there is no better way to describe him, was the French ambassador, Cardinal François Joachim Pierre de Bernis. With a large budget at his disposal, almost every day saw a long procession of his *dapiferi*—the household servants used by the cardinals to transport meals and other comforts to and from their Roman residences—bringing lavish buffets of food and drink to the whole assembly. After weeks of leisurely negotiation, principally involving de Bernis and Cardinal Cristoforo de Migazzi de Valle a Soletturin, archbishop of Vienna and Maria Theresa's representative in the conclave, Giovanni Angelo Braschi was chosen on February 15, 1775, and assumed the name Pius VI.

The new pope, a gentle dilettante who preferred the company of his books and manuscripts to anything else, might have had a reign as physically undisturbed as those of his recent predecessors, but the French Revolution dramatically changed forever the relationship of the pope to the world in which he lived.

The Civil Constitution of the Clergy signaled the beginning. After all, the pope and the Church were as much emblems of the *ancien régime* as were Louis XVI himself or the aristocracy of France. Pius resisted the onrush of revolutionary events but feebly, and without success. Soon, the revolution was exported and arrived in Italy. With it also arrived the newly-discovered and empowered genius of Napoleon Bonaparte. He entered Italy at the beginning of the spring of 1796, and his military brilliance brought him victory after victory over both Austrian and Piedmontese forces—Montenotte, his first triumph, on April 12; Dego on April 14–15; Mondovi on April 21; Fombio on May 8; Borghetto on May 10; Second Montenotte on May 30; Lonato on August 3; Castiglione on August 5; Bassano on September 8; First Caldiero on November 12; Arcola on November 15–17; and, finally, Rivoli on January 14, 1797. Now all of northern Italy, including the Papal States and the pope himself, was at Bonaparte's mercy.

The last, slight hope for rescue was extinguished when the last Austrian commander in Italy, the seventy-two-year-old Dagobert-Sigismond, Graf von Würmser, surrendered his forces at Mantua on February 2, 1797. Napoleon accorded him the honors of war and allowed him to return to Vienna. By April 21, his fifty-year career destroyed, he was dead from humiliation.

Pius did what he could to avert disaster. He sent a delegation to treat with Napoleon. Headed by Cardinal Alessandro Mattei, archbishop of Ferrara, and Luigi Braschi Onesti, duke of Nemi, the pope's nephew, the little embassy met with the triumphant French general at Tolentino on February 17. Two days later, the cardinal and the duke subscribed to a treaty that embodied the complete collapse of papal government. The major articles tell the whole story in brief:

Articolo VI. – Il Papa rinuncia puramente e semplice mente a tutti i diritti che potrebbe pretendere sopra le città e territori di Avignone, Contado Venassino e sue dipendenze, e trasferisce, cede e abbandona i diritti suddetti alla Repubblica Francese.

Articolo VII. – Il Papa rinuncia similmente per sempre, cede e trasferisce alla Repubblica Francese tutti i suoi diritti sopra i Territori conosciuti sotto il nome di Legazioni di Bologna, di Ferrara e della Romagna. Non sarà fatta alcuna innovazione alla Religione cattolica nelle suddette Legazioni.

Articolo VIII. – La Città, Cittadella e i villaggi che formano il territorio della città di Ancona, resteran no alla Repubblica Francese fino alla pace conti nentale.

Articolo IX. – Il Papa si obbliga per sé e i suoi successori a non trasferire ad alcuno i Titoli delle Signorie annessi al territorio da lui ceduto alla Repubblica Francese.

Articolo X. – Sua Santità si obbliga di far pagare e con segnare in Foligno al Tesoriere dell'Armata francese prima dei 15 del mese di ventoso corrente (li 5 marzo prossimo) la somma di quindici milioni di lire tornesi di Francia, dei quali dieci milioni in con tanti e cinque milioni in diamanti e altri effetti preziosi per conto della somma di circa sedici milioni che restano di debito secondo l'articolo IX dell'armistizio firmato a Bologna li 5 Messidoro anno 4, e ratificato da Sua Santità li 27 giugno.

Articolo XI. – Per sodisfare definitivamente ció che resterà a pagarsi per l'intera esecuzione dell'Armistizio segnato a Bologna, Sua Santit farà somministrare all'Armata ottocento cavalli di cavalleria bardati, ottocento cavalli da tiro, bovi, bufali ed altri oggetti prodotti del Territorio della Chiesa.

Articolo XII. – Indipendentemente dalla somma enunciata nei due articoli precedenti il Papa pagher alla Repubblica Francese in contanti, diamanti e altro valore la somma di 15 milioni di lire tornesi di Francia, dei quali dieci milioni dentro il mese di Marzo e cinque milioni nel mese di Aprile prossimo.

Articolo XIII. – L'articolo VIII del Trattato d'armistizio segnato a Bologna, riguardante i manoscritti e gli oggetti d'arte, avrà la sua intera esecuzione al più presto possibile.

In one stroke, everything was gone—most of the Papal States and with them the temporal power of the papacy, millions in money, diamonds, works of art, manuscripts, privileges, power, prestige, prerogative. The precise text of the Treaty of Tolentino is reprinted here because it formed the model for so many parts of other treaties and concordats which Pius's successors signed. Its echoes can be seen even in the Lateran treaties in 1929.

The final acts that completed the ruin of the life and reign of Pius VI began on the late afternoon of December 28, 1797. A group of Roman Jacobins demonstrated in front of the Palazzo Corsini, then the French embassy, and attempted to force their way into the embassy's precincts. Joseph Bonaparte, Napoleon's brother and the future king of Spain, was now the ambassador of the Directory in Rome. He ordered the expulsion of the enthusiastic supporters of French ideas from the embassy's grounds, and then duly informed the cardinal-secretary of state, Giuseppe Doria Pamfili, about the incident. Later on the same day, a second group of Jacobins appeared before the Palazzo Corsini and carried their demonstration into the gardens of the embassy. Here, they were pursued by a small force of papal dragoons which was acting under orders to expel them, prompted by the disorder that had occurred earlier in the day. By the time they arrived, however, the Jacobins had been joined by some of Bonaparte's house guests.

The ambassador was entertaining a rather large party of visitors during the Christmas season in Rome, including his sister-in-law, Désirée Clary; her fiancé, General Jean-Pierre Duphot; and the sixteen-year-old Eugène de Beauharnais, Josephine's son, who would become prince of Venice and viceroy of Italy.

It was Duphot who assumed the leadership of the Jacobin demonstrators in their ensuing fight with the dragoons. He led his suddenly-acquired command in a headlong charge which drove the dragoons out of the gardens and down the street in the direction of the Porta Settimiana. Suddenly, a shot rang out and Duphot fell dead in the street. Joseph Bonaparte wrote a full explanation of the incident, portraying the young French general as entirely blameless. He rejected the prodigious apologies of Cardinal Giuseppe Doria Pamfili, and then departed from the city.

The riots of December 28 were momentous in many ways, not the least of which was that the death of Duphot left Désirée once again unattached. Within a year, she married Jean-Baptiste Bernadotte and began the journey that would see her die as queen of Sweden and maternal foundress of the dynasty that reigns in that nation to the present day.

In Paris, the report of the incident caused the Directory to decide to eliminate the States of the Church and to eradicate papal temporal power. Napoleon, who had just returned from Italy, was not willing to assume command of the new expedition—he was already in the midst of planning the invasion of Egypt. The command, therefore, devolved on Louis-Alexandre Berthier, another general who would rise to become a marshal of France. Berthier moved at once, and by the evening of February 9, 1798, his forces were immediately outside Rome. His orders were clear: occupy Rome; remove the pope physically from the city; and establish a Roman Republic. But Berthier dissembled cleverly to the embassy that Pius VI sent to him. He told the cardinal-secretary of state, Giuseppe Doria Pamfili; the pope's nephew, Luigi Braschi Onesti, duke of Nemi; and the Spanish ambassador, José Nicolás de Azara, that he would respect the safety and integrity of the Catholic Church, the pope, and the Papal States. The three reported to Pius that Berthier presented no immediate danger.

Meanwhile, Berthier waited for the right moment to carry out his commission with the least amount of bloodshed and trouble. That moment came six days later, when all the cardinals in Rome gathered with the pope for the celebration of the twenty-third anniversary of Pius's election. During the consistory, French forces swept into the city without resistance. The pope and all the cardinals were arrested. The fox took his scarlet-clad chickens, gabbling and squawking, to a brief imprisonment in Rome, and then he transported them to more secure cells at Civitàvecchia. Pius was informed that his reign was over and that he had three days to prepare himself to be taken from Rome to a place of exile. Pius used some of his last three days to establish a commission of seven, under the presidency of Cardinal Leonardo Antonelli, to administer the affairs of the Church. He had no way of knowing whether this step would be effective, but, in the end, it proved a sufficient bridge from his reign to that of his successor.

In the night of the twentieth of February, Pius, who was so afflicted with paralysis in his legs that he had to be supported on each side in order to take a few steps, was half dragged to a carriage which took him speedily to Siena. From the time of his expulsion from Rome, Pius took no further real interest in the government of the Church. Occasionally, he would rouse himself when he received some document which could not be ignored—as when he received letters from both Cardinals Tommaso Antici and Vincenzo Maria Altieri asking him to grant them permission to resign the cardinalate. Pius refused them, but the cardinals resigned in spite of him: Antici on March 7, 1798, and Altieri on September 7, 1798. Antonelli, who secured his freedom from the French and tried to establish an interim, rump curia with staff from the Dataria and the secretariat of briefs, wrote several times to try to persuade Pius to allow this tiny court to rejoin him, but Pius refused.

On June 1, 1798, Pius was moved again, this time to the Certosa near Florence. Here, amid the solitude of the Carthusians, he withdrew even further from outside associations. He refused to consider the creation of new cardinals, even though membership in the College had fallen below fifty; and he refused to consider issuing a bull or other apostolic command with regard to the holding of the next conclave at Venice, safely outside French control. Finally, when it was borne in on him that the French might try to arrange a conclave of their own after his death, he did issue a bull, on November 13, 1798, which ordered that the true conclave would be the one attended by the largest number of cardinals in a place that was under the protection of a Catholic ruler.

Meanwhile, French excesses in Italy, of which one was the kidnapping and sequestration of the pope, prompted a vigorous series of unconnected local revolts throughout the peninsula. The rebels, collectively called the *Sanfedisti*, were remarkably successful in a short time. Perhaps the most remarkable accomplishment was the reconquest of nearly all of the kingdom of Naples, and the collapse of the Parthenopean Republic that the French had created in its place, at the hands of Cardinal Fabrizio Ruffo and his rag-tag army, which he called the Armate della Santa Fede (hence *Sanfedisti*, a term soon applied to all the counter-revolutionary movements). Within weeks of his appointment as vicar general of the kingdom by Ferdinand I on January 25, 1799, Ruffo had overcome almost all French resistance in the south of Italy.

The *Sanfedisti* and their sympathizers already had been heartened by the news of the victory of Vice-Admiral Horatio Nelson over the French at the Battle of the Nile on August 1, 1798. There was no lack of understanding that Nelson's great deed had trapped both Napoleon himself and a very large French army amid the sands of Egypt—thus removing both as threats to the unfolding Italian successes in the Peninsula. As Nelson himself had predicted before the battle, he was raised to the peerage as Baron Nelson of the Nile and of Burnham Thorpe in the County of Norfolk. But Ferdinand I had a better idea. The ancient Greek stem *bront*, meaning "thunder," appeared in a number of Sicilian words, which may have dated from the period of ancient Hellenic colonization. The king found a village whose name embodied the appropriate stem and created Nelson a noble of the kingdom with the title duke of Brontë. Nelson, who had arrived with his fleet soon after the battle, was delighted. Ever afterward, to the end of his life at Trafalgar, he signed himself "Nelson and Brontë." Soon afterward, an impecunious, Irish-born Anglican clergyman named Patrick Brunty decided that Ferdinand's title was a much more magnificent-sounding name than his own, so he adopted it as his style and passed it on to his three daughters who stamped it indelibly on English literature.

For Pius VI, none of these events had any meaning other than the decision by the French to move him yet again, and again, to places under their control. In March, 1799, he was taken to Bologna, then to Parma, then Piacenza, then up through Turin and over the Alps to Briançon, then to Grenoble, and finally to Valence. By now, he was paraplegic and close to death; he could not be moved further lest he die in his carriage, like George I of England. He was taken into the shabby Hôtel du Gouvernement, overlooking the Rhône. Tended only by his faithful manservant, Father Giuseppe Spina, later cardinal, he died on August 29, 1799. At the end, he was eighty-one years, eight months, and two days old, and had reigned for twenty-four years, six months, and fourteen days. Without considering the traditional stay of Saint Peter of twenty-five years in Rome, Pius VI had the longest reign of any pope up to his time; and remains the third longest-reigning pope, after Pius IX and Leo XIII.

Beginning in late 1798, the Emperor Franz II and his chancellor, Johann Amadeus Franz de Paula Thugut, had sent letters to the cardinals which urged them to assemble at Venice, under imperial protection, to await the necessity of the next conclave. Pius VI, as has been mentioned, was urged to support this plan, but declined to do so. Cardinal Giovanni Francesco Albani da Urbino, the cardinal-bishop of Ostia e Velletri and dean of the College, held the greatest power of decision in the matter by virtue of his office. He, together with several other cardinals, was at Naples and continued to hold out hope that the next conclave could be held in Rome. The arrival of the French and the establishment of the Parthenopean Republic forced this small assembly to flee, and brought an end to Albani's plans to hold a conclave in the traditional place.

Most of the cardinals were now entirely dependent on charity, their benefices either taken as prizes of war or abolished altogether. In order to attend the next conclave, some of them applied for loans from the leading financial house in Rome at the time, the bank founded by Giovanni Torlonia, duke of Bracciano—a bank which would later attain literary fame in book II, chapter XV, of Charles Dickens's *Little Dorrit*. The necessity to reach safety, and to go quickly, made Venice seem more attractive than other potential sites, including Rome. By the time Pius died, approximately twenty cardinals already were in Venice, and thus the site of the election was decided. It would be the last conclave to be held outside Rome.

At first, Franz II and Thugut were delighted at the outcome of events. They now hoped that the cardinals would elect a new pope who would be beholden to Austria for physical protection and who thus could be counted on to cede, once again, the bulk of the territories of the Papal States to Austria, as Pius VI had done when, in the treaty of Tolentino, he gave them up to France.

Most of the preliminary preparations for the election were carried out by Monsignor Ercole Consalvi. Originally a protégé of

Henry Mary Benedict Clement Stuart, the Cardinal-Duke of York, Consalvi had risen in Roman administration through his own merits. He was, in fact, the prelate in charge of the military commission that controlled the dragoons who were involved in the death of General Duphot. Consequently, his name appeared prominently on the list of those whom General Berthier was empowered to arrest when he assumed control of Rome and the Papal States. He was arrested and taken to Civitàvecchia to await transportation to French Guiana. But he negotiated his way out of this dangerous fate and eventually made his way to Naples. From thence, he went to the Certosa near Florence where he had at least two audiences with Pius VI. Denied permission to stay near the pope, he arrived in Venice in September, 1798. In cooperation with the Austrian authorities, he persuaded the Benedictines of the monastery of San Giorgio to lend their house and their island, opposite the Piazzetta, for the conclave. The Emperor contributed 40,000 ducats to cover the costs of the electoral meeting.

The conclave opened on November 30, 1799, just twenty-one days after the *coup d'etat* of 18th Brumaire that overthrew the Directory and placed all real power in the hands of Napoleon as First Consul. Thirty-four of the forty-five living cardinals were present for the proceedings. The absence of the three French cardinals, Louis de Rohan, Domenic de la Rochefoucauld, and Louis-Joseph de Laval Montmorency, was expected; and the absence of the ordinaries of far-distant dioceses also was understood: Jean-Henri de Frankenberg, archbishop of Malines; Joao Francisco de Mendoza, patriarch of Lisbon; and Antonino de Sentmanat y Cartella, archbishop of Toledo. Four Italians were hindered from appearing by local troubles of their own, beginning with Giuseppe Capece Zurlo, the Theatine archbishop of Naples, and including Vincenzo Ranuzzi of Ancona, Muzio Gallo of Viterbo, and Carlo Livizzani. Also strangely absent from an event of such concern to his emperor was Cristoforo de Migazzi de Valle a Soletturin, archpriest of the College and archbishop of Vienna. The first act of the electors was to confirm Monsignor Consalvi as the secretary of the conclave.

Within a few days, a majority of the cardinals was voting for the elevation of Carlo Bellisomi, bishop of Cesena. The official candidate of Giovanni Francesco Albani, the dean of the College, Bellisomi, a robust sixty-three, was seen as a vigorous defender of the rights of the popes to temporal power who would defend papal claims to the States of the Church. Opposing him were Cardinal Leonardo Antonelli, the favorite of Pius VI, and the Austrian ambassador, Cardinal Franz Herzan von Harras (who had Germanized his Czech surname, Hrczan). Both favored the elevation of Alessandro Mattei, archbishop of Ferrara, who had signed the treaty of Tolentino that ceded most of the Papal States to the French in 1797. The Austrian partisans believed that what he had done once, he would do again, this time in their favor.

Soon, Bellisomi was receiving so many votes that it seemed certain that he would be elected in a short time. Herzan von Harras now pleaded with Albani to suspend the voting while he wrote to Vienna for further instructions. The degree of fright that permeated the walls of the conclave can be judged by the fact that Albani, who was the captain of Bellisomi's forces, agreed to this suggestion. If Herzan von Harras hoped that the reply from Vienna would contain Franz II's veto of Bellisomi's candidacy, he was gravely disappointed. The reply contained only the Emperor's restatement of his support for Mattei, without any mention of his opposition to Bellisomi.

The conclave was now deadlocked. Bellisomi received eighteen or twenty votes on each ballot, while Mattei received about ten, with the remaining four or six being scattered among others. The first attempt to break this impasse saw the proposal of Cardinal Giacinto Sigismondo Gerdil, a Savoyard and a Barnabite who had been prefect of the Index of Prohibited Books and a prominent member of the Congregation of the Holy Office. Herzan von Harras promptly announced Austria's veto of this austere and inflexible monk. Soon, Consalvi and the Spanish ambassador, Monsignor Antonio Despuig y Dameto, later a cardinal, devised a clever compromise. They proposed that a leader of Mattei's party select a suitable candidate from among the cardinals who supported Bellisomi. Step-by-step, this plan won the support of the electors. Leonardo Antonelli was chosen to select the compromise candidate. Now, Consalvi worked to get him to choose Barnabà Chiaramonti, who had chosen the name Gregorio when he joined the Benedictines in 1756. To do this, Consalvi had to use all of his superb diplomatic and persuasive skills, because Chiaramonti had three notable deficits. As bishop of Imola, he had cooperated, rather willingly, with the French; he was young for a pope—only fifty-nine—and another long reign was not necessarily to be desired after the nearly quarter-century tenure of the last pope; and he was a cousin of Pius VI. Although the cardinals often had chosen two or more popes from the same family, they had never before chosen one in direct succession to another. In the end, Consalvi had his way. Antonelli announced that Chiaramonti was his choice. Antonelli quickly won over the adherents of Mattei, while Albani persuaded the cardinals of Bellisomi's party to switch their votes. Herzan von Harras, having no exclusion to pronounce against so unexpected a candidate, was weaponless in his efforts to defend Mattei's candidacy. On March 14, 1800, after one hundred and five days of wrangling, Chiaramonti was elected. As expected, he chose the name Pius VII in memory of his cousin and patron, Pius VI.

Herzan von Harras was not about to yield in his efforts to place Austria in the most influential position in the new reign. Three days after the election, he was pressing Pius VII to name Cardinal Luigi Flangini, a native Venetian and an Austrian adherent who had supported Mattei in the conclave, as cardinal-secretary of state. Pius replied that he had no state, so there was no need for a cardinal-secretary. A few days later, he created the position of secretary of the pope and named Consalvi to that office. A little later, when he felt himself more secure in Rome, he created Consalvi a cardinal on August 11, 1800, in the first cardinalitial consistory of the reign, and later did name him secretary of state.

Having failed in his push to have Flangini as secretary of state, Herzan von Harras now importuned Pius VII to go to Vienna himself. Both the pope and his loyal secretary realized that such a journey could only end with great pressure to cede the territories of the Papal States formally to Austria, so the pontiff graciously declined.

Meanwhile, Franz II and Thugut were affronted by the conclave's failure to elect Austria's candidate, so they retaliated with a petty denial to allow Pius to be crowned in the great basilica of San

Marco. Instead, the coronation was held in the much smaller monastic church of San Gregorio, adjacent to the site of the conclave. The doors of the church were thrown open, so that those crowded into the little piazza outside could perhaps glimpse something of the ceremony; while the Piazzetta opposite was lined with people with telescopes who also hoped to catch a brief sight of the ancient rite. The tiara was a tawdry affair, largely of plaster, and was ornamented with a few jewels donated by the noble ladies of Venice. It reposes today, an honored relic of a troubled time, in the Vatican treasury.

Once elected, enthroned, and crowned, Pius's wish was to journey to Rome as quickly as possible. Haste was made more necessary by the arrival of a new Austrian envoy, the Marchese Ghislieri, a descendant of a nephew of Pope Pius V, who demanded that the pope immediately surrender all those portions of the States of the Church north of Rome. Pius VII bluntly refused. The Austrians in Venice quickly realized that, if Pius were to travel to Rome, it could not be through the very territories he had refused to cede, lest there be uprisings in his wake. Consequently, Pius was told that transportation would be provided for him by sea as far as Pesaro and that he could journey by land from there. He, and a small entourage of Consalvi, four cardinals, and a few servants, was taken out to Malamocco by gondola. Here, he boarded a leaky and ill-equipped old frigate, the *Bellona*, for the voyage down the Adriatic to Pesaro. The trip, which should have taken little more than a day, stretched out to twelve days because of storms and the incompetence of the crew. Since there were no cooking facilities aboard, the pope and his small company were forced to survive on meager cold rations, which became smaller and more distasteful day by day. Marchese Ghislieri, who accompanied the party, probably had not been instructed to bring about Pius's death, as is sometimes reported, but he may almost have accomplished that in any case thanks to the miserable conditions to which the slight and rather delicate pope was subjected. After landing at Pesaro, the small party traveled by coach to Ancona, where they received momentous news. On June 14, Napoleon had won the greatest victory of his career up to that time, the battle of Marengo. While the battle may not have given the modern world a famous poultry dish, it did place nearly all of the Italian peninsula into the hands of the First Consul. Austrian forces were in full retreat from all of their garrisons and Ghislieri's ability to coerce the pope was at an abrupt end. By the time Pius had reached Foligno, Ghislieri was anxious to join his compatriots in flight. He hastily staged a little ceremony in which he surrendered formally to the pope some of the territories that had lately been occupied by imperial troops; then he was gone.

Pius VII made his formal entry into Rome on July 3, 1800, going immediately not to his palace, the Quirinale, but to Saint Peter's, where he prayed for the protection of the "fisher of men" for his pontificate. After this, the only thing the pope could do was to wait and meditate on how Napoleon would deal with both papacy and Church from the summit of his power. Pius already had to consider the rashness of his decision to send the official notification of his election not to the First Consul but to Louis XVIII. Pius's tensions were eased materially, a few hours after he arrived in Rome, when he received a letter, dated June 26, 1800, from Cardinal Carlo Giuseppe Martiniana, bishop of Vercelli. In the letter, Martiniana, newly returned to his diocese from the conclave in Venice, recounted how he had met with Napoleon twice; first, as he passed through Vercelli with his forces on the way to Marengo; and, second, on June 25, after the victory. The cardinal informed his superior that, in the second meeting, Napoleon had expressed his strong wish to rectify Church affairs in France and to establish peace generally. Napoleon also promised that a successful suite of negotiations with him would lead to the restoration of all the territory of the States of the Church. Pius's hopes soared with the expectation that Napoleon was someone with whom he could deal, someone he could trust. In some fashion, Pius kept a fast hold on those hopes for most of the next fourteen years, in spite of Napoleon's perfidy time and again. Napoleon, in turn, learned quickly that Pius VII was a malleable instrument who was powerless to thwart his will. The Concordat of July 16, 1802, completed after more than a year and a half of negotiation, did re-establish the Church in France, though with far less privilege than it had enjoyed before 1789. It was perhaps the zenith of Pius VII's relations with Napoleon.

If Pius had not yet discovered that Napoleon regarded the papacy as an ornament to his style and as a pawn in his policy, the imperial coronation on December 2, 1804, surely left him with few illusions. The invitation itself, the studied insults the pope received in Paris—not just that the pope was forced to make his entrance into Paris at night, that Napoleon came an hour late to the ceremony, that he crowned himself and Josephine, but rather that he refused both confession and communion from Pius's hands—and the precipitous departure of Napoleon for the Lombard coronation in Milan, all served to indicate how low the emperor rated the pope. It seems almost amusing today that Pius VII, in accepting Napoleon's invitation to the coronation, had stipulated that the emperor make no attempt to detain him in France. Of course, Napoleon accepted the stipulation, and honored it on the occasion. But the emperor knew that he could do with the pope whatever he pleased, and whenever he pleased.

Between the French occupation of Ancona on October 18, 1805, and the stationing of French troops in Rome in 1808, Napoleon gradually nibbled away at the Papal States until almost nothing was left. Finally came the imperial decree of May 17, 1809, issued at Schönbrunn just four days after the occupation of Vienna, which abolished the Papal States. On June 10, General Sextius Alexandre François Miollis, comte de Miollis, the French commander in Rome, lowered the papal flag from Castel Sant'Angelo and assumed complete control of the city. Pius retaliated with a bull of excommunication against the emperor, which was liberally posted throughout the city. Napoleon, fresh from another triumphal victory at Essling (May 21) and on the threshold of another at Wagram (July 6), was informed of the excommunication. On June 20, he wrote to Joachim Murat, now the king of Naples, "he [Pius VII] is a raving madman (*fou insensé*) who must be locked up." How different this reaction was from the fright which once had been produced by the mere threat of excommunication.

Murat, commander of all of Napoleon's forces in Italy, communicated the emperor's wishes to Miollis at once. The latter, recently reinforced by troops under the command of General Etienne Radet, seems to have had some qualms about seizing the pope. Radet, however, was unhesitating. In the early morning hours of July

6, 1809, treating his task as a full military operation, he had troops surround the Quirinale, some equipped with scaling ladders to enable them to enter the palace through windows or from the roof, if that were needed. Without resistance of any kind, however, he entered the papal apartments, where he found Pius VII, his current cardinal-secretary of state, Bartolommeo Pacca (for whom Radet also had an arrest warrant), and four other cardinals. Radet told the pope and Cardinal Pacca that they had just half an hour to prepare themselves to be taken to the headquarters of General Miollis. At four in the morning, pope and cardinal were put into a traveling carriage with locked doors and hastened away. The carriage moved from the palace's entrance on Monte Cavallo through the Via Pia (now the Via Venti Settembre), then exited the city through the Porta Salaria. Carriage and escort now passed along the Aurelian Wall to the Porta del Popolo, where the horses were changed, and then onward, through Viterbo and Siena, to the Certosa near Florence, where Pius VI had been detained little more than eleven years before.

As soon as the carriage had passed out of the Porta Salaria, Pius realized that he was being taken not to the French military headquarters in Rome but rather to some place of exile, if not imprisonment, distant from Rome. While he remonstrated with Radet for his perfidy, he tried, as well, to mitigate the situation by pardoning Napoleon, thus effectively lifting the excommunication. But it was too late.

Throughout the day on July 6, the carriage moved swiftly through a stifling summer heat. Radet had ordered the windows of the carriage to be sealed, so that the pope and the cardinal were trapped inside a dark, sealed, swaying box, without ventilation. By the evening, when the party arrived at Radicofani, the pope was seriously ill with dysentery. This onset of illness, far from bringing any consideration or relief from Radet, merely persuaded the general that he needed to move his charges even more swiftly. The pace of the journey was increased so much that at Poggibonsi the carriage overturned, throwing Radet, who was riding with the driver, to the ground, although both Pius and Pacca escaped serious injury. On the evening of July 8, the general ensconced his charges at the Certosa. By now, Pius was suffering severely from fever and chills, as well. He asked to be taken to a room where he could remain undisturbed through the night and the next day.

By now, the news of what was happening to the pope had begun to spread. One of those who discovered that the pope now was being held at the Certosa was Elise Bonaparte Baciocchi, sister of Napoleon. She and her husband, Felice, had received a revived grand duchy of Tuscany from the hands of the emperor in 1808, so she was the ruler of the territory in which Pius was now a prisoner. Frightened by the possible consequences of the papal imprisonment, she ordered Radet to move his charge out of her lands immediately. Consequently, with only a few hours rest, Pius was awakened and rushed back into the carriage at four in the morning of July 9. Pacca was placed into another carriage to be transported to Bologna.

Pius was now taken in the direction of Genoa, but the same embarrassment, or worse, which had threatened the grand duchess now presented itself to Prince Camillo Borghese, husband of another of the emperor's sisters, Pauline, into whose possessions the carriage now passed. He reacted much as his sister-in-law had done and ordered that the pope not be permitted to stop in Ligurian territory. The pope was taken to a small village on the coast and ferried across the Bay of Genoa at night. He was then placed in another carriage and taken over the Alps, by way of Mont Cenis, to Grenoble, where he arrived on July 21.

By this time, Pius, gravely ill and debilitated, was convinced that Napoleon was trying to kill him by keeping him on the move to the point of fatal exhaustion. He was heartened, however, by the growing crowds that gathered to watch his carriage pass by—by the time he reached Grenoble and was lodged in the prefecture there, his journey had assumed something of a triumphal tour.

Napoleon now learned of Radet's actions and their consequences. With perhaps feigned anger and ferocity, he protested that he had never desired the arrest and transportation of the pope, he had merely wanted to arrest Cardinal Pacca. On July 23, he wrote to Jean Jacques Régis de Cambacérès, once the second consul and now prince-duke of Parma and archchancellor of the empire: "It is without my orders and against my will that the pope has been removed from Rome." But something had to be done at once, to avoid further troubles. The emperor instructed the head of his state police, Joseph Fouché (who would be made duke of Otranto on August 15), to get the pope out of France as soon as possible. In the earliest hours of August 2, the pope was bundled once more into a carriage and taken back over the Alps to Savona. He arrived there on August 17 and was lodged in the episcopal palace under the watchful care of Louis de Chabrol de Volvic, prefect of the department of Montenotte—later, in 1815 after Waterloo, it was de Chabrol who would coin the term "the hundred days" to describe Napoleon's brief restoration.

Here Pius would remain, almost sequestered, for nearly three years. During the first months of his imprisonment, he managed periodically to obtain paper and pen, with which he sent some messages, including a small number of bulls, that were smuggled out by a valet. When this was discovered, de Chabrol quickly closed even this small trickle of communication. During this time, Napoleon tried a number of administrative and diplomatic expedients to rectify his relationship with the Church, but Pius steadfastly rejected the proposals of the various staged councils, assemblies, and conferences of which he was not a part.

By the spring of 1812, Napoleon became convinced that an English fleet would soon descend on the Gulf of Genoa to rescue the pope from Savona. Already preparing for the invasion of Russia, he apparently thought that the English might be able to use the pope as a destabilizing instrument while he was away on his great northern adventure. His response to this idea was to order Pius to be removed and taken to the palace of Fontainebleau, outside Paris, where he could be kept under immediate imperial control.

The whole operation was conducted swiftly and most secretly— only about a dozen imperial officials, including Prince Camillo Borghese, knew of the plan. At 5:30 P.M. on the afternoon of June 9, 1812, Pius was informed that he was to be taken away. At midnight, he was placed in a closed carriage for the journey to Paris, dressed in plain black as a common priest. Once again, he quickly became ill, this time from acute urinary distress, but, in spite of this, the carriage pressed forward. He arrived at he great palace of François I on June 19, once again in a condition which might have heralded his death. The speed and secrecy of the whole endeavor was so great that the staff of the palace did not know the pope was coming until the carriage arrived. For weeks afterward, Pius lay bedridden.

For Napoleon, the safe lodging of the pope near Paris seemed to close one more political problem, as the evolution of his plans in the north unfolded. Three days after Pius's arrival, on June 22, the emperor formally declared war on Russia. Soon would come the costly victory at Borodino (September 7), the imperial entrance into Moscow (September 14), and then the disastrous retreat from Russia which signaled the beginning of the end of the Napoleonic Age.

When the emperor was once again in Paris, he decided to end, forever, his difficulties with pope and Church. On December 29, 1812, he wrote to Pius in his own hand. His letter expressed respect and affection for the pope himself, and a desire to close the difficulties between them at last. This letter was followed by the arrival of Jean-Baptiste Duvoisin, bishop of Nantes and almoner to the Empress Marie Louise, with orders to negotiate a new concordat with the pope.

The terms that the bishop had to offer were harsh in the extreme and represented, in fact, France's complete control over the Catholic Church. The pope was to agree to take up permanent residence in Paris, to allow the Catholic rulers of Europe (in reality now almost all relatives and companions of Napoleon) to nominate two-thirds of all new cardinals, to agree to the final abolition of the States of the Church, and to yield virtually all power in the appointment of bishops, among other requirements of papal government. Pius VII was to become the almost silent figurehead of a new Napoleonic Catholic Church. After days of wrangling, Pius finally pronounced his definite refusal. On January 18, 1813, Napoleon himself came to Fontainebleau to join the discussions. Over several days, he harangued the pope, screamed at him, threatened him with every dire consequence if he continued his refusal. Finally, Pius collapsed and signed the new treaty on January 25. Napoleon had made a few concessions, which included dropping the demand with regard to the nomination of new cardinals, but the document was a complete humiliation of both Pius and the papacy. By this time, twenty-five of the thirty-five living cardinals were in Paris or its vicinity. The overwhelming majority of them also acquiesced to the agreement.

Once the concordat was concluded, the emperor gave orders for the release of a number of imprisoned prelates, including Bartolommeo Pacca, who hurried to rejoin his master. From the pope, he learned the story of the final days which led to Pius's capitulation. The pope told him, "In the end, I was defiled . . . they [the cardinals who supported Napoleon] dragged me to the table and made me sign." Pacca once more resumed officially his office as cardinal-secretary of state, but Consalvi, too, was finally at liberty and began to function once again as Pius's principal advisor. Pacca's great loyalty during the past years restrained the pope from reinstalling Consalvi immediately as secretary of state—he was given the title as well as the power on May 17, 1814, once Napoleon's fall was complete.

In the meantime, it seemed as if Napoleon's success was absolute. Although he had agreed that the new concordat was to be kept secret, he ordered its publication on February 13 together with a decree that the terms were now to be regarded as a law of the state. Pius responded to this with a letter that repudiated the concordat, but Napoleon seized the document. However, the emperor's delight was short-lived. The campaign of 1813 was yet another disaster. Although punctuated with enough victories—Dresden on August 27, Hanau on October 30, and Hochheim on November 2—to allow him to retain the imperial crown for a little longer, his tremendous defeat at the Battle of the Nations at Leipzig on October 18–19 foretold the inevitable end.

With the armies of the Allies now pressing hard on him from the north, Napoleon, on January 22, 1814, instructed Captain Lagorse, who had escorted Pius from Savona to Paris and who had remained in charge of Pius's security, to remove the pope from Fontainebleau and take him toward Italy. Once more, for the last time, Pius was stripped of his associates and companions and bundled into a carriage. Although Napoleon had ordered that the carriage travel in secrecy and by a devious route, the journey was far from that. It became a slow, triumphal procession back to Italy. The unhurried pace allowed Pius to rest frequently and, consequently, to avoid the nearly-mortal illnesses which had accompanied his earlier forced journeys. On February 6, 1814, with Napoleon's collapse at hand, Pius arrived in Savona once more. While there, on March 10, Louis de Chabrol, still functioning as prefect of the department of Montenotte, received the emperor's orders to conduct Pius to the safety of the Austrian garrison at Piacenza. The pope was to be restored to liberty with full sovereignty over the States of the Church. Incredible as it may seem, apparently Napoleon did this in the hope that Pius might be moved to intercede with the Allies on his behalf. If that was the case, it was far too late. On April 4, at Fontainebleau—which surely must have seemed a comic irony to Pius VII—Napoleon abdicated, and was soon on his way to Elba.

From Savona to Rome, Pius made a grand progress through towns lined with cheering crowds. He remained two weeks at Imola, where he had once been the bishop, and still more time at Cesena, where he had been born almost seventy-four years earlier, and where Pius VI also had first seen the world. Here, he was met by Joachim Murat, the king of Naples, whose troops still controlled Rome, though now in the name of the Allies rather than that of the fallen French emperor. Murat, whose position as a turncoat against Napoleon had left him politically weak, apparently tried to get Pius to agree to some arrangement which would leave him in control of most of central as well as southern Italy. Pius abruptly refused.

Consalvi, now traveling with the pope, soon became aware of the negotiations that were taking place in Paris between the restored Louis XVIII and the Allies. Fearing that some disposal would be made of Italian territory without any recognition of papal rights, he hastened to Paris. He arrived just too late to prevent the loss of Avignon and the Comtat Venaissin, which were now indissoluably joined to France in the treaty signed on May 20. He was, however, able to meet and to negotiate with the kings and ministers who had gathered for the first post-Napoleonic settlement. From Paris, he went on to London for further talks with the Prince Regent. All of this prepared the way for Consalvi's participation at the Congress of Vienna, which led to the full restoration of the Papal States.

Pius VII made his grand entrance into Rome, with Cardinal

Bartolommeo Pacca at his side, on May 24, 1814. Though the Hundred Days was yet to come, it would not affect Italy, other than to lead to the final destruction of Murat; in practical terms, the arrival in Rome signaled the end of Pius's political and ecclesiastical ordeals.

The triumph of pope and papacy in 1814 was due not to the general obstinacy and stolidity of Pius VII, nor to the brilliance of Consalvi, Pacca, and others who worked for a complete restoration, but rather simply to the fact that Pius had survived. Had he died at any time during the years of Napoleon's power, he would have been replaced by a puppet in Napoleon's hands, if he had been replaced at all. That this is true may be seen by reflecting that there were only thirty-four living cardinals when Pius VII finally achieved his liberty. Of these, twenty-five had been resident in Paris during most of the pope's time at Fontainebleau, and all the remainder were in territories under Napoleon's control.

The final phase of the reign of Pius VII began in the summer of 1817 while the pope was enjoying a brief summer vacation at Castel Gandolfo. He fell heavily and was so badly bruised and shaken that he was bedridden for a month. Although he would live another six years, he never fully recovered from his injuries. As is so often the case when elderly popes suffer a sudden debilitation, the pace of Pius's activities and government slowed and the cardinals began in earnest the informal, opening stages of the *prattiche*. The evolution of their discussions soon revealed two strong competitive parties; those in favor of Ercole Consalvi's slightly liberalizing policies and those archconservative ultramontanists who favored a radical return to the vision and style of papal government as it had been before the French Revolution. These latter, called *zelanti* (zealots), were strengthened by the elevation of several new conservative cardinals, especially among the thirteen who were created on March 10, 1823.

Four months after that consistory, Pius VII, now eighty-two, fell again in his apartments and broke his thigh. His physicians thought that he was too old and feeble to withstand any attempt to set the fracture, so he languished in ever-heightening misery until he finally succumbed to a heart attack six weeks later on August 20.

Forty-nine of the fifty-three living cardinals participated in the twenty-six-day conclave that met to elect Pius VII's successor on September 2, 1823. Two cardinals, Giulio Maria della Somaglia, cardinal-bishop of Ostia e Velletri and dean of the College, and Fabrizio Ruffo, the archdeacon and the last cardinal to command an army in the field, survived from the reign of Pius VI; all the remaining cardinals were creations of Pius VII.

From the opening days of the election, the two opposing factions placed themselves firmly behind their respective official candidates—Antonio Gabriele Severoli for the *zelanti* and Francesco Saverio Castiglione for the moderates—a mild-mannered scion of the noble family which had given Pope Celestine IV to the Church in 1241. As the month of September wore on, more and more of the undecided cardinals—perhaps ten of them—were drawn into supporting Severoli's candidacy. The Austrian foreign minister, Metternich, had anticipated this possible outcome. He certainly did not want the rigid and unforgiving Severoli on the throne—he remembered all too well Severoli's uncooperative days as nuncio to Vienna. In consequence, Metternich had confided Austria's veto of Severoli's candidacy to the imperial agent in the conclave, Cardinal Giuseppe Albani.

On the afternoon of September 21, Severoli received twenty-six of the thirty-four votes needed for election. Albani concluded that Severoli would be elected in the first voting of the next day, and publicly pronounced the exclusion of Severoli. In earlier conclaves, the exercise of the *jus exclusivæ* or veto, especially on the threshold of the election of the excluded candidate, usually caused a period of confusion while the partisans of the failed candidacy regrouped behind another choice. In 1823, however, the *zelanti* moved swiftly to repair the damage Albani's action had done to their cause. Severoli himself chose a substitute candidate, Cardinal Annibale Francesco Clemente Melchiore Girolamo Nicola della Genga Sermattei, the cardinal-vicar of Rome. Consalvi, the leader of the moderate party and the architect of most of the successes of Pius VII's reign, regarded della Genga's intelligence as inversely proportional to the length of his name. The two had clashed openly on several occasions, notably in the summer of 1814, when Pius had sent the frail della Genga to Paris to convey official papal congratulations to Louis XVIII on the restoration of the French monarchy. Consalvi, already hastening to Paris himself to engage in the most delicate negotiations with the throng of monarchs then in the city concerning the restoration of the States of the Church, saw della Genga make several false steps which jeopardized the plans of the cardinal-secretary of state. In a swift note, he asked Pius to recall his new envoy as quickly as possible, a request with which the pope complied at once.

In the conclave, however, Consalvi could do little to stop della Genga's candidacy from moving forward with sure steps. The *zelanti* capitalized on the fact that Metternich's veto was a deliberate, illegal, and unjust interference by a secular power in the governance of the Church and that Severoli, the injured party, now wanted della Genga elevated to the throne as a rebuff to the Austrian foreign minister.

On September 28, the *zelanti* carried the day. Della Genga received thirty-four votes, precisely the number needed for election. While protesting his ill-health and the infirmities of age—"You are electing a dead man," he said, again and again—he accepted the throne and chose the name Leo XII, in honor of Leo XI, who had ennobled the della Genga family during the few days of his reign in 1605. During the first obedience of the cardinals which followed, he consoled Castiglione by assuring him that one day he would be Pius VIII.

As the moderates had anticipated, Leo XII suddenly dismantled the policies of Pius VII. Consalvi was dismissed as secretary of state and the pope gave the post to the octogenarian and reactionary della Somaglia. The collapse of the moderates was so complete that Consalvi, the chief intellectual and champion of the cause, fell into a profound depression and, by the following January 24, was dead.

Leo, who soon earned the sobriquet "pontiff of the *ancien régime*," quickly alienated nearly the whole population of the States of the Church with new, repressive laws and regulations—some of which seemed remarkably silly, such as imprisonment for men who walked too closely behind women; while others were understood to be highly dangerous, such as the suppression of the pontifical commission for vaccination, whose disappearance was soon followed by a rise in the incidence of smallpox. Meanwhile, the major European powers found themselves appalled by Leo's excessive ultraconservatism in diplomatic and ecclesiastical matters. To counteract this growing disenchantment with Leo's policies, the pope dispatched a rising young moderate, the forty-six-year-old Tommaso Bernetti, to tour the major capitals to assure the powers that the pope was not an ultramontanist. Bernetti's success was rewarded with the cardinalate on October 2, 1826, and by his appointment to succeed della Somaglia as secretary of state on June 17, 1828, when the latter, now nearly ninety, retired because of the infirmities of his age.

The appointment of Bernetti may have signaled some moderation in Leo's archconservative views, since the *zelanti* had pressed him to name the hard-line Cardinal Giacomo Giustiniani instead. Leo could not have been unaware of the failures of his domestic policy in the States of the Church and of the disquiet his diplomatic policies had caused, especially in Vienna where Metternich had emerged as the chief protector of the papacy and papal interests among the great powers.

If it was his intention to craft a new, more moderate general policy, he had little time to do it. On February 5, 1829, after concluding an audience with Bernetti, Leo collapsed in his apartments. His vital signs spiraled downward. On the eighth, he received the *viaticum*; on the ninth, he lost consciousness for the last time; and, on the tenth, he was dead.

Nearly forgotten today, Leo XII was certainly deeply religious but he remained to his last breath utterly unconscious of the developments—social, political, and economic—that were changing the face of Europe, and the world, in his time. Indeed, he seems more of a seventeenth century man in his outlook. His offhand rejection of vaccination as a necessary public policy to reduce the scourge of smallpox—even while Edward Jenner's discovery was being hailed as the medical miracle of the age elsewhere in Europe, and even though Pius VII had established a commission to promote vaccination in the Papal States—shows the extremely limited scope of his intellect and his imagination.

In spite of the brevity of the reign—only five and a half years—the College of Cardinals had undergone a substantial change in personnel in Leo's time. Fabrizio Ruffo, the grizzled old general against the forces of Napoleon's Parthenopean Republic, died on December 13, 1827, leaving only Giulio Maria della Somaglia as a survivor of the creations of Pius VI. Only thirty-two cardinals survived from the creations of Pius VII; but all twenty-five of Leo's creations survived him, although one, Francesco Maria Marazzani Visconti, died on February 18, two days after the conclave opened. Ultimately, the membership in the College stood at fifty-seven.

The *zelanti* had learned from the failures of Leo XII that an ultramontanist crusade was doomed to failure and that perhaps, after all, there had been some merit to Consalvi's policies of reconciliation and moderation. Consequently, the ideological gap between the *zelanti* and the moderates narrowed somewhat; and the politics of the College as a whole had moved slightly to the left. At the same time, both France and Austria were anxious to ensure the election of a conciliatory and moderate pope.

Early in March, the doors of the conclave were opened—a not unusual occurrence in this period—to admit the French ambassador, Vicomte François-Renè de Chateaubriand. The famous soldier, diplomat, gourmet, and author, now little more than a year away from the July Revolution of 1830 that would sweep him from the corridors of power forever, addressed the cardinals in the last great oration of his career. He urged them to elect a pontiff who would not spend his reign looking backward, but rather a man who would bring the Church into harmony with the "spirit of the age." The author of *Le Génie du Christianisme*, a lifelong and ardent royalist, was now at the zenith of his personal and political liberalism. His speech was impassioned, but he was preaching to the converted; and it is unclear how many votes he swayed to the cause of the official candidate of France—and Austria—Francesco Saverio Castiglione.

Whatever the effect of Chateaubriand's speech, Castiglione was chosen on March 31, 1829, forty-nine days after the death of Leo. He chose to be called Pius VIII, just as Leo had predicted he would at the conclusion of the 1823 election.

The brief, six-hundred-nine-day reign of Pius VIII seems to the modern observer to be almost as reactionary and unimaginative as that of Leo XII, but to contemporaries it was like a short day of sunshine when compared with the administrations and policies of both his predecessor and his successor. Like Leo, Pius VIII also fulminated against indifferentism—the intellectual and moral toleration of other religions—Freemasonry, and other "modern errors." On the other hand, he did abrogate quickly most of Leo XII's most draconian laws and regulations in the States of the Church, most notably the restriction on the sale of wine and other alcoholic drinks.

While the citizens of the States of the Church enjoyed a brief respite from the ardors of zealotry, elsewhere in Europe Catholics often found themselves feeling betrayed by the policies of the Vatican. In Belgium, where Catholics were, for the most part, ardent supporters of the revolution that brought the country into existence in 1830, they were condemned by the new cardinal-secretary of state, Giuseppe Albani, for opposing the order of Europe that had been created by the Congress of Vienna. Later, in Poland, patriotic Catholics also found themselves rebuffed by Rome when they opposed the established authority of the tsar. Both groups were fighting, in part, for a greater freedom for Catholicism and both were seriously disappointed and bewildered by the failure of Rome to support them. Both peoples, however—like the Irish during the time of Gregory XVI, who were similarly condemned for opposing the authority of the English—failed to understand that the papacy was now reduced to dependence on the great powers for its continued territorial existence and that the pope was now completely marginalized in his role in the affairs of Europe.

One symbol of the papacy's powerlessness passed at the time as a great victory. On April 4, 1829, George IV gave his assent to the Roman Catholic Relief Bill, better known today as the Catholic Emancipation Act. The law, introduced into Parliament by Sir Robert Peel, the home secretary, removed most of the legal obstacles under which Catholics in Great Britain and Ireland had labored for centuries. Consalvi had begun the process that led to the law's passage more than a decade before, and the work of Daniel O'Connell had materially furthered the progress of the movement. But the passage of the bill itself arose from a general understanding among the members of Parliament, as well as throughout Britain, that not the pope, nor the papacy, nor the Catholic Church was in any position to threaten or upset the British state, society, or religion in any way. Why not let the Catholics have their legal Church, and why not let Catholics enjoy the full rights of citizenship, so went the argument, since the leader of their Church is now so powerless in the affairs of Europe as to represent no power at all. The fact that the bill had so little serious opposition testifies to the strength of this argument, when compared to the uproar caused by the similarly-intentioned Declaration of Indulgence issued by James II in 1687—also on April 4—when the power of the Church was still seen as a menace and while the vigorous Innocent XI occupied the papal throne.

The summer of liberal unrest in 1830, that saw the disappearance of Charles X in France and the arrival of Leopold I in Belgium, manifested itself in Italy with some signs of unrest in Parma, Modena, and other towns in the States of the Church. While Metternich and Pius VIII worked to contain these troubles, Francesco I of Naples died on November 8. The accession of his son, Ferdinando II, was accompanied by a plea from the influential journalist, Luigi Settembrini, that the new king seek at once to become king of a united Italy. Metternich, fearful of how a twenty-year-old, impressionable monarch might react to such a solicitation, was greatly alarmed. He pressed Pius VIII to permit Austrian troops to cross through the Papal States for a preemptive strike at the new Neapolitan monarch. Pius VIII was able to thwart this plan, which, in the end, came to nothing; but the event proved to be only the beginning of a siege of troubles.

Pius VIII, like Leo XII before him, had not been a well man when he was elected. Throughout his reign, he had been beset by episodes of ill health which did not signal a long pontificate. Suddenly, on the evening of November 30, 1830, he was overcome by a series of dramatic convulsions in his apartments in the Quirinale. Just before midnight, he died.

His end came so quickly and the fermentation of political instability was so great that several of the cardinals who attended the early meetings of the general congregation thought it almost certain that he had been poisoned. The convulsions that presaged his end lent further support to the theory. Consequently, for the first time in modern history, the cardinals voted to have an autopsy performed on Pius's corpse. This procedure, of which we have extensive notes in the handwriting of Agostino Chigi, the prince marshal of the conclave, suggested that Pius had died of repeated strictures of the throat. At this distance, the best conclusion that can be drawn from the narration of the physical signs is that he died from several asthmatic attacks in quick succession.

The *sede vacante* of 1830–1831 was the most turbulent and dangerous in recent centuries, except for that of 1799–1800; but this time there was no brilliant and able Ercole Consalvi to keep order and to calm the fears of the cardinals. As soon as the cardinal-legates had left their posts in the Papal States to come to Rome for the funeral of Pius VIII and the conclave, armed uprisings broke out in most of the major cities of the States. While Rome itself remained generally quiet, as did most of the Campagna, everywhere else papal government was soon driven out or seriously compromised.

In the conclave, two parties quickly formed: one under the leadership of Pius VIII's cardinal-secretary of state, Giuseppe Albani, Austria's perennial friend; and the other under the leadership of Tommaso Bernetti, who had served Leo XII in the same office, and who believed that Austrian help in suppressing the revolts should be sought only as a last resort. In general, the cardinals of the curia and the administration of the Papal States were eager to elect a pope who would summon Austrian aid quickly. Within a few days, a consensus was reached in both parties to elevate Cardinal Giacomo Giustiniani to the throne. But this plan came to naught when Ferdinand VII of Spain vetoed his election, apparently because the king resented the fact that Giustiniani had advised Leo XII to appoint new bishops in Latin America, particularly Colombia, after the continent had broken with Spain and formed a constellation of new nations.

After the sudden defeat of Giustiniani's candidacy, Albani named as his official candidate Cardinal Bartolommeo Pacca, the cardinal-bishop of Ostia e Velletri and dean of the College. Bernetti turned his attention to promoting the election of Mauro Cappellari, a Benedictine monk of the rigid Camaldolese reform who had served both Leo XII and Pius VIII as cardinal-prefect of the Congregation for the Propagation of the Faith.

In his electioneering, Bernetti emphasized Pacca's age—the cardinal-dean passed into his seventy-fifth year on Christmas Day—and the consequent probability that Pacca would become the third pope in succession to suffer from severe ill-health. By contrast, Cappellari was ten years younger and physically vigorous. Gradually, as the political situation outside the conclave worsened dramatically, Bernetti persuaded a few more cardinals to join his cause. On February 2, 1831, Cappellari was elected and chose the name Gregory XVI, in honor of Gregory XV (1621–1623) who had founded the Congregation for the Propagation of the Faith (*de Propaganda Fide*).

Today, hindsight shows us that Gregory XVI was the last man who should have been chosen to lead the Church, just as the industrial revolution was making its effects felt throughout the developed world and as the press for liberal political reform was gathering increasing momentum almost everywhere in Europe. Gregory, who had been baptized Bartolommeo Albert Cappellari, and who is the last member of a religious order to be elevated to the papal throne, had become a monk in the Camaldolese house of San Michele di Murano in the Veneto when he was eighteen. His talents soon led his superiors to have him trained in philosophy and theology, after which he became a teacher of those subjects to younger members of his order. In 1795, he left for Rome and joined the ancient monastery of San Gregorio al Monte Celio. Four years later, in 1799, he published his principal theological work, *Il Trionfo della Santa Sede e della Chiesa contro gli Assalti de' Novatori Respinti e Combattuti colle Stesse loro Armi* (Roma: Stampato Pagliarini). This work of more than four hundred pages was a highly-charged, polemical defense of both papal infallibility and the rights of the popes to temporal sovereignty.

During the *sede vacante* of 1799–1800, he was elected abbot-vicar of San Gregorio. Pius VII confirmed the election and made him abbot of the house in 1805. Though he had to flee Rome when Pius was taken to France and French authority prevailed in Rome, he quickly returned when Pius was firmly replaced on the throne in 1815. From that time forward his rise in the Church was fairly rapid. Pius made him consultor to several congregations and an examiner of bishops, and twice offered him episcopal consecration, which Cappellari refused. Leo XII created him a cardinal, but reserved his name *in pectore* in the consistory of March 21, 1825. His name was published and he was assigned the rank of cardinal-priest of the title of San Callisto one year later, in the consistory of March 13, 1826. It was at that time that he was made cardinal-prefect.

Now pope, Gregory reappointed Bernetti, the grand elector of 1831, to his old post as secretary of state; and authorized his new second-in-command to open a policy of negotiation with the various parties of rebels in the Papal States. Quick decisions were vital, since Bologna—the second largest city in the Papal States, after Rome itself—fell into the hands of the revolutionaries on February 3, the day after the election. Bernetti secured the appointment of Cardinal Giovanni Antonio Benvenuti as legate *a latere* to conduct the negotiations, but, as soon as the cardinal fell into the hands of the rebels, he was arrested and no parleys of consequence took place. It has often been said that Bernetti also gave Benvenuti a letter which authorized him to "provoke a counter-revolution" whenever and wherever he could. This document, which was reprinted a number of times in the nineteenth century, no longer survives. It was almost certainly a forgery concocted to embarrass Rome and derail Benvenuti's efforts, however—both Bernetti and Benvenuti were too clever to consign such instructions to written form, had they existed.

The failure of Benvenuti's mission caused Bernetti to fall back to a second plan for the defense of the Papal States. He formed a small army of volunteers and mercenaries to spearhead a counter-revolution. Within days, however, the mercenaries fled and many of the volunteers joined the revolutionaries. Meanwhile, the cardinal had appealed to both France and Naples for assistance, in the hope that he could avoid intervention by the Austrian army, now poised on the northern frontier for an advance toward Rome. Bernetti's cries for help were ignored. Meanwhile, the provisional government that had been established in Bologna issued a declaration which announced the abolition of papal temporal power. This was accompanied by the mobilization of an army under the command of General Giuseppe Sercognani, an old veteran of Napoleon's armies, for an immediate advance on Rome. Bernetti was left with no choice but to appeal to Metternich for rescue. By the end of February, an informal message from Gregory was received in Vienna, followed two weeks later by a formal request for Austrian intervention. By that time, Austrian troops already had occupied Modena. On March 19, four days after the official plea for help, the Austrian army advanced on Bologna, and the revolution collapsed. The remnants of the revolutionary army, now under the command of Carlo Zucchi, another Napoleonic veteran, retreated toward Ancona, with Cardinal Benvenuti as their prisoner. Soon this force, too, fell into Austrian hands, and Zucchi was captured.

Although many of the revolutionary leaders escaped to France, including Sercognani and, later, Zucchi, those who remained were subjected to swift and powerful retribution. Exile was the punishment meted out to many who had sympathized with the revolutionary cause, including Count Terenzio Mamiani, who would become prime minister in the reformed government created by Pius IX in 1848, and Count Pietro Ferretti, a cousin of the future Pius IX.

The sad and inauspicious beginning of the reign of Gregory XVI was a true harbinger of the rest of his pontificate. In a few weeks, Austrian troops were withdrawn from the States of the Church in response to French pressure, but they returned when unrest soon broke out again. On this second occasion, French troops occupied Ancona, ostensibly to preserve some balance of influence in the Papal States.

By the end of the reign, whether troops were present or not, Gregory had lost all real semblance of independence. He willingly joined the ministers of the major powers in an archconservative opposition to the changes that were sweeping through Europe and the New World. In his two encyclicals, *Mirari vos* (August 15, 1832) and *Singulari nos* (June 23, 1834), he condemned almost every liberal movement both inside and outside the Church. In the former, he condemned the enemies of God who concealed their "evils" under such spurious causes as liberty of conscience and freedom of the press. He also condemned the "impudence of science" and its new "monstrous opinions." In the latter, directed completely against the thought and writings of Félicité Robert de Lamennais, he ordered all Catholics to reject any efforts at religious toleration and to reject calls for greater liberty of thought and action.

In the real world of his time, Gregory cost the papacy nearly all its credibility as a moderator of morality and Christian ethics. In continuing the policy of Leo XII that forbade resistance to constituted political authority, he alienated the affection and loyalty of thousands of Poles, Irishmen, and Germans. In the United States, he responded to an effort by the lay trustees of the cathedral of the diocese of New Orleans to have some voice in choosing a new rector of the cathedral in 1842 by reprimanding them severely for their "arrogance" and threatening the city with ecclesiastical censure. In 1844, his condemnation of the "evils" of Bible societies and his prohibition of any association between Catholics and other Christians added fuel to the growing distrust of Catholics by America's non-Catholic population. He was, in one sense, the best friend the Know Nothings and other anti-Catholic movements in the United States ever had. Gregory's only real success was his vigorous espousal of the cause of the Immaculate Conception, which was proclaimed a dogma of the Church by Pius IX on December 8, 1854.

By late 1845, the recurrent pain and distress that Gregory experienced in his face was finally diagnosed as an inoperable cancer. He died in agony on June 1, 1846, lamented only by the most reactionary and unregretted even by many of those closest to him.

The ensuing *sede vacante* of sixteen days was the shortest since the thirteen-day-vacancy that followed the death of Gregory XIV on October 16, 1591, and led to the election of Giovanni Antonio Facchinetti as Innocent IX on October 29. This speed was achieved because of the exceptional length of the *prattiche*, the informal discussions among the cardinals about the succession, which began as early as Christmas, 1845. Haste also was dictated by the parlous condition of the Church's finances and by a growing spirit of political unrest in Europe in general and the Papal States in particular, which would soon manifest itself in the revolutions of 1848. It can be postulated that not one of the sixty-two living cardinals believed that the reign which had just ended was other than a failure, in spite of the fact that all but nine of these cardinals had been elevated by Gregory XVI—only two cardinals, Carlo Oppizzoni and Tommaso Riario Sforza, survived from the creations of Pius VII; while seven, including the hardy Tommaso Bernetti, remained of the creations of Leo XII. All of the creations of Pius VIII were gone. Fifty of these cardinals were present as electors.

The opening of the conclave saw the cardinals organized into three distinct parties. The largest consisted of progressives who wished to elect a pope who would come to terms with the developments of the age. They supported Cardinal Ludovico Micara, an enlightened Capuchin friar who had been created a cardinal *in pectore* by Leo XII in the consistory of December 20, 1824, but whose name had not been published until March 13, 1826. Now the cardinal-bishop of Ostia e Velletri and dean of the College, Micara was president of the Supreme Council of the Apostolic Chamber. In addition, he also was prefect of the Congregation of Ceremonies and Rites. Had he not been in his eighty-first year, he might have been hastened to the throne in a near-universal reaction to Gregory's pontificate. In spite of his vigor and acumen, the question of age hindered his candidacy.

The second group, staunch conservatives, supported the cardinal-bishop of Sabina, Luigi Lambruschini, who had become cardinal-secretary of state on January 20, 1835, when Gregory finally lost faith in Bernetti's abilities. Lambruschini, a great favorite of Gregory XVI, had been the premier cardinalitial creation of his reign, on September 30, 1831. A Genoese and a member of the Clerks Regular of Saint Paul, Lambruschini also was eighty years old, just seven months and four days younger than Micara. Age worked against him in his open efforts to reach the throne; although Metternich—now virtually the sole diplomatic and military prop of the papacy—had chosen him as Austria's official candidate.

The third and smallest group had coalesced rapidly behind the candidacy of Cardinal Tommaso Pasquale Gizzi. A native of Ceccano in the diocese of Ferentino, he was a dozen years younger than his rivals. His career had been steady but unspectacular until Gregory appointed him to be the first papal nuncio to Belgium in January, 1838. In that post, he proved spectacularly successful in conciliating many who had become alienated from the Church during and after the independence movement in 1830. When he returned to Rome, Gregory created him a cardinal on July 12, 1841, but did not publish his name until January 22, 1844. As cardinal, Gizzi served ably as prefect of the "Consulta" and as president of the Special Congregation for Public Health—the *Sanitaria*. His work attracted the admiration of the noted diplomat and commentator, Massimo Tapparelli d'Azeglio, Marchese d'Azeglio, who made Gizzi the paradigm of good government in his tract *Degli Ultimi Casi di Romagna*, which had been published a few months before (Lugano: Tipografia della Svizzera Italiana, 1846). D'Azeglio's work was a sensation in its time, offering a cogent and reasoned consideration of the maladministration of the Papal States and arguing against the temporal sovereignty of the popes. The author himself, in the service of Carlo Alberto di Savoja, was something of a hero to progressives in Italy—his first wife, Giulia, was the beloved daughter of Alessandro Manzoni, Italy's greatest novelist.

Gizzi's partisans, however, were unable to mount a successful campaign on his behalf based solely on the admiration expressed for him by one author in one small book. When they saw that he had no chance of reaching the throne, they swiftly regrouped around Cardinal Giovanni Maria Mastai-Ferretti, the bishop of Imola. The name of Imola's bishop already had circulated among the cardinals as a possible compromise candidate who would be acceptable to both the supporters of Micara and those of Gizzi's party. Moreover, he was only fifty-four and in robust health. He had made no secret of his dissatisfaction with papal government under Gregory XVI, in spite of the fact that it was Gregory who had elevated him to the cardinalate on December 23, 1839; publishing his name a year later on December 14, 1840. On June 16, 1846, on the fourth ballot, the progressives united behind him and rushed the election. Mastai-Ferretti received thirty-seven of the fifty votes. He chose the name Pius IX, in honor of Pius VII who had allowed him to have an ecclesiastical career in spite of the fact that he was epileptic—a disease then regarded as an absolute bar to ordination. Metternich, who had feared a strong liberal reaction to Gregory XVI's reign, confided Austria's veto of several candidates, including Mastai-Ferretti, to the hands of his electoral agent, Cardinal Carl Cajetan Gaysruck, archbishop of Milan. Gaysruck arrived just too late to pronounce his master's exclusion of the man who was now Pius IX.

It seemed to be the dawn of a new and freer age. After a few interim days in which Monsignor Giovanni Corboli-Bussi acted as secretary of state, Gizzi was appointed to the office. On July 16, Pius issued a universal amnesty for political prisoners. In 1847, the pope granted further concessions to the spirit of the age: on April 19, he formed a new State Council which included laymen drawn widely from the whole extent of the States of the Church; on July 5, he created a Civic Guard for Rome under lay command; and, on December 29, he created a new cabinet for the government of the Papal States that included lay representation. But these reforms were too little for the need. On February 8, 1848, revolution broke out in Rome. Pius hastened to act to relieve the public's dissatisfaction with papal government—on March 14 he granted a constitution. But popular fury spread too fast for any of these measures to be successful. On the day that the new parliament was to open, November 15, the prime minister, Pellegrino Rossi, was stabbed to death as he entered the Cancelleria, where the new assembly was to meet. On the next day, Pius himself was besieged in the Quirinale by a throng of outraged demonstrators. On the seventeenth, the Guardia Civica occupied all of the posts and duties of the Swiss Guard, virtually without resistance. No help for the pope seemed to be available anywhere. Metternich was being swept away by the revolution in Vienna; Naples was in chaos; Milan was in the throes of the aftermath of its Five Days (March 18–22). The collapse of papal government was complete.

On the night of November 24, 1848, with the help of the French, Bavarian, and Spanish ambassadors, Pius fled in disguise to Gaëta in the Kingdom of Naples. Here, he soon was joined by some of the cardinals and other functionaries of the papal court. On February 9, 1849, the revolutionary assembly in Rome proclaimed the end of the temporal power of the papacy, following a resolution introduced by Giuseppe Garibaldi, who had come to the city to assist in its defense.

The pope's situation was grave indeed. A number of plans were floated, including one which would have seen him as a refugee in the United States, and another which offered him British protection at some location outside Italy. The ultimate solution was a conference at Gaëta at which the representatives of Spain, Austria, France, and Naples agreed on a joint expedition to restore Pius to the government of Rome. Once decided, the result was achieved quickly. The Austrians, fresh from their victory over the Savoyards at the Battle of Novara on March 23, marched swiftly to secure the bulk of papal territory north of Rome. On April 24, a French army landed at Civitavecchia for a rapid march on Rome itself, while Neapolitan and Spanish forces pushed northward from Gaëta to secure the southern parts of the Papal States.

Meanwhile, the revolutionary government, under the leadership of Giuseppe Mazzini, nationalist patriot and the founder of "Young Italy," defied its many opponents. Garibaldi's forces succeeded in defeating an early assault by the French on the Janiculum as well as a Neapolitan force that approached the city from the south. But the allies were too strong and, on June 29, the French forces under General Charles Oudinot captured the city—He was the son of Napoleon's marshal, Nicholas Charles Oudinot, duc de Reggio. Garibaldi evacuated his troops in a brilliant retreat to San Marino, and the victory of the allies was complete. Pius IX, however, did not re-enter Rome until April 12, 1850. Like Louis XVIII before him, he returned to his capital in the baggage of the allies.

The pope's experience had changed him, politically and spiritually. His conservatism now was scarcely less than that of Leo XII or Gregory XVI. His administration during this time reflected his growing disenchantment with liberalism and his new mistrust of any action which sought to curtail papal temporal power. Gizzi had been dismissed on July 17, 1847, in favor of the pope's cousin, Gabriele Ferretti, who had been created a cardinal by Gregory in 1838. At the first signs of unrest, Ferretti fled his post and the city, to be replaced on January 21, 1848, by Giuseppe Bofondi, a conservative who was among Pius IX's first four creations on December 21, 1846. He failed to stem the tide of revolution and was happy to yield his place to Giacomo Antonelli on the following May 4. Antonelli, an archconservative who had been made a cardinal on June 11, 1847, would remain as cardinal-secretary of state for more than twenty-eight years.

After his return to Rome, Pius would rule the city and the Papal States nominally for another two decades, but every moment of that rule was supported by the presence of foreign troops; and it was everywhere understood that the withdrawal of this soldiery would be followed almost immediately by the disappearance of Pius's government. The proponents of a united Italy had only to wait.

In the meantime, Pius began to devote more and more of his attention to matters of ecclesiastical government and policy, leaving the problems of administration strictly in the hands of Antonelli. The showpiece of Pius IX's reign would be the First Vatican Council, which opened on December 8, 1869, and approved the doctrine of papal infallibility on July 18, 1870, by a vote of four hundred thirty-three to two—although many bishops either disapproved of the doctrine or considered it inexpedient to proclaim it, because of the troubles of the papacy, only Ludovico Riccio, bishop of Cajazzo, and Edward Fitzgerald, bishop of Little Rock, Arkansas, had the courage to vote against it, with the pope sitting before them. The council closed on October 20, 1870, after Rome already had been occupied by Italian troops.

Pius IX had the longest reign of any pope in history, thirty-one years, seven months, and seventeen days. Nearly all of it was an unrelieved disaster for the papacy and the Church.

The last years of Pius's reign saw the *Kulturkampf* in Germany and other attacks on the authority of both pope and Church, but the aged and feeble pontiff could do nothing to resist these assaults. Would the papacy even continue to exist when Pius was gone? It was a serious question posed by many, including many Catholics, during the 1870s. If it was to continue, it would be up to the cardinals in the next conclave to elect a pope who would chart an altogether different course for the institution.

II
THE SOCIALIST POPE

FROM THE MOMENT the Royal Italian Army entered Rome, in September, 1870, until the death of Pius IX, seven and a half years later, many people doubted whether there would ever be another conclave. Pius responded to Victor Emmanuel's occupation of Rome by retiring within the Vatican Palace and permitted virtually no intercourse between the members of his court and the bureaucracy of a newly united Italy.

During the last years of his life, no one was more aware than Pius that attempts might be made by the Italian government to thwart the choice of a new pope. Therefore, he put into effect several policies designed to ensure that his death would be followed speedily by the election of his successor. He secretly prepared no fewer than three papal constitutions dealing with conclaves to be made public only at his death.

The first of these, *In hac sublimi*, dated August 21, 1871, was the most far reaching. In it, he abrogated all the laws regarding conclaves established by his predecessors during the preceding six centuries, should any interference be offered to the cardinals after his death. He directed that the meeting of the conclave need not necessarily take place at the site of his death but rather that a general congregation of cardinals should meet immediately to decide the time and place of the papal election and inform absent cardinals of its decision. Further, Pius instructed that the electoral process was to begin when one-half plus one of the living cardinals should meet, even if this were in the first general congregation assembled after his death. Any person who received the adherence of two-thirds of those present would be elected canonically as the new pope, though that might represent the votes of as little as one-third of the living cardinals.

In the second constitution, *Licet per apostolicas*, September 8, 1874, Pius confirmed the earlier document but forbade the cardinals to break, in any way, with those traditions which could be observed safely. In addition, he expressly prohibited the Sacred College from exercising papal powers, thus forcing them to a quick election, and he demanded strongly that the cardinals maintain secrecy about the electoral proceedings.

In the third and last electoral constitution, *Consulturi*, dated October 10, 1877, Pius ordered that the cardinals should be prepared to break up the conclave and move at once to a new site if their work were impeded in any way. They were empowered to take this action, even if the balloting already had begun. Moreover, though he had wished formerly that his constitutions be first considered by a tribunal made up of the dean, archpriest, and archdeacon of the College of Cardinals, he now desired that all the cardinals be informed of their provisions at once by a public reading immediately after his death.

These regulations were, however, far from the limit of the steps Pius took to ensure the successful meeting of the next conclave. Numerous regulations and traditions barred the cardinals from private meetings among themselves to discuss the next pope during the current reign. Pius cancelled all these, and indeed encouraged the cardinals to such discussions, in the hope that many disagreements and campaign details would be resolved by the time of his death, in order to shorten still further the lapse of time before the next enthronement.

Of all the steps he took, however, the most far-reaching was his intentional broadening of the membership in the College to include wider representation for non-Italian Catholics. He hoped to reduce, thereby, the possibility that the Italian government would interfere with the deliberations of a body which included, among others, English, French, German, and Spanish nationals. The importance of this policy cannot be overstated, since the steady increase in non-Italian membership has led to a gradual diminution of Italian influence in the selection of the pope from that time to our own, even though the Vatican bureaucracy remains chiefly Italian. When Pius IX was elected, in 1846, there had been sixty-two cardinals of whom only nine were not Italian, and one of these was of Neapolitan birth though of English ancestry. By the dawn of 1878 there were sixty-four cardinals, but no fewer than twenty-five were non-Italian, and eighteen of these had been elevated to the cardinalate after 1870. Among them was the Church's first non-European diocesan cardinal, John McCloskey of New York.

By early 1877, it was clear that the eighty-five year old Pius would not live much longer. The members of the Vatican diplomatic service in the various European capitals were instructed to inquire of representatives of their host governments regarding the possibility of holding the next conclave outside Rome. The consensus they received was that the electoral assembly should be held in the Eternal City, if at all possible, for if the cardinals were to meet elsewhere there was a distinct likelihood that they would not be allowed to return to the Eternal City in the company of a new pontiff. Bismarck, for example, was strongly of this opinion. Meanwhile, the Italian government gave every assurance that the next conclave could be held without the slightest interference. But these guarantees were much distrusted by the pope and many cardinals.

During the fall of 1877, Pius IX was gravely ill but, from the standpoint of the next reign, the illness of the influential Cardinal Domenico Bartolini was of greater moment. Endowed with a loud, coarse voice, and immensely fat as well, the sixty-four-year-old Bartolini had risen to become prefect of the Sacred Congregation of Rites. By virtue of his office, as well as his considerable intellectual ability, he had become one of a small handful of powerful cardinals who actually made the day-to-day decisions by which the Church functioned. His reputation among his fellow cardinals was not enhanced, however, by his notoriously vile temper—it often led him to sudden outbursts which both embarrassed and discomforted his friends and delighted his enemies. Bartolini, however, like many urban peasants who grow up in the streets, had an unerring sense of political manipulation. At the heart of this skill was his staunch protection of everyone whom he called friend. He carefully abided by every arrangement and compromise he ever made and was famous for never breaking his word.

While he recuperated from his illness in his Roman residence, Bartolini astutely took advantage of the courtesy calls that other cardinals made on him to sound them out carefully regarding their plans for the next election, a freedom given him by Pius's lifting of the prohibition on electioneering. Cardinals who came to inquire after the patient's health were skillfully drawn into discussions of the relative merits of their colleagues. During the long beginning of this political orchestration, the scarlet-clad Friar Tuck artfully concealed both his motives and his choice for the throne. By the Christmas season, however, Bartolini had decided that he would expend every effort to secure the elevation of Gioacchino Pecci, a senior cardinal who had recently been elevated to the vitally important position of chamberlain of the Church.

The sixty-seven-year-old Pecci was, ironically, by appearance and personality, Bartolini's opposite. Sprung from the minor nobility, this tall and spare intellectual had begun his rise in the Church's bureaucracy when he had served a term as papal ambassador to Belgium under Gregory XVI. Though Pius IX had made him bishop of Perugia in 1846 and cardinal in 1853, he had been for years *persona non grata* at the papal court as a result of a deep and long-standing antipathy between him and Cardinal Giacomo Antonelli, secretary of state for most of Pius's reign. After Antonelli's death in the autumn of 1876, however, the way was clear for Pecci to appear more often in Rome. His talents, long hidden away in provincial administration, now quickly won him preferment. The office of chamberlain was, and is, one of the most powerful in the Church. Among other functions, this prelate, who is always a cardinal, is the interim administrator of the entire Church during a vacancy of the papal chair. After the death of Cardinal Filippo De Angelis, on July 6, 1877, Pius IX allowed the office to remain vacant for some weeks while he meditated on his choice of the man who would be responsible for ensuring a smooth change of reigns in the near future. Two of the cardinals personally close to Pius, Anton Maria Panebianco and Alessandro Franchi, repeatedly urged the aging pontiff to appoint Pecci. On September 21, the pope yielded to their wishes. This expression of papal confidence in a prelate who had been absent from the corridors of power for more than two decades did not go unnoticed by the other cardinals, Bartolini among them.

At the end of 1877, however, the name most often mentioned as the successor of Pius was the smooth-faced, slightly balding Franchi, who had developed a large following during the course of a long Church career that included a brilliant tour as papal ambassador in Spain. His abilities had now brought him to the prefecture of the Congregation for the Propagation of the Faith, an office which gave him direct superintendence over all the Church's far-flung missionary activities. Bartolini, among many others, would have been eager to support his candidature for the papacy, had Franchi not denied, often and strongly, his availability for the office. Franchi was not alone in publicly refusing to be considered for the throne. Luigi Bilio, the cardinal-bishop of Sabina, was another popular prelate who ruled himself out.

Late in December, 1877, Bartolini, now fully recovered, gave a small dinner party for a select group of powerful cardinals with the intention of creating a party to work for Pecci in the next conclave. The five cardinals who dined that evening at Bartolini's began to plan actively for the next reign over brandy and cigars were Franchi; Bilio; Raffaele Monaco La Valetta, the cardinal-vicar of Rome; Lorenzo Nina, an able bureaucrat who had been made a cardinal only in the preceding March; and Henry Edward Manning, the primate of England, who exercised a great influence among the non-Italian cardinals. At the conclusion of the evening's discussions, four of the six agreed among themselves to begin at once to lay the foundation for Pecci's elevation—Bilio was lukewarm towards Pecci, and Monaco was opposed to his candidacy in the strongest terms. The six did agree, however, to keep the results of their deliberations secret, and, when Pecci heard of the meeting a little later, he was miffed not to have received an invitation, confiding to his brother, Giuseppe, that this clearly indicated Bartolini's want of confidence in him. Only much later would he learn that he himself had been the topic of debate.

While these discussions were in progress, elsewhere in Rome Victor Emmanuel II, the founder of a united Italy, was slipping into his final illness. His death on January 9, 1878, plunged the Italian government into momentary disorganization which precluded any strong action for several weeks until the next king, Umberto I, took hold of the machinery of state. The Vatican was in no position, though, to take advantage of the temporary disruption; Pius IX was too old and ill, and limited himself to a protest against Umberto's assumption of the title King of Italy on January 17.

Toward the end of January, it became very clear that Pius IX was at the end of his reign; indeed, one Roman paper already had published an erroneous notice of his death. The pope was able to give a public audience on February 2, but, on the following day, he could stand and take a few steps only with assistance. By the night of the sixth, he was feverish and slightly delirious. On the morning of the seventh, he suffered a brief attack of fever after which he regained his full faculties; but, by this time, the physicians in attendance on him confirmed his own sensations, which indicated his last day. During the course of the morning, the pope was visited by numerous cardinals and prelates. At noon, the pope sent for Cardinal Bilio, so that he could begin his recitation of the prayers for the dying. When the cardinal reached the prayer which begins "Depart, Christian soul," Pius spoke his last words in a firm, strong voice, "yes, depart." Almost immediately afterward the final agony began and, at 5:40 P.M., the pope was dead. Within twenty minutes the final medical formalities were concluded, and the cardinal-vicar Monaco had issued a public circular officially notifying Rome that the pope who had ruled the Church for longer than any other man in history was gone. Two hours later, Pecci, who as chamberlain was now the administrator of the church, left his apartments in the Vatican and went to Pius's deathbed to begin the long series of funeral ceremonies.

The chamberlain already had ordered the members of his staff to secure the papal apartments and to take an inventory of all the documents and valuables they found there. Now he approached the body of Pius IX. The old ceremony of tapping the pontiff's forehead three times with a silver hammer, while calling out his baptismal name, recounted frequently in tales of the deaths of popes, had not been used since the passing of Clement X in 1676; rather the veil covering the face of Pius was lifted three times as Pecci softly said, "Giovanni, Giovanni, Giovanni." After this the chamberlain retired to his own quarters to inspect the documents discovered by his staff and to issue orders that the first general congregation of cardinals would be held on the following morning.

Early on the next day, the cardinals then in Rome began to assemble at the Vatican. Each paid a visit of mourning to Pius and then proceeded to the Consistorial Hall for their first meeting. The principal question to be considered was the site of the conclave. By nine o'clock, all but one of the thirty-nine cardinals resident in the Eternal City were united together. The sole absentee was the dean of the Sacred College, Luigi Amat di San Filippo e Sorso, who was too ill to leave his apartments. Since he, as the most senior prelate, would normally have presided over the meeting, he authorized the next senior cardinal-bishop, Camillo Di Pietro, to act in his stead.

When Pecci appeared, guarded by a troop of the Swiss guards, as was now his privilege, he brought with him the texts of the three election constitutions of Pius IX which were then read to the Sacred College. As president of the congregation, Di Pietro now spoke, both for himself and for the absent Amat, in favor of holding the conclave in Rome. Considerable opposition to this program appeared at once, and the spokesman for the opposition, Cardinal Anton Maria Panebianco, argued that to hold the meeting in Rome was contrary to the spirit of Pius IX's constitutions. Di Pietro replied that he had been assured by a representative of the Italian government that no interference would be offered to the cardinals in performing their duty of papal election and that the conclave would have complete security, freedom, and independence.

The question of where to hold the conclave produced six hours of debate. Several cardinals, including the cardinal-bishops Filippo Maria Guidi and Carlo Luigi Morichini, and, ultimately, Di Pietro himself, voted to abide by the decision of the majority. All the others, however, had definite opinions that they were willing to back with votes.

In the course of the debate, the opposition to Rome as the site for the conclave quickly won the adherence of most of the cardinals, sparked by fear that the Italians would find some way to interrupt the election or embarrass the College. Pecci himself voiced such an opinion and he was joined by many of the most influential members, including Monaco, Franchi, Antonino De Luca, and the cardinal-bishop Carlo Sacconi. Manning of England advanced the proposition that the cardinals should retire to Malta where, he assured them, the British governor would offer protection. Even the Polish cardinal, Mieczyslaw Halka Ledochowski, no stranger to harassment, was of the opinion that Rome was too dangerous. In this first meeting, only eight cardinals supported the idea of holding the conclave in the Vatican. Flavio Chigi, of the noble Roman family that had given Pope Alexander VII to the Church, was for staying, as was Gustav Adolf von Hohenlohe, the German cardinal who had corresponded with Bismarck on just this question. Innocenzo Ferrieri, the resident wit of the College, probably joined them simply because his particular brand of perversity always led him to support the minority loudly. Prospero Caterini, the archdeacon, who was eighty-two, and Teodolfo Mertel, the next junior cardinal-deacon, ten years younger, both opted for Rome simply because they felt themselves too old to undertake any kind of journey in this atmosphere of crisis. Enea Sbarretti gave no reason for siding with Chigi and the others, but Giuseppe Berardi said that he did so because he trusted the word of the Italian government. Finally, Lorenzo Randi supported the idea that the conclave should be held in Rome because his old enemies, Bartolini and Pecci, did not. At the conclusion of the meeting, Di Pietro kept alive the hopes of those who favored Rome by persuading the cardinals to put off a final vote on the question for one more day. Meanwhile, the cause of Rome was being aided in a number of meetings with papal ambassadors and cardinals abroad. In Vienna, the Emperor Franz Josef met privately on the morning of February 8 with the cardinal-archbishop of his capital, Johann Rudolf Kutschker, and promised him Austria's active interest in the liberty and security of the conclave. Later in the day, the Austrian chancellor, Count Julius Andrassy, called at the nunciature with similar assurances for Ludovico Jacobini, the pope's representative, and told him, as well, that Italy had given specific guarantees to Austria that the conclave would have complete liberty. In the evening, Jacobini telegraphed the substance of both meetings to Di Pietro. In Rome itself, Marchese Filippo Berardi, brother of the cardinal and a close associate of Pietro Mancini, the Italian minister of justice, called on both Pecci and Monaco to promise, once again, Italian protection for the conclave; he even conveyed an offer of troops to protect the cardinals during the vacancy.

At nine on the following morning, the cardinals once more met in the Consistorial Hall. During the night, Lucido Maria Parocchi, archbishop of Bologna and, at forty-four, the youngest cardinal, arrived. This brought the number of cardinals in Rome to forty. Three were absent from the second general congregation, however. Caterini had found the previous day's debate too strenuous and had taken to his bed. Amat was still too ill to attend; and, to the surprise of nearly all the College, Berardi also absented himself. Di Pietro again spoke first. He pointed out to his colleagues that, thus far, no government had invited the cardinals formally to come elsewhere for the election, and he added that the potential difficulty of returning in the company of a new pope, as well as the danger of a journey to the health of the elder cardinals, made the Vatican the best possible choice. This speech made a profound impression on many of those present, and, when the debate began, it was plain that opposition to Rome had weakened considerably. Vocal defenders of the departure were still heard, however. Sacconi urged the cardinals to retire to the principality of Monaco, of all places, at which Ferrieri stage-whispered to Hohenlohe that this was because Sacconi appreciated the feminine company to be found there. Guidi, on the other hand, now espoused Manning's original proposal to hold the election in Malta. A number of cardinals, including Bilio, Franchi, Ledochowski, and Eduardo Borromeo, now spoke in favor of going to Spain, but added that they hoped for an invitation from Alfonso XII before the cardinals made a final decision. Monaco, who for some reason had gotten into a panic overnight, urged the cardinals to conduct an election on the spot, as Pius IX had provided they might—but his suggestion was quietly ignored.

The most prominent cardinals, however, were now convinced of the suitability of the Vatican—Pecci, Bartolini, Manning, Giovanni Simeoni, and eventually even Franchi, came to this opinion. Near the end of the session, Luigi Oreglia di Santo Stefano rose and began to deliver a long, rambling monologue favoring any site outside of Italy. After some moments, Ferrieri could contain his impatience no longer, "Let's go up in a balloon, Eminence, and hold the conclave there," he shouted. The resulting laughter silenced Oreglia, and concluded the debate. Di Pietro formally proposed the Vatican as the site, and the proposal was then voted on in the time-honored consistorial procedure of dropping a white ball into an urn for acceptance, black for rejection. Thirty-two of the balls were white, only five were black. Rome had been chosen.

Vincenzo Martinucci, an architect close to Pius IX, had been asked by the pope, in the preceding December, to design plans for a secure conclave in the Vatican, just in case the cardinals decided to assemble there. Pecci now told him to go forward with construction. Meanwhile, telegrams were dispatched in Pecci's name to the twenty-four absent cardinals pressing them to reach Rome as quickly as possible.

On the following day, February 10, there was a third meeting of the Roman cardinals. The first order of business was the display of the Fisherman's Ring, Pius's signet, which had been removed from the corpse by Pecci. The ceremony of shattering the ring to prevent its misuse was then performed by Di Pietro. The French cardinal Frederic de Falloux de Coudray asked that he might be given a small fragment, but his request was refused. After the conclusion of this rite, the cardinals began an open discussion on how advisable it was to decide in advance to choose another Italian for the papal throne. Only seven of the cardinals present were not Italian, but they were among the strongest supporters of the opinion that an Italian pope was an asset to the Church during a long period of difficulty with the Italian government. They represented some of the finest minds and longest experience in the College—Hohenlohe, Manning, Ledochowski, De Falloux, Johann Franzelin, Jean Baptiste Pitra, and Edward Howard. Since, collectively, they could be said to speak for the non-Italian Catholic world, the others tacitly joined them in determining to restrict the voting to Italian candidates.

Following this debate, Cardinal Bartolomeo D'Avanzo, bishop of Calvi and Teano, delivered an address in which he urged the cardinals to speed the selection of a new pope. Then the cardinals voted into office a committee of five to supervise the preparation of the conclave's quarters. Besides Pecci, the other members were Di Petro, Sacconi, Borromeo, and Giovanni Simeoni, Pius IX's last secretary of state.

Later that evening, Bilio, Panebianco, Manning, Monaco, and Nina, all went to dine with Bartolini. The latter escalated his attempts to get firm pledges of support for Pecci's candidacy; and, by the end of the reunion, all but Monaco agreed. The latter, a deeply conservative bureaucrat devoted to the policies of Antonelli, was one of a small number of cardinals, including Bilio and Oreglia, who were unwilling under any circumstances to have Pecci as pope.

Of those who attended Bartolini's dinner, Nina was the most enthusiastic convert. He volunteered at once to canvass the other cardinal-deacons on Pecci's behalf. By the following morning, he reported to Bartolini that three more cardinals had been won to the cause: De Falloux, Mertel, and Domenico Consolini.

At the fifth congregation, which met on the eleventh, Pecci announced that forty-one cardinals already were in Rome and that another nine were expected shortly. Consequently, since they foresaw no further delay, the cardinals voted to enter the conclave on the eighteenth, an earlier day than the maintenance of tradition permitted. While this meeting was in progress, more than five hundred workmen were busy in the Vatican putting up the walls and partitions that would isolate the College from the outside world during the course of the papal election. They completed the entire construction in one day.

The next six days were filled with the lengthy and elaborate funeral ceremonies for Pius, as well as with the smoothing of small details in the preparations for the conclave, including the nomination by each cardinal of two conclavists, one clerical and one lay, who would act as his personal attendants.

By the fourteenth, six more cardinals had arrived, including Joseph Guibert, the archbishop of Paris. He had taken up residence at the Palazzo Borghese and, since he was perhaps the most influential French member of the College, Bartolini hastened to call on him as soon as he arrived, in an attempt to obtain further support for Pecci. As soon as the two met Guibert bluntly asked, "Well, who's to be the pope." When the Roman replied that the chamberlain was the obvious choice, the Parisian was startled. He was for Bilio, he explained, because Pius IX had once gestured in the latter's direction when Guibert was present, saying "That is my successor." Guibert was sure that the elevation of Bilio was in keeping with the wishes of the dead pontiff, whom he revered. Moreover, the Parisian knew Bilio and found him congenial, but he was virtually unacquainted with Pecci. Bartolini informed Guibert that

Bilio had taken himself out of the running altogether. Still, Guibert supported him and withheld any offer of aid to Bartolini. After this meeting, Bartolini moved on to the Palazzo di Spagna, where Juan Ignacio Moreno y Maisonave, the archbishop of Toledo and primate of Spain, had just arrived. Moreno also got right to the point. Spain's cardinals were all solidly behind the candidature of Franchi, whom they knew and respected for his long tenure as nuncio in Madrid. Moreover, the Spaniard continued, the cardinals of his nation had met with representatives of the Spanish government, who likewise were in favor of Franchi. Bartolini stated that Franchi, like Bilio, was not a candidate by his own wish and that both of them were partisans for Pecci. Moreno, to put it softly, did not believe his Roman colleague. Bartolini left, leaving the task of persuading the Spanish to Franchi himself. The other Spanish cardinals, Paya y Rico, García-Gil, and Benavides y Navarrete, meanwhile also had arrived. Together, they paid a courtesy call on Franchi after which they repaired to their temporary Roman residences.

At nine in the morning of Friday the fifteenth began the first of the three principal funerals of Pius IX, which all the cardinals attended. Two hours later, forty-eight of them met in the Consistorial Hall to receive formally several members of the diplomatic corps who came to offer their official condolences. Once the ambassadors had departed, a general conversation ensued in which it was revealed that both France and Austria had made tentative arrangements to exercise their right of veto. Marshal MacMahon, the French president, had confided his country's right to Henri Boisnormand de Bonnechose, the archbishop of Rouen; while Franz Josef had given a similar privilege to Johann Simor, the Hungarian archbishop of Esztergom. Neither cardinal was willing to disclose whose election was to be thwarted, but rumor had it that both vetoes were against Bilio because of his rôle in helping Pius prepare the "Syllabus of Errors," a document most unpopular with several governments. Spain, the other nation with the power of exclusion, did not care to raise the issue in 1878.

Though Bartolini knew that Guibert exercised considerable influence over his compatriots, he felt it wise to call on three of them later that evening. How much he was able to persuade François

Auguste Ferdinand Donnet, René François Regnier, and Louis Marie Joseph Eusebe Caverot of Lyons, to his view is uncertain, but each of them doubtless felt flattered that so important a prelate as Bartolini would single him out for a visit during the crucial final days before the conclave began. This was perhaps particularly true of Regnier, the eighty-three-year-old archbishop of Cambrai, who, though he had been a cardinal for but four years, had been a bishop for thirty-five, and so felt that his age and experience were not receiving the consideration they deserved.

Bartolini was not, however, the only cardinal campaigning for his favorite candidate. The Austrian Jesuit, Johann Franzelin, was scurrying around feverishly trying to form an Austrian national party to spearhead the candidacy of Monaco. The latter, meanwhile, met with Oreglia and Randi, who agreed to begin a serious drive for the saintly and retiring Augustinian monk, Cardinal Tommaso Maria Martinelli. At the second requiem for Pius, on the sixteenth, signs of considerable strain began to appear in several of the cardinals, occasionally manifested in rude remarks addressed to each other. When Pecci stepped forward, flanked by Franchi and Guibert, to bless with holy water the temporary tomb of the dead pope, the waving of his hand over the cavity prompted Oreglia to call out, "Look at this one beat the bass drum," an allusion to Italian comedians announcing a performance. This rude jeer visibly disturbed the sensitive Pecci, and Guibert also was noticeably upset; Franchi, however, only laughed.

After the ceremony, fifty-four cardinals met in the last general congregation before the conclave, in which the principal order of business was the assignment of cells to the electors and their conclavists. All four floors of the ancient palace had been walled off for use as quarters, and so those cardinals who already had been given apartments by Pius IX found themselves back in their own rooms. To this class belonged Pecci, Simeoni, and Randi. Amat, now gravely ill, was given the cell closest to the Sistine Chapel, where the balloting was to take place. Ferrieri, on the other hand, perhaps in revenge for his caustic barbs which spared few of his colleagues, was given an isolated cell at the far end of the third floor, overlooking the Court of Gregory XIII. Most of the cardinals were content with their assignments; only a few sought to exchange with others. Pecci, for example, was at first given the rooms he had occupied during the last hours of Pius IX rather than his own apartments, which had been given to Bilio. The two met and effected an exchange. Oreglia complained that his allotted cell, number seventeen, was too humid and asked for another. He was then given number forty-one, right next to Pitra, so that the two most intransigent of the conservative cardinals were now together. Borromeo was now assigned seventeen, and uttered no complaint at all—but then Oreglia did not have to maintain the image of one who came from the family of a saint.

After these allotments had been made, the cardinals dispersed through the Vatican to examine their new quarters. They found each cell partitioned into four tiny rooms. The first was the cardinal's bedroom, the second for the clerical conclavist, the third for the lay attendant, and the fourth was a small dining area where visitors also might be received. Within the general enclosure, a set of kitchens had been constructed so that the cardinals no longer had to have food brought from their residences, as had been the case in former times. The cardinals pronounced themselves highly satisfied with this innovation, except Hohenlohe, a considerable gourmet, who insisted on having his meals catered from his residence. To some of the electors, this seemed too prideful, but those of his colleagues who knew him were aware that Hohenlohe had a deep abhorrence of pasta that amounted to a mania.

Within the reserved area, the cardinals found that facilities and quarters also had been provided for two doctors, a druggist, a number of maintenance men, and several prelates who were in charge of various aspects of daily ceremonial.

The inspection tour was not without dismay or amusement for some. Simeoni, glad to be assigned to the suite he had occupied while he served as Pius's cardinal-secretary of state, was nonplussed to find his apartments subdivided beyond belief and that he was now sharing his familiar space with no fewer than nine other cardinals. De Falloux, as the junior cardinal-deacon, had received the last allotment. He found cell number two permeated with a fetid stench that would not abate, no matter how much airing it was given. The next day, he thoughtfully provided himself with a large store of perfume as an antidote. Later, when this failed, he had his bed moved out into a nearby corridor—his poor conclavists simply had to endure.

At ten o'clock on the morning of Sunday, the seventeenth, the last of the funerals of Pius IX was celebrated in the Sistine Chapel. After the dispersal of the cardinals for lunch, Bilio encountered Bartolini. The latter asked the cardinal-bishop why he was now supporting Martinelli for the throne. Bilio responded that the present times were like those when Pius VI had died. Then, in Venice in 1800, the cardinals had bypassed the most influential and intellectual among themselves to elect Barnabà Chiaramonti as Pius VII. Bilio characterized Chiaramonti as a humble monk of no great education who had been made a cardinal simply because he was a cousin of Pius VI, and yet Pius VII had proven the most able of the popes of the preceding century. Bartolini countered this argument by pointing out that Chiaramonti was not ignorant—he had taught philosophy at the University of Perugia—and had governed his diocese of Imola very well indeed. Moreover, Pius IX recently had acquired the correspondence of Chiaramonti when a cardinal, and the letters showed that he was a man who was very able to deal directly and competently with persons of every social and political position. Bilio remained unmoved by this indirect comparison with Pecci and continued his support of Martinelli's cause.

By this time, additional politicking could have but little effect on the cardinals who had been in Rome during the preceding two weeks. Their private deliberations had produced a clear definition of a number of parties that adhered to favored candidates. The party supporting Pecci, lead by Bartolini, included Franchi, Manning, and Nina, as well as De Falloux, Mertel, and Consolini. Martinelli was the favorite of Randi, Monaco, Bilio, and Oreglia. Between these two extremes were a number of smaller groupings. The four Spanish cardinals were united in their support of Franchi, and Hohenlohe leaned towards him as well. A number of cardinals with no declared candidate were united in opposing Pecci, including Amat, Chigi, Pietro Giannelli, and Pitra; while Howard supported Simeoni, and Franzelin was for Monaco. The two imponderables which ultimately would decide the issue were whether or not the cardinals who were opposed to Pecci could settle among themselves on one major candidate, and to whom the foreign cardinals eventually would give their votes, since their views on the election were still unrevealed to the cardinals who resided in Rome.

On Sunday evening, Pius was entombed, and then the cardinals returned to their residences for a last night's rest in their own beds before they began the task of supplying the Church with a new head. On Monday morning, all the electors entered the Vatican and went directly to the Pauline Chapel for the Mass of the Holy Spirit, chanted by Cardinal Friedrich von Schwarzenberg, the most senior of the cardinal-priests. They then adjourned to the Sistine for a formal oration on their duties and responsibilities, delivered by Monsignor Francesco Mercurelli, Pius IX's secretary of Latin letters to princes. Once these ceremonies were concluded, a little after noon, the cardinals were given a chance to return to their normal quarters and pack for their stay in the conclave. Pecci remained in the Vatican, with De Luca for company, as did Simeoni, Randi, and Ledochowski, whose belongings already were in the palace. Borromeo hastened off to establish a checkpoint at which to examine the credentials of the conclavists and other servants who were now beginning to enter the Vatican in great numbers.

A little before four o'clock, the cardinals began to return. A considerable crowd of sightseers had gathered to see them go in and to speculate, as the violet-robed figures passed, on which of them would emerge as the next pontiff.

In the popular imagination, Pecci was not an important figure. Yet, a number of the most farseeing had indicated in print that he was clearly the best choice for the job. In 1877, for example, Ruggiero Bonghi, a keen political commentator on Church affairs, had written in his volume, *Il conclave e il papa futuro*, that Pecci would, in fact, be the next pope. More recently, a number of newspapers, including the London *Times*, also had devoted space to mentioning the suitability of the chamberlain. Tradition, however, was against him. It was held generally that it was unthinkable that either the chamberlain or the secretary of state of the last pope should be elevated to the throne, for to do so would seem too strong a tie to the policies of the reign that had just ended. No matter how wise or astute the policies of the dead pope might have been, the College was mindful that the maintenance of any policy for too long was likely to lead to political and intellectual sterility, and of this opinion the populace in the Eternal City was well aware. In the fairly recent past, as the Church measures time, a secretary of state had ascended the throne—in 1667, when Guilio Rospigliosi became Clement IX; but no chamberlain had been elected pope since Cencio Savelli became Honorius III in 1216.

At four o'clock, the Sacred College once again assembled in the Pauline Chapel in an atmosphere of considerable confusion, occasioned in part by the fact that the Roman residents had been accompanied to the Vatican by many members of their families, their staff, and their retainers, all of whom had to be urged away gently. The formal procession of the College into the conclave then began, as the cardinals walked, two by two, into the Sistine. In keeping with tradition, the Sistine had been furnished with a throne for each of the sixty-four potential electors. Four of these, those of Amat, Schwarzenberg, Fabio Asquini, and Domenico Carafa, were covered with green serge upholstery and provided with green canopies of the same material, which indicated that they had been made cardinals before the time of Pius IX. All of the remainder were provided with violet fittings, which told that they were cardinals who owed their rank to the favor of the recently-deceased pope.

At thirty-five minutes past five, the secretary of the Sacred College, Monsignor Pietro Lasagni, announced "extra omnes," the signal that everyone who was not to be immured must leave. The external guardian of the conclave's security, the Marshal of the Conclave, Prince Mario Chigi, a brother of the cardinal, together with Pecci then concluded the final formalities by locking the doors on each side. The conclave had begun.

The first task was a thorough inspection of the entire premises to ensure that no unauthorized persons had secreted themselves in the area. Then came a final inspection of the credentials of those present. This set of chores took nearly two hours and was conducted under the personal supervision of Pecci.

This conclave was the largest one held thus far in the history of the Church, not because there were sixty electors—other conclaves had seen as many—but because the staff of cooks and servants were for the first time included within the conclave walls. In spite of this, and the confusion that was engendered by the fact that this was the first papal election to be held in the Vatican in more than a century, security was perfect. Not a few of those present were impressed by the excellent job done by the chamberlain in preparing the conclave so swiftly.

At eight o'clock, the cardinals dined on soup, boiled meat, pasta and vegetables, accompanied by white and red wines of good vintages, followed by a large dessert. Meanwhile, in another hall, the conclavists and valets were dining from a buffet of cheese, salads, and fruits, washed down with ample quantities of wine. Everyone seemed satisfied with the culinary arrangements, except, of course, Hohenlohe.

Because of these arrangements, the Roman crowds were deprived of the long, colorful procession of servants who, in former vacancies, had brought meals to the cardinals three times each day. They had now to be content with the vision of Hohenlohe's butler passing a single large tray through the windowless revolving door, the *ruota*, which was the only means of communication between the College and the outside world. This curious device, which was invented by Paris de Grassis, papal master of ceremonies, for the second conclave in 1503—which saw the election of Julius II—was used in every conclave afterward, although some Renaissance and Baroque elections were so open that the device was a decoration. Since it was the obvious symbol of the official isolation of the cardinals during a conclave, it often was described by commentators on Rome and the papal elections. Thomas Jefferson, probably while he was ambassador in Paris, read an account of the *ruota*. Always eager for new knowledge and how it could be applied to the circumstances of the day, he had one installed between his dining room and the adjacent corridor at Monticello, so that servants need not pass into the room while he was entertaining his guests— he served them from his side of the door by himself. In this way, conversation over dinner at the Sage's home could be infinitely more open and revealing, without any danger of being overheard by the household staff, who placed meals on the shelves while the *ruota* faced the passage and then turned it a half-rotation, thus ensuring complete privacy—turning each Jeffersonian dinner into a little conclave.

At the end of the dinner, the cardinals and their attendants retired to their cells for rest. Silence did not pervade the area, however, as conclavists scurried from cell to cell carrying messages from their masters, and, occasionally, a bit of purple could be seen in the candlelight as the cardinals visited one another.

When they arose, at seven thirty, the College went to Mass, after which they were served cocoa and cafe-au-lait. They then entered the Sistine for the taking of the first ballot. In front of each throne they found a small flat desk, upon which had been placed a case that contained large sheets of notepaper stamped with the signet of the papal palace, an inkwell, pens, pencils, and a list of the cardinals in large type.

In the center of the chapel stood a long table covered with a stiff cloth on which stood two large gold vases. One, a chalice covered with a small plate, was the depository for the ballots. The other, similar to a pyx, was a counting receptacle, in which each cardinal deposited a small wooden ball after voting. During the actual canvass, both urns reposed on the chapel altar after which they were taken to the central table for the counting of ballots and balls together, a formality which ensured that each elector had voted only once. On the same table, on one side, stood a small black lockbox provided for the committee of three cardinals, called infirmarians, who were to go to the cells of cardinals who were too sick to come to the chapel and obtain their ballots. Amat, who had to be carried in a litter from his residence to his cell, made use of the services of the infirmarians at each vote, while, at the first canvass, Giannelli was also absent. The central table also was provided with supplies for another board of three cardinals, called scrutators, who counted the ballots and announced the results, as well as with blank ballots for distribution during the two votes held each day.

Each vote was divided into two separate procedures. The first, the scrutiny, was a vote by secret ballot. The second, the *accessus*, allowed each cardinal to change his vote once in favor of another candidate, if he chose to do that.

In addition, the chapel had two small retiring rooms, one of which contained a buffet of wine and crackers for the suddenly famished.

Just before the balloting began, the three infirmarians and the three scrutators were chosen by lot. The former were Pecci, Oreglia, and Luigi Di Canossa; the latter were Borromeo, Antonio Antonucci, and Luigi Serafini. This process, and the seating of the cardinals, was attended by considerable uproar and confusion, since all but four of the electors had never participated in a conclave before and were uncertain what to do or where to place themselves.

The actual voting began at eleven and was concluded in an hour. Each cardinal stepped forward, in order of seniority, and announced to his colleagues that he was about to vote for the candidate he believed best suited to occupy the papal office. After this declaration, he placed his ballot first on the chalice cover, and then tipped the lid so that the paper fell into the urn. Turning slightly to one side, he then dropped his counter into the second urn and resumed his throne.

While the procession to the altar continued, many members of the College, impressed with the drama of both the occasion and their surroundings, chatted in low voices with their neighbors. A number of them were impressed with the theatrical effect of the tall, aristocratic Howard, in his violet robes, enthroned between the short, dark forms of Paya y Rico and García-Gil, who wore the black and white robes of Dominican friars despite their rank as cardinals.

The counting began after De Falloux, the junior cardinal-deacon, had voted. The scrutators announced almost immediately that the whole procedure would have to be voided because two cardinals had violated the mandatory secrecy. One had not sealed his ballot at all, and another had used his personal signet for that purpose, so that his coat of arms was stamped visibly on the paper. The latter was François Auguste Ferdinand Donnet, the archbishop of Bordeaux. Nevertheless, it was decided to announce the results, to give the College a chance to see if any pattern was emerging. The results were:

| Filippo Maria Guidi | 1 |
| Luigi Bilio | 7 |

Gioacchino Pecci	19
Anton Maria Panebianco	4
Antonino De Luca	5
Innocenzo Ferrieri	3
Raffaele Monaco	4
Alessandro Franchi	5
Tommaso Maria Martinelli	1
Mieczyslaw Ledochowski	1
Giovanni Simeoni	4
Luigi Di Canossa	1
Vincenzo Moretti	2
Prospero Caterini	1
Lorenzo Nina	1
Teodolfo Mertel	1

Because the vote was voided, the cardinals did not hold an *accessus*. Bartolini exploded! His huge frame shook, and his bellowings were clearly audible to the conclavists who were gathered in the Ducal Hall, some distance away. The cardinal's first available target was the master of ceremonies nearest to him. Why, he wanted to know, had the non-Roman cardinals not been instructed fully in the correct procedure for voting. The errors which produced an invalid scrutiny were clearly the fault of Lasagni and his staff, who had not fulfilled their responsibilities. The blushing staff of the Sacred College did not dare to venture a reply. The next portion of Bartolini's tirade was vented on his brother cardinals. Had they not sworn before God, he raged, to vote for the best man. How could any of them vote for a wag like Ferrieri or for candidates who already had excluded themselves publicly, like Bilio and Franchi. If they had indeed voted for the best man, Pecci would not have received only nineteen votes. Bartolini screamed that he had been betrayed by so many who had promised their votes to the cause. In silence, Borromeo burned the ballots in the little stove that had been installed at the entrance to the chapel, and the ensuing black smoke told the Romans they did not yet have a new pope.

After Bartolini's outburst, the cardinals dispersed, and the infuriated Roman's principal conclavist, Father Generoso Calenzio, tried to soothe his master's rage by pointing out that the chamberlain's opponents had made no headway, that Bilio had kept his promise of non-candidacy, and that Martinelli's candidacy was foundering.

At three o'clock, after a light lunch, the College was once more in the Sistine for the second ballot. In this session, Giannelli appeared, so the infirmarians had to leave the chapel only to retrieve Amat's ballot. On this occasion, the infirmarians were Sacconi, Serafini, and Jozef Mihalovic; while the scrutators were Berardi, Simeoni, and Consolini.

Considerably sobered by Bartolini's outburst, the cardinals carried out the ritual of voting in silence. The results were:

Filippo Maria Guidi	1
Luigi Bilio	7
Gioacchino Pecci	26
Anton Maria Panebianco	4
Innocenzo Ferrieri	1
Raffaele Monaco	4
Alessandro Franchi	3
Antonino De Luca	3
Tommaso Maria Martinelli	2
Mieczyslaw Ledochowski	1
Giovanni Simeoni	2
Luigi Di Canossa	1
Lucido Maria Parocchi	1
Vincenzo Moretti	1
Prospero Caterini	1
Teodolfo Mertel	1

The issue was becoming clearer. In spite of the official secrecy, many of the cardinals knew who was giving each candidate support, thanks to their extensive evenings of gossip and debate. Amat was voting for Canossa, Randi for Martinelli, Howard for Simeoni, and some of the Spanish for Franchi; but Pecci had picked up seven more votes, primarily at the expense of De Luca, Ferrieri, Franchi, and Simeoni. Bartolini's sheep were returning to the fold. Pecci's increase would have been greater still had not one voter written "Picchino" for the chamberlain's name thus invalidating that ballot. Somewhat snidely, the Roman cardinals laid the blame for this slip on one of the German or Spanish cardinals.

Enea Sbarretti, curiously enough, was voting for the aged and decrepit cardinal-archdeacon Caterini, because he felt that the latter was the one possible pope who could never leave Rome, for whatever reason, because of his physical condition.

The *accessus* was then performed. In it, the chamberlain received eight more votes, bringing his total to thirty-four. Simeoni received three additional votes; Bilio, Monaco, Franchi, and Caterini each got two more, while Mertel found another adherent.

The cardinals then left the Sistine for dinner. Bartolini was cheered considerably by the progress made by Pecci in the afternoon's voting, as were his friends, Nina, Franchi, and De Falloux. On the other hand, there was no cheer at all at the tables of the archconservatives, Sacconi, Monaco, Randi, Oreglia, and Franzelin.

During the course of the afternoon scrutiny, Pecci had carried on a rambling conversation with Donnet, who occupied the adjacent throne. As his name was called by the scrutators more and more frequently, the chamberlain became agitated and confused visibly, and finally dropped his pen on the floor as his hands began to shake. Donnet leaned toward him and quietly said, "Courage, there is no question here of you; but rather the question of the Church and the future of the world." At one point Hohenlohe passed quite close to Pecci, who said to him, "Don't give me your vote, Eminence." The German prince replied, "Your Eminence was a papal delegate and understands temporal government; was a nuncio and knows diplomacy; and is a bishop and understands the government of the Church," thus affirming that the chamberlain was indeed his choice.

In the early evening, a message was passed through the grate for the chamberlain from Prince Chigi which stated that Cardinal Ignacio do Nascimento Moraes y Cardoso, the patriarch of Lisbon, had arrived and desired to enter. The doors were unlocked on either side, and the primate of Portugal entered with his attendants. When it was time for Moraes to be shown to his quarters, after a formal reception in the Pauline Chapel, Pecci had become so agitated that he had lost the key to the cell of the Portuguese primate, and the door had to be forced by a servant. Moraes's arrival brought the total number of cardinals in conclave to sixty-one, its final number. The three not in attendance were Geoffroy Brossais Saint-Marc of Rennes, who was too ill to come; and both Paul Cullen of Armagh and John McCloskey of New York, who were en route to Rome during the conclave.

Few of the cardinals or their servants could sleep at all during the night of the nineteenth. All of them were aware that the denouement was near and that Pecci likely would preside over the Church on the morrow, perhaps leading her on a very different course from the one charted by Pius IX in his third-of-a-century reign. For the Roman princes, it was the acme of their clerical lives, for the election of a pope was the highest privilege of their office and, since only four of the sixty-one now present had ever performed that function before, most of those who now voted were aware that they were unlikely ever again to be present at such a meeting.

Whatever feverish activity had taken place the night before was now eclipsed, as cardinals and conclavists alike gathered together in twos and threes to consider their rôles in the conclave and in history.

A number of the more powerful cardinals, including Bilio, Monaco, Ferrieri, Franchi, and Hohenlohe, repaired to the cell of Amat to give him all the gossip from the Sistine. Most of the crowd in the dean's cell eagerly expected the election of Pecci in the morning. But Bilio could not stomach the chamberlain at all, and his dissatisfaction was evident in his manner. Amat, with considerable irony in his tone, told Bilio, "You must not have any fear, Eminence."

In Bartolini's cell, a number of conclavists gathered together with Lasagni and other members of the conclave's staff, chatting at length over what name the new pope would choose. One or two of the more knowledgeable or prescient called attention to Pecci's fondness for Leo XII and predicted he would select the same name.

Generoso Calenzio was not at that meeting. Bartolini's convivial, well-known conclavist was searching for the cell of Ferrieri in the dim light but could not find it. In his wanderings, he came upon the staircase which led to the apartments of the secretary of state, near Pecci's cell. There he met Canon Frederico Foschi, the chamberlain's conclavist, who had a truly woebegone appearance. Calenzio, surprised at his demeanor, asked, "What's the matter? You should be happy, since tomorrow you will have as pope your bishop and father." "So I hear," responded Foschi. "And the cardinal, what is he doing?" continued Calenzio. Foschi replied, "He is in the next room. He has received no one and is completely agitated and pensive; he trembles and sighs, and calls on God. He is like a ship overtaken by an unexpected storm. I am so distressed about him." Calenzio then asked to be allowed to speak with the chamberlain. As soon as Pecci was made aware of the presence of the conclavists outside, he called out, "Come, good Father Calenzio." Pecci was sitting with his back to a window which overlooked the Piazza di San Pietro. The cardinal's emotional near-collapse was readily apparent. Calenzio stepped forward, "Your Eminence, and in such a state."

"Do you know what they want of me?" responded the chamberlain. "I know everything, and you have all too much reason to be troubled. The Church today is a vineyard full of thorns, surrounded by death-dealing serpents, and the hand of the vigilant husbandman risks being torn or bitten wherever he touches. In the place of Your Eminence, I, too, should shudder, even as you do, or rather more. But what does such shuddering avail the Church? Peter's ship is without a pilot, and unless Your Eminence takes the helm, who else can do so? No one has received as many votes as Your Eminence."

"But I am advanced in age, and not too strong in health. I cannot accept so enormous a burden. I shall fall under it in a few days. It is not the papacy, but death, that is offered to me."

"Your Eminence, the present position of the Church has come about through no faults of ours. God willed that it should reach us in this state. It is the wish of God, and not of men, that Your Eminence should be pope. Is it man's work that in one day nearly forty votes should fall on one person? Is it a man's work that the foreign cardinals, in number greater than has ever been known in any conclave, should vote in unison? Therefore, the exaltation of Your

Eminence is an act of God. Beware how tomorrow you refuse a dignity that comes from Him. The burden is immense, the condition of the Church lamentable, the chalice most bitter, but Your Eminence will not have forgotten the solemn promise made to the Church when you received your first tonsure: 'The Lord is the portion of mine inheritance and of my cup: thou maintainest my lot! (Ps 16:5).' Would you have the heritage without the bitterness? The chalice is indeed most bitter, but it is God's will that you should drink it. The divine will must not be gainsaid."

"But I have wholly resolved to renounce the papacy."

"Let Your Eminence beware how you give such scandal to your colleagues. I will say to Your Eminence what on a similar occasion was said by a French conclavist to Cardinal Albani, unanimously elected pope, and resolved not to be so: 'The renunciation of the highest honors is not a sign of humility but a manifest sign of vainglory.' That is a sentence from the Pastoral Rule of Gregory the Great. Would you give way to vainglory and refuse to yield to the divine will that would have you pope? You have certainly never intrigued for votes. Does not your conscience bear witness that you need have no remorse for sacrilegious ambition? God, not men, assembled so great a number of votes. Accept, obey, edify the Church, or else the conclave will go on for ages, and you and the whole of the Sacred College will be ill-spoken of among the faithful. So you must obey, and that's all there is to it."

"But our life is so short," the chamberlain said.

"Possibly. But it is God who makes the weak strong, and many popes elected in poor health governed the Church for years. Paul III was weak and old, and he governed well for more than fifteen years. Our life is not in our power. It is God who shortens or lengthens our days."

"But do you not see my feeble strength? My pontificate will be very short, and the conclave will have to be held again immediately, and difficulties will increase. My pontificate will be as short as that of Marcellus II."

"Your Eminence, that depends on God, and if God for His glory wishes you to be pope even for only a few days, what does it matter? When He judges pontificates, He does not measure the years a pope has lived, but his good intentions and the good he has endeavored to do. Even were you to be like Leo XI, who lived an even shorter time than Marcellus II. But the Church was edified by that brief government, so that today we read upon his tomb: 'Having shown greater things than the time that was given him.' Religious culture, the only thing which remains to aid us, needs support, and, finding in yourself one who loves it, may restore to us that which we have lost. Alexander VII, too, did not wish to accept, and yet he had to submit to the heavy burden. Alexander VII was a friend of literary men, and Pallavicini who received Flavio Chigi into the academy he had founded, when he had become a Jesuit and a famous author, was chosen a cardinal by Chigi to that office he so adorned rather by the friend than by the pontiff. Those times must return."

"So there is nothing for it but for me to give way?"

"Your Eminence, it is God's will."

"Well, then, I will repeat the two lines that fell from the lips of Alexander VII, whom you have mentioned, when he was in the same distress as myself: 'Already, unless I err, the day is here, which, as you wished, O gods, ever to me, shall be to honor and to bitterness.'"

Calenzio, at this point convinced that he finally had swayed Pecci to accept Bartolini's plan, took his leave and continued his search for Ferrieri, whom he discovered at last in the middle of the night. The usually sarcastic cardinal greeted Calenzio with the blunt summation, "In brief, they say Pecci for pope." Calenzio responded that it was God's will, but Ferrieri was not so willing to bow quickly before another man's elucidation of the divine plan. He carefully reviewed for the conclavist all the reasons which militated against choosing the chamberlain, but concluded his monologue by agreeing that Pecci was the best candidate and promised to vote for him in the morning.

Just about everyone was moving about in the darkness. Among those trying to forward the election of Pecci was De Falloux. Driven from his cell by the foul stench, he spent most of the night conversing with Amat in the hope that he could win the dean of the College to his cause, but he had no success.

The morning of Wednesday, February 20, 1878, dawned clear and surprisingly warm in Rome. The cardinals had their usual hot chocolate or cafe-au-lait and then made their way, in various states of exhaustion, to the Pauline Chapel where Mass was said at eight o'clock. Afterwards, sixty of them went to the Sistine to begin preparations for the morning scrutiny, which nearly all concerned believed would be the last. The final thrust by the conservatives occurred just when Randi entered the chapel and saw Bartolini on one side. He grimly marched up to Pecci's major campaigner and bitterly stated, "You take sides for Pecci. Why such a hurry for an election, everything should be done with deliberation." Bartolini replied, "I stay as I am, and I follow my conscience." "No," replied the other, "you drag the others after you." "No, I stay as a I am," boomed Bartolini. Randi began to stutter: "You. . . you. . . ." "Anyhow, don't bother me again," concluded the pope-maker.

Antonio Pellegrini was given the task of drawing the names of the scrutators and the infirmarians. The first three were Regnier, Mihalovic, and Moraes y Cardoso; the latter were García-Gil, Mertel, and Oreglia. During this process of preparation, Pecci entered the chapel, the last cardinal to do so. Every eye turned towards him for some clue to his reaction to the knowledge that within two hours he would be the new pope. His face seemed drained of all color, and his evident agitation gave every appearance of fright. He made his way stiffly to Bartolini's side and said, "Since you want it, Eminence, and many others will vote to have me as pope, are you pleased with the name Leo XIII, in memory of Leo XII, whom I always esteemed?" Bartolini calmly replied, "Call yourself Leo XIII, Eminence, by all means."

A number of the cardinals seeing the exchange importuned Bartolini to know the subject of the conversation. The latter, however, steadfastly refused to reveal what had taken place. Franzelin guessed that the future papal name had been the topic and asked Bartolini if the chamberlain would be Pius X. The latter said no, at which point Simor joined them, saying that he was sure Bartolini knew the chosen name. He knew it, confided the Roman, but had promised secrecy. Simor insisted on the knowledge, offering Pius X, Clement XV, and Benedict XV, as possible options. Now Franzelin chimed in again with John XXV. "Oh, let it go," chided Bartolini, turning away. A little afterward, after reflection, Bartolini did confide to Simor that Pecci was to be called Leo XIII.

The Socialist Pope

At eleven the voting began. The infirmarians went to Amat's cell to collect his ballot and, on their return, the ceremonial of the long march to the Sistine altar was enacted once more.

During the counting of the ballots which followed, a ripple of chuckles ran through the chapel when the scrutators read one which was marked "for no one." As the enumeration continued, the chamberlain stood silently at his throne, staring straight ahead. At the conclusion, he had received forty-four votes, three more than the number necessary for election, and the scrutators concluded their work by announcing, "Pecci—electus." The chamberlain's nearest rival, Bilio, had received four votes; Panebianco, Monaco, and Simeoni had two each; while Schwarzenberg, Ferrieri, Martinelli, Di Canossa, Moretti, and Caterini each had one.

Pecci sank back onto his throne and closed his eyes. Immediately, the other cardinals lowered the canopies over their thrones so that only the one above number eleven remained elevated. Franchi shattered the silence by beginning to applaud vigorously. Soon, he was joined by others, many of whom began to cheer loudly. Di Pietro, performing the duty of the absent Amat, ordered the doors of the Sistine opened, so that Lasagni and Martinucci could enter to witness the formal interrogation of Pecci's acceptance. When they had arrived, Di Pietro, accompanied by Schwarzenberg, the senior cardinal-priest, and Caterini, the senior cardinal-deacon, approached Pecci's throne and asked him, "Do you accept the lawfully held election of yourself as sovereign pontiff?" Pecci rose, and silence fell in the Sistine. "Since God wills that I assume the papacy, I will not contradict." Di Pietro continued, "By what name will you be known." "That of Leo XIII, out of the deference and gratitude I have always had for Leo XII and the veneration of Saint Leo I have had since my youth," responded the new pope. It was just a few minutes short of one o'clock.

Consolini and Mertel then came forward to conduct the pope to a small robing room, where Foschi and Baldassari, the conclavist and valet of the former chamberlain, were admitted to help Leo into one of the three sets of papal robes prepared in advance. Outside the chapel, meanwhile, the other inhabitants of the conclave learned of Pecci's election when Lasagni poked his head outside the door and said, "So we have Pecci, who's calling himself Leo

XIII." The conclavists and servants broke into applause. Calenzio tried to quiet them, saying that such behavior was not seemly for ecclesiastics, and urged them to congregate in the Pauline Chapel to pray. He was largely ignored.

Inside, all semblance of order broke down as well. The cardinals gathered in little groups to speculate openly on the voting in the last ballot. Amat was identified readily as having given his vote to Cannosa, while Sbarretti's vote for Caterini and Di Pietro's for Schwarzenberg were fairly well known, too. The general speculation decided that D'Avanzo and Martinelli had voted for Panebianco. It was uncertain, as rumor and discussion mounted, whether Bilio or Monaco had given the one vote to Martinelli. Pecci voted always for Bilio. Among the other cardinals who did not vote for Pecci, Oreglia, Chigi, Randi, Sacconi, and Franzelin were identified easily. Thus the thirteen principal cardinals who opposed the elevation of the chamberlain were settled in the minds of the College. The other four who did not vote for Leo XIII were cardinals who never revealed their intentions during the course of the conclave, and remain unknown today.

Leo, who, during the robing, had been given some wine and a few crackers to help to restore his color, now emerged to receive the first homage of the Sacred College. Bartolini, Franchi, and De Luca came forward in their turn with obvious demonstrations of unaffected joy. Randi, Monaco, Oreglia, and Sacconi, on the other hand, were hard pressed to simulate satisfaction. Guibert took the opportunity to ask that the first papal blessing be sent to his beloved Paris, while Asquini was so moved that he could only grasp Leo's hand and repeatedly kiss it.

Outside in the Piazza, the crowd already knew of the election of a new pope from the white smoke which appeared when the ballots were burned. The distinction of announcing a papal election to the people belongs to the archdeacon, and Caterini, in spite of his eighty-two years and feebleness, was not about to yield this privilege to Mertel, his immediate junior. Preceded by the masters of ceremonies and accompanied by a crowd of conclavists, the old man made his way slowly through the halls and stairs to the balcony in the interior façade of the basilica, whose windows had been opened. At 1:20 P.M., he stepped onto the balcony and began the age-old formula, "Annuntio vobis," and then stopped, physically drained and overcome with emotion. One of the masters of ceremonies, Antonio Cataldi, whispered to him, "Courage, Eminence," and Caterini drew himself up for another attempt but the effort had been too much and the archdeacon could only stammer, "Annuntio. . . annuntio. . . ." Impatient voices in the crowd now began to shout up demanding the name of the new bishop of Rome, and in some areas of the crowd their were signs of disturbance. At that moment, Bartolomeo Grassi-Landi, Oreglia's conclavist, shouted down to the throng in Italian, "Cardinal Pecci with the name of Leo XIII." Then the people began to cheer and the bells of Saint Peter's to peal.

Leo did not break up the conclave at once, however, but rather ordered everyone to lunch while he retired for a brief rest. During this time, a number of cardinals debated whether the first public papal blessing should be delivered from a window facing inside the basilica, because they feared hostile demonstrations from radical anti-clericalists in the crowd if the outer loggia were used. This opinion, which Bartolini, for one, supported, prevailed. At four, Leo left his cell for the last time and ordered the conclave disbanded. A little more than a half hour later, he gave his blessing, *urbi et orbi*, to a gathering of more than 30,000 who had crowded into the world's largest Christian church.

The reign of Leo XIII had begun. When it ended, a quarter century later, Gioacchino Pecci had led the Church firmly, with clear and measured steps, into the modern world, while raising the spiritual prestige of the papacy to a height it had not enjoyed perhaps since the thirteenth century. His reign, second in length only to that of Pius IX in the history of the Church, fully justified the confidence and enthusiasm of Domenico Bartolini, the Roman peasant boy risen to cardinal, who was chiefly responsible for engineering Pecci's rise.

III
VETO

Leo XIII was one of the outstanding popes in the Church's history, but the conduct of the conclave after his death was marred by several political and procedural blunders which virtually suspended, for more than a decade, much of his forward-looking policy of political modernization.

As in 1878, the Sacred College had ample time to consider their duty of election while Leo yet lived. In March, 1899, the pontiff underwent surgery for the removal on an enlarged cyst in his side, and from then on his health steadily declined. By the early spring of 1903, it was evident that the ninety-three-year-old pope had but a short time to live. Throughout the next several months, Leo was well aware that preliminary negotiations among the cardinals over the choice of his successor were underway. In June, a substantial number of cardinals, prompted by a rumor that the pope was near death, hastened to Rome. Leo used the occasion to summon a general consistory on June 22, at which seven new cardinals were named. At the outset of this session Leo glanced over the assembled College and grimly remarked, "Dear brethren, I am happy to announce to this consistory which I have summoned that this is to be a consistory, and not a conclave." Nevertheless, the pope's pale, emaciated form and his feeble voice gave every indication that the reign soon would end.

During his pontificate, Leo gave no hint to the cardinals of his own choice for a successor, but his complex conciliatory political policy, which seemed everywhere successful in raising the popular estimation of the papacy, was administered during the last decade and a half of the reign by one of the ablest of modern cardinal-secretaries of state, Mariano Rampolla del Tindaro. By 1903, the forty-nine-year-old Sicilian, who had once been papal ambassador to Madrid, was generally regarded as the logical choice to follow in the footsteps of Leo. Rampolla's sixteen years in the cardinalate made him one of the more senior members of the college, and his like term as secretary of state had given him wide experience in dealing with every sort of problem facing the Church in the modern world. As Leo passed into his nineties, his increasing infirmity led the pace of papal government to slow materially, yet the pope maintained the clarity and vigor of his mind and his grasp of affairs until the last moments of his life. Since the pope left more and more of the daily affairs of the Vatican in Rampolla's hands during this period, and seemed in every way satisfied with the results, it is possible to conclude that Rampolla was indeed the cardinal whom Leo most desired to have on the throne after him.

Side by side with the wisdom of discovering and advancing Rampolla, however, was Leo's great blunder, in May 1885, in raising to his own former office of chamberlain Luigi Oreglia di Santo Stefano. Oreglia was one of the most reactionary of the arch-conservative cardinals under Pius IX and had vehemently opposed Pecci's elevation to the papal chair in 1878. Perhaps Leo did not expect Oreglia to outlive him, or perhaps pressure within the highest levels of Church administration was brought to bear on the pope to advance an arch-conservative to so lofty an office as a political counterpoise to Leo's own progressive policy. In any case, Oreglia lived on, rising to become cardinal-bishop of Ostia and Velletri and dean of the Sacred College, as well as chamberlain, by the summer of 1903. He was, by this time, the only cardinal not elevated to the College by Leo himself. The powers which he would exercise as chamberlain and as dean during the next vacancy were so considerable as to represent a threat to the continuation of Leo's policies.

By late June, the pope was growing visibly more feeble day by day, and quiet but active preparations began for the coming conclave. The Italian government placed two provincial regiments on alert as a reinforcement to come to Rome in case force was needed to maintain public order.

On July 3, the Vatican's semi-official newspaper, *Osservatore Romano*, published a notice that all the pope's audiences and receptions had been abandoned; this statement was interpreted by many members of the College as the signal to begin preparing for a journey to Rome. On the following day, public word was issued that the pope was indeed seriously ill. On Tuesday, July 7, Oreglia ordered that telegrams be dispatched to all the absent cardinals asking them to prepare for the conclave. This decision, probably made without Leo's knowledge, was reached in a conference held two days before between Oreglia, Rampolla, and Girolamo Maria Gotti, the powerful cardinal-prefect of the congregation for the propagation of the faith.

In spite of every expectation, Leo held on to life with a serenity and an exercise of will that passed the imaginations of those about him. Several crises during the next two weeks were overcome successfully, and some began to voice the hope that the pontiff might recover. But his strength was exhausted, his constitution shattered, and at 2:45 P.M. on Monday, July 20, he suffered a heart attack which heralded the end. A few minutes before four o'clock, the majordomo of the palace, Gaetano Bisleti, bent over Leo and asked for a blessing. The pope, lucid still, raised his arm in benediction and quietly said, "This is the end," after which he sank back and lost consciousness. It was four o'clock. Four minutes later, without any disturbance at all, he was dead.

As soon as the physicians had certified that Leo was truly gone, Oreglia, who also was present, ordered the Swiss guards to shut all the gates of the Vatican. Then he dismissed all those present from the papal apartments.

At 9:30 on the following morning, the chamberlain returned to the deathbed to secure the Fisherman's Ring so that it might be shattered before the assembled cardinals in the first general congregation, which was to meet later in the day. Leo, departing from custom, had not worn the ring during the last years of his reign but had left it in the care of one of his private chamberlains. Now it was discovered to be missing. Not being able to resolve the question of the ring before the arrival of the other cardinals, Oreglia simply let the matter lapse. An hour afterwards, the nineteen other cardinals in Rome made a formal visitation to the death chamber, after which they assembled in the Consistorial Hall for the first congregation.

The major business to be settled at once was the voting into office of a new secretary of the Sacred College, since the former incumbent had died a few days before Leo. The choice of the cardinals was Raffaele Merry del Val, a young Anglo-Spanish prelate who, at thirty-seven, was already titular archbishop of Nicea. The elevation of Merry del Val, with the support of Oreglia, would prove to be of great importance for the coming reign.

The second congregation, held on July 22, saw the number of cardinals present rise to twenty-seven. At this session, the program of Leo's funeral ceremonies was agreed upon. The third congregation, on the next day, elected a committee of three cardinals to superintend the physical preparation of the conclave. This committee, consisting of Giovanni Battista Casali del Drago, Francesco Salesio della Volpe, and the archdeacon, Luigi Macchi, ordered that the plan developed by Martinucci in 1878 be used once again, and that construction begin at once. The twenty-nine cardinals in the third congregation also gave out appointments to various functionaries of the conclave, including the major confessor, physicians, surgeons, and the resident druggist.

By Friday the twenty-fourth, thirty-four of the sixty-four cardinals were in Rome. A sufficient number were now present so that real negotiations among them could begin. A substantial majority of the progressive wing had already determined upon advancing the candidacy of Rampolla. This group, having more than twenty adherents, was by far the largest bloc and included most of the non-Italian cardinals. A second group, only slightly smaller at about fifteen members, favored Gotti for the papacy. Everyone conceded that he had unparalleled intellectual qualifications, as well as considerable diplomatic experience. But Gotti, a sixty-nine-year-old Carmelite monk, was never able to win friends or rally around him a devoted following. His demeanor was cold and distant by nature, and without humor. This aloof and unsmiling manner won him the epithet of "The Marble Cardinal" from colleagues and subordinates alike.

The general impression in the College during the days of Leo's funeral rites was that the conclave would see a duel for the throne between the partisans of Rampolla on the one hand and the supporters of Gotti on the other. It was expected that the presence of most of the twenty-five non-Italian members would materially increase Rampolla's chances; the conservatives, greatly outnumbered, were thought likely to support Gotti in the absence of a candidate of their own.

Thirty-seven cardinals were present for the last of Leo's funeral Masses, on Saturday morning, July 25. Afterwards, they adjourned to the Consistorial Hall to receive formally the representatives of the diplomatic corps who came to offer condolences. The magnitude of Leo's success in pursuing an enlightened diplomatic policy was nowhere more evident than on this occasion. The presence of emissaries from Russia, Prussia, and Bavaria contrasted with the rather furtive condolences that had been offered only by Catholic ambassadors in 1878. The wider diplomatic representation testified to the broadening of papal influence. After the diplomatic reception, the cardinals went to their residences for dinner and then returned to St. Peter's for the entombment of the pope. This ceremony, which began at seven o'clock, lasted throughout the greater part of the evening.

Most of Sunday, as well as Monday morning, July 27, was occupied in further commemorative Masses for the dead pontiff, but by the seventh general congregation, which met at 10:30 A.M. on Monday, the cardinals were ready to devote their time exclusively to preparations for the conclave.

In this session, Felice Cavagnis, the junior cardinal-deacon, drew lots for the assignment of cells to all the cardinals except Oreglia, Rampolla, and Mario Mocenni, prefect of the palace. These three were invited formally to retain their own apartments in the Vatican as their cells. Rampolla and Mocenni did so, with the understanding that they would share their commodious quarters with others, but Oreglia insisted on maintaining his full quarters uncluttered by any temporary construction.

On the following day, the committee on construction reported that the physical requirements had been met, and they then distributed to the others copies of the ground plan of the conclave showing where each cell was located.

The next congregation met at noon on the twenty-ninth. During this meeting, the cardinals reviewed the pending business of the Vatican, settling those affairs within their power, and appointed three new committees of cardinals. The first of these was instructed to inspect the conclave area thoroughly to verify that it was secure from all outside interference. The second was to supervise the cleanliness of the conclave, while the third was empowered to examine the credentials of all those attendants who would be immured with the cardinals during the election.

On the next day, the cardinals met for the last time before entering the conclave, to settle a few last-minute details. Oreglia, remembering the confusion of the first day's balloting in 1878, distributed sample ballots for both the scrutiny and the *accessus* and then conducted a little lesson on the procedure to be followed when the cardinals cast their votes.

All the preparations for the election were now complete, and in the evening messengers carried an official notice from the principal master of ceremonies, Monsignor Francesco Riggi, that the conclave would open at ten o'clock in the morning of the next day. Sixty-two of the sixty-four cardinals were in Rome to receive the notice. Only Pietro Celesia, the decrepit eighty-nine year old archbishop of Palermo, and Patrick Francis Moran, the Irish-born archbishop of Sidney, Australia, were absent. Celesia was too ill to leave his palace; Moran was still at sea on his 10,000 mile voyage to Rome.

At the appointed hour the cardinals assembled in the Pauline Chapel for the Mass of the Holy Spirit, said on this occasion by Serafino Vannutelli, the sub-dean of the college. The public was strictly excluded from this rite except for Prince Sixtus of Bourbon-Parma. After Mass the cardinals heard the traditional discourse on the election of a new pope, delivered on this occasion by Monsignor Vincenzo Sardi, one of the assistants to the cardinal-secretary of state. After this, all the laws relating to the holding of the conclave were read, and then the participants took an oath to obey those regulations fully. These ceremonies lasted about two hours. At noon, the cardinals returned once again to their Roman residences to enjoy one final lunch "on the outside" and to pack for their stay in the Vatican, five hours being given them for that purpose. All the cardinals availed themselves of this opportunity except Sebastiano Herrero y Espinosa de los Monteros, the archbishop of Valencia, who was so ill that he was helped to his bed in his cell at once and remained there during the entire election. His cell, number fifty-four, was one of six set up in the apartments of the secretary of state and was quite close to the Sistine Chapel so that the *infirmarii* (infirmarians) did not have to journey very far to collect his ballot. Herrero also was given permission to have his special diet catered into the conclave.

By four in the afternoon, large crowds had begun to gather outside the Vatican to watch the procession of carriages bringing the cardinals to the palace. Some came in vehicles with shades drawn, while others sat by open window returning gestures to the cheers of the people. Most of the electors chose to come without pomp, but Klaudius Vaszary, the cardinal primate of Hungary, made his appearance in true princely splendor with full equipage.

Among the first to arrive was the only French cardinal in the Vatican bureaucracy, François Desiré Matthieu, who wished to make himself available to his six countrymen colleagues as a guide, because of his familiarity with the papal palace.

Cardinals Guiseppe Melchiore Sarto, patriarch of Venice, and Victor Lucien Sulpice Lecot, archbishop of Bordeaux, arrived at the same time and entered together. Lecot spoke to Sarto in French, "Of which diocese is Your Eminence the archbishop?" Sarto, whose colloquial French was quite poor, responded that he didn't understand the question and Lecot rephrased it in Latin. Sarto informed him that he was the cardinal of Venice. Lecot, who had conferred with his French colleagues earlier on the possibility of Sarto's candidacy, continued, "You are indeed the patriarch of Venice?" "I certainly am," assured the white-haired, somewhat plump Italian. "Well," observed Lecot, "if you do not speak French, you cannot become pope." To this comment Sarto responded cheerfully, "Then, Eminence, I am not a candidate, and for that I thank God."

Shortly after this exchange, Cardinal Gotti arrived, and the crowd pressed forward for a closer look at the man many supposed would be the next pope. At the sudden press, the carriage's horses reared and plunged in fright and in so doing dealt the carriage a violent kick. Gotti had given a lift to another cardinal who now emerged, thoroughly frightened, and scurried inside before he could be identified by the onlookers.

By five o'clock all the cardinals were in the Pauline Chapel, while their conclavists and servants wrestled bundles of luggage of all shapes and sizes into the conclave area. The members of the College then marched, two by two, in procession to the Sistine

Chapel, where Prince Mario Chigi took the public oath of office as marshal of the conclave, just as he had twenty-five years before.

When this was over, the cardinals retired to their cells to receive a few well-wishers before the doors were sealed. Among those receiving visitors was Cardinal Michael Logue, the archbishop of Armagh, whose cell was located on the top floor, up some two hundred eighty steps from the level of the Sistine. Logue arrived late only to find no furnishing in his cell for either his conclavist or his servant, yet he remained unoffended, and commented that he was impressed with the distinction of being the first Irishman ever to participate in a conclave.

Another who entertained visitors in the early evening was Francesco di Paola Cassetta. He was one of the most popular members of the College since he devoted the bulk of his large private fortune to charitable work in the Eternal City. A huge, jolly man with protruding eyes and an infectious laugh, Cassetta conversed genially with many callers.

Just before eight o'clock, the masters of ceremonies began to go through the cells ringing bells and calling "extra omnes," the signal that the doors were to be closed. The last visitors left amid shouts of farewell and good fortune, and Prince Chigi came from his apartments accompanied by the governor of the conclave, Monsignor Ottavio Caggiano de Azevedo, and a large retinue of other attendants. In procession, they proceeded to made a thorough inspection of the external walls and partitions to make sure there was no breach of the conclave's security. Meanwhile, Cardinal Serafino Vannutelli, in place of Oreglia, and Cardinals Jose Sebastião Netto and Luigi Macchi, the senior cardinal-priest and cardinal-deacon, respectively, made a similar inspection of the interior to ensure that no unauthorized person remained in the conclave. These two tours took about an hour and a half, then, at nine thirty, Chigi met with the three cardinals at the main gate of the conclave, outside the Sala Regia. This entrance was duly locked by the cardinals and the marshal on their respective sides. The election had begun.

After the sealing of the doors, most of the cardinals retired to their cells to rest; although a few chose to have some warm milk or chocolate in the communal dining area before retiring.

Though the day had been an exciting one, filled with crowds

and ceremony, few of the cardinals had any reason to think that the conclave itself would present many surprises. The progressive wing of the college was firmly behind the candidacy of Rampolla. All seven of the French cardinals, for example, were thought to be his supporters, and they made up the largest single bloc of non-Italians. The conservatives, led by Oreglia, knew they would be unsuccessful with a candidate drawn from their own ranks, but they hoped that by supporting Gotti, a man of long and able diplomatic experience, they would be able to draw enough neutral and progressive cardinals to their side to thwart Rampolla's chances, and perhaps bring off an ultimate *coup strategique* and elect "The Marble Cardinal." Almost every other candidate discussed during the days preceding the conclave was considered only half-heartedly. Vincenzo Vannutelli, for example, had little success in his efforts to persude many of his colleagues that his older brother, Serafino, would be an outstanding pope. Sarto of Venice attracted some attention because of the special sanctity of his life, but his complete lack of diplomatic experience and intellectual interests did not seem to fit him for the rôle of successor to Leo XIII. From their discussions among themselves, most cardinals surmised that Rampolla already could count on nearly thirty of the forty-two votes he needed to be elected; and many knew that in most of the conclaves in the preceding two centuries any candidate who had started the balloting with anything like that kind of support eventually achieved the throne, including Pecci in 1878. It was true, of course, that no one had been elected pope directly from the position of cardinal-secretary of state since Guilio Rospigliosi became Clement IX in 1667, but Leo's farsighted policies of diplomatic rapprochement had brought both Church and papacy too far in the preceding two decades and a half to be lightly discarded. Oreglia, leader of the conservatives and, as chamberlain, director of the Church's affairs during the papal vacancy, supported Gotti. But neither of them could be considered great favorites with their colleagues, though both were respected for their considerable intellectual and administrative talents. Oreglia, for example, won few friends in the College by his constant reference to the pope during the last years of the reign as "His Eternity, Leo XIII." This, and other gibes at the aging pontiff, created no good impression among the cardinals, every one of whom, except Oreglia himself, owed his elevation to Leo. Nevertheless, Gotti was in many ways a formidable candidate. His antecedents as a monk in a rigorous order debarred any sniping at his religious fervor, and his success as a diplomat, as well as his well-received theological works, demonstrated his capacity for the throne. Yet "The Marble Cardinal" would not unbend enough to attract support by even a touch of human warmth.

Upon arising on the morning of the first of August, the cardinals attended Mass together, after which they had a small breakfast and then entered the Sistine for the first ballot. They found the furnishings in the chapel much the same as those described in discussing the conclave of 1878, except that there was only one throne on this occasion with green rather than violet hangings, that of Oreglia.

The first order of business was an official calling of the roll by Monsignor Riggi, principal master of ceremonies. When this was completed, Cardinal Cavagnis placed slips of paper with the cardinal's names into a violet sack so that the drawing could be made for the three *infirmarii* and the three scrutators. A buzz of interest was audible in the chapel when Rampolla was chosen first among the latter.

Immediately afterward, the *infirmarii* went to the cell of Herrero and collected his ballot. Meanwhile, the other cardinals were filling out their ballots and sealing them with plain signets. One by one, they advanced to the chapel altar and deposited the ballots in the ornate chalice which stood in its center. At the end of the procession, Rampolla, the senior scrutator, removed the chalice to the counting table in the center of the Sistine and emptied it. After verifying that just sixty-two ballots were there, he opened the first of them, showed it to his two colleagues, and then read it aloud. It was a vote for Gotti. At the end of the counting the results confirmed the expectations of most of the members of the College:

Mariano Rampolla del Tindaro	24
Girolamo Maria Gotti	17
Guiseppe Melchiore Sarto	5
Serafino Vannutelli	4

Luigi Oreglia di Santo Stefano	2
Alfonso Capecellatro	2
Angelo Di Pietro	2
Antonio Agliardi	1
Domenico Ferrata	1
Francesco di Paola Cassetta	1
Gianuario Portanova	1
Agostino Richelmy	1
Francesco Segna	1

At the conclusion of the count, Sarto turned to Lecot, who occupied the adjacent throne, and remarked on his five votes: "They are amusing themselves with my name."

There were no surprises, save perhaps that every one of the twenty-five non-Italians had voted for an Italian candidate. Cavagnis then stepped forward and asked Oreglia if the preparation for the *accessus* should now begin. The dean and chamberlain replied no, that such a procedure gave rise to the possibility of error and surprises were very easy. Oreglia almost unquestionably opted to exclude the *accessus* because the "surprise" he feared was a sudden stampede to Rampolla; nonetheless the *accessus* was abandoned and has never been used again in a papal election. Subsequent legislation abolished this tradition, which was established at least as early as 1458, when Pius II was elected in the manner.

Monsignor Riggi then carried the ballots to the small stove in the chapel's entranceway where they were burned with a few handfuls of damp straw, to increase the volume of black smoke which announced to the people in St. Peter's Square that there was no election. The doors of the chapel were then opened and the cardinals returned to their cells for a few minutes rest before lunch. About twenty of the cardinals ate in the common dining hall, set up in a nearby enclosed balcony, while the remainder were served in their cells by their servants. The servants themselves ate later in a dining area set up in the Vatican's Lapidary Museum.

During the early afternoon, several cardinals took their free time to call on other members of the college to discuss the morning's vote. Serafino Vannutelli visited his brother, Vincenzo, and the others who had voted for him, James Gibbons of Baltimore, Antonio Agliardi, and Francesco di Paola Satolli, and urged them to support Sarto instead. All except Gibbons immediately accepted the admonition and dispersed to seek support for the patriarch of Venice. Meanwhile, Lecot called on Georg Kopp, the prince-bishop of Breslau, and asked him if he and the other German cardinals were amenable to voting for Rampolla. Kopp, a confidant of Kaiser Wilhelm II, noncommittally replied that he desired only that the duration of the conclave be short. This response indirectly informed the French they could expect no support from the Germans in their maneuvering for Rampolla.

When the cardinals assembled in the Sistine for the afternoon voting, every aspect of the procedure went smoothly. The results of the scrutiny were:

Mariano Rampolla del Tindaro	29
Girolamo Maria Gotti	16
Guiseppe Melchiore Sarto	10
Agostino Richelmy	3
Alfonso Capecellatro	2
Serafino Vannutelli	1
Francesco Segna	1

The supporters of Rampolla were most encouraged. Their candidate had advanced five more votes from the morning total, while Gotti had lost one. Such a narrow shift in some earlier conclaves had signalled the rise of the gaining candidate to the throne. Since more than half the minor candidates were no longer in consideration, it seemed to the College that the following day would see the beginning of balloting on the simple question of Rampolla's swift or slow rise to the papal chair. If Gibbons, for example, were to switch from Serafino Vannutelli to Rampolla, since it seemed he was not converted to Sarto, and if the Germans could be persuaded to accede to the Sicilian in order to bring the conclave to a speedy close, by forming a solid non-Italian bloc, then the cardinal-secretary of state might be elevated on the morning ballot.

Sarto, the principal minor candidate, seemed of the opinion that his candidacy, a profound personal surprise, would fade by the next ballot. One cardinal, who asked his opinion on having doubled his morning total from five to ten, received the reply, "I hope tomorrow nobody will think of me any more. Today it was a mistake. Well, one can understand, they do not know me."

The night of August 1 passed quietly in the conclave, for only one man knew that he would, in the morning, explode a political bombshell that would halt Leo's policies for a decade and bring about a stunning coup for Oreglia and the conservatives. That man was Cardinal Jan Puzyna de Kozielsko, and the bombshell was the specific exclusion of Rampolla from the throne by the Emperor Franz Josef.

The *jus exclusivae*, or right of exclusion, traditionally claimed by Spain, France, and Austria, developed in the sixteenth century when Philip II unofficially informed the cardinals, in several of the conclaves during his long reign, of candidates he found unacceptable. The cardinals of his time, in acceding to his wishes in his self-proclaimed rôle as protector of the Catholic Church, established a dangerous precedent by tacitly recognizing Philip's right to a voice, however indirect, in the choice of a pope. After Philip's death in 1598, no more was heard of any "right" to exclude a cardinal from the papal throne for almost half a century until, in 1644, Philip IV of Spain revived the pretensions of his grandfather by opposing Cardinal Guilio Sacchetti, a trusted confidant of the recently deceased Pope Urban VIII. Eleven years later, in the next conclave, Sacchetti was again excluded by Spain. On both occasions, many cardinals were troubled by this interference and appealed to their more theologically minded colleagues for opinions on the validity of Spain's actions. In 1655, the Spanish Jesuit, Cardinal Juan de Lugo, wrote a dissertation on the subject while the conclave was still in progress. In it, he affirmed Spain's right to the veto. Apparently, few in the conclave cared that the skilled theologian was a Spanish subject himself. By the end of the century, France had risen to the position of international prominence enjoyed by Spain in the time of Philip II. The French monarch, Louis XIV, expected to receive the same consideration for his wishes as had been granted to former Spanish kings. At the same time, the German emperor was not to be upstaged by either of his southern neighbors, and likewise advanced a claim to the "right of exclusion." Since these three monarchs represented the bulk of the political power that was in the hands of Catholic sovereigns, the members of the College silently agreed to the right of veto being in the hands of these monarchs, and, in 1721, it was formally exercised in writing for the first time, when Cardinal Michael Friedrich von Althaan notified the conclave that the Emperor Charles VI opposed the elevation of the cardinal-secretary of state of Clement XI, Fabrizio Paolucci de' Calboli, although the latter had, at that time, received only fourteen votes out of fifty-eight cast. During the next century and a half, the "right of exclusion" was invoked five more times; by Spain in 1730 and 1830, by Austria in 1800 and 1823, and by France in 1758. Whether the *jus exlusivae* was a valid right or not, it is the case that no cardinal who was subjected to the exclusion ever rose to the throne. In 1878, it was known that Cardinal Luigi Bilio was opposed by both France and Austria but, as he specifically excluded himself from consideration for the throne before the conclave ever began, both of the cardinals who were entrusted with their master's vetoes kept silent. By 1903, most members of the College did not give the prospect of a veto very much thought. Though the *jus exlusivae* was not mentioned, as such, in the legislation of Pius IX concerning the possible coercion of the cardinals, they considered that the legislation banished the question forever. The key error was, of course, that Pius, and some earlier popes as well, had not specifically abolished the "right of exclusion" in their general electoral pronouncements.

On the morning of August 2, the cardinals followed the same routine as they had on the first day of the meeting. Early in the day, Puzyna had drawn Oreglia aside and tried to present a written memorandum to the dean which contained the Emperor's exclusion. Oreglia realized at once what the College would think if he accepted the document officially—namely that he himself was launching an attack to prevent Rampolla's rise. And though stopping Rampolla was his highest ambition for the conclave, Oreglia foresaw that acceptance of the note might well bring about his greatest dread, a backfire of opinion that would lead to a Sicilian Leo XIV.

Following his rebuff by Oreglia, the Polish cardinal-prince then approached the secretary of the conclave, Monsignor Merry del Val, and asked him to take official receipt of the memorandum, but the newly-appointed secretary was horrified at the thought and refused categorically to have anything to do with the matter. Puzyna then went to the Sistine, and when his colleagues arrived he began to read his statement aloud. In the conversation and confusion which accompanied the entrance of the cardinals, many could not hear the Pole, while others paid no attention. Puzyna raised his voice considerably, and a sudden silence pervaded Michaelangelo's room as the stunned College listened to the text of the note Oreglia had rejected: "I consider it an honor to have been called by highest command to this commission, to inform Your Eminence, as dean of the Sacred College of the most eminent cardinals and chamberlain of the Holy Roman Church, so that Your Eminence may become aware of, and deign to note in an official manner, in the name and by the authority of His Apostolic Majesty, Franz Josef, Emperor of Austria and King of Hungary, that he wishes to use the ancient rights and privileges of exclusion against my most eminent lord Cardinal Mariano Rampolla del Tindaro."

In the welter of voices which rose following this reading, Oreglia stepped forward and clearly announced, "This communication is not accepted by the conclave in any official manner. No cardinal is to give any consideration whatever to this 'veto' and all are to continue to vote their conscience." Rampolla himself then rose to speak, "I regret that a grave attempt has been made in the matter of a pontifical election against the liberty of the Church and the dignity of the Sacred College by a lay power, and therefore I protest it energetically. As far as my humble person is concerned, I declare that nothing more honorable nor more pleasing to me could have happened." As Cardinal Matthieu later remarked, at that moment Rampolla could not find one enemy in the conclave.

A blow had been struck against Rampolla's candidacy, however, which assuredly doomed it to fail. Franz Josef, the patriarch of Europe's monarchs and a general supporter of the Church, could not be ignored. There was a frenzy of activity in the chapel. Some thought the action of the Austrian emperor was taken upon the request of the Italian government, others thought that Kaiser Wilhelm II might have importuned Vienna for the exclusion of Rampolla. Not one cardinal was sure what his position should be, but all of them knew the that the papacy of Leo's chief servant would be compromised from its beginning, were he to be elevated. The conservatives could only be elated, however secretly. They could now abandon Gotti altogether and turn to someone more fully in accord with their views—but who? Hurried consultations settled the matter—Sarto. He had already received ten votes in the previous scrutiny, so why could not the simple priest with the anti-liberal views attract still more support, now that Rampolla's chances were doomed? The hurried switching of votes, because of the change in conservative orientation, was quickly revealed in the morning ballot, their force clearly seen behind a surge of sympathy for Rampolla.

Mariano Rampolla del Tindaro	29
Guiseppe Melchiore Sarto	21
Girolmano Maria Gotti	9
Luigi Oreglia de Santo Stefano	1
Angelo Di Pietro	1
Alfonso Capecellatro	1

After the count was concluded, the cardinals dispersed for lunch and long consultations with others on this latest development. By four thirty, all seven of the French cardinals had congregated in the cell of Benoit Marie Langenieux, the archbishop of Reims, where they decided to continue to support Rampolla firmly. The conservatives did not take the morning's advantage for granted, however. They recruited a squad of northern Italian cardinals from among themselves to circulate among the other cardinals and answer questions about the personality and background of their neighbor, the cardinal of Venice. Bartolomeo Bacilieri of Verona, Giulio Boschi of Ferrara, Agostino Richelmy of Turin, and Andrea Ferrari of Milan freely gave favorable opinions about Sarto, as the swing toward the Venetian's candidacy began to gain momentum. Gibbons of Baltimore was converted and joined the Vannutelli brothers, Agliardi, and Satolli in campaigning for Sarto. The Germans, too, began to consider the saintly patriarch a possibility worthy of consideration for the throne.

Absent from all this scurrying and confederation was Puzyna, whose lean, chiseled aristocratic features were nowhere to be seen—he had shot his bolt, and now became as self-effacing as possible.

When the cardinals were assembled for the second scrutiny of the day, they found themselves confronted by Cardinal Louis Adolphe Perraud, the bishop of Autun, who delivered a vigorous tirade against the veto of Rampolla from the middle of the chapel, but his remarks were greeted with silence, and nobody rose to second his opinion. Delayed far past the scheduled hour by the unexpected events of the day, the count was not completed until nearly six thirty. The results were:

Mariano Rampolla del Tindaro	30
Guiseppe Melchiore Sarto	24
Girolamo Maria Gotti	3
Luigi Oreglia de Santo Stefano	2
Angelo Di Pietro	2
Alfonso Capecellatro	1

This ballot marked Rampolla's high tide—but all were convinced that it stood as much for sympathy as for hope. Sarto was nonplussed. After springing from ten to twenty-one votes in the morning scrutiny, he now added three more; and he was the only candidate whose strength was growing from vote to vote. At the end of the count, he turned to Lecot and said in Latin, "My election will be the ruin of the Church." Later, he wandered around the chapel, almost in a daze, saying to various cardinals, "God knows that I am not worthy of the papacy and not fitted to the enormous task; give your vote to someone else. . . I am not worthy. . . I am not capable. . . forget me." Clearly, he had become panic stricken. This was no pose. Sarto was so frightened and overwhelmed that he broke down and wept publicly during the course of the evening. This exhibition did not deter the cardinals who supported him. Indeed, one or two who hesitated were now won to his cause by his unfeigned humility, including Anton Fischer of Cologne. Yet there was a danger. In spite of the traditional assurances from the other cardinals that his election was God's will, Sarto persisted in saying that he would never accept the crown. His voice carried so much conviction that Oreglia spent much of the night of August 2 bustling through the conclave, telling the conservatives that they should prepare themselves for a last-minute switch to Domenico Ferrata, an important Vatican conservative bureaucrat, should Sarto's insistence on refusal threaten their position. But the momentum was now too strong for even the architects of Sarto's candidacy to have any further effect. Matthieu occupied his night closeted with Di Pietro, inquiring about Sarto's background for the benefit of his French colleagues; other non-Italian cardinals also were seeking information about the Venetian before the morning vote.

The first scrutiny on Monday, August 3, clearly revealed the new trend:

Mariano Rampolla del Tindaro	27
Guiseppe Melchiore Sarto	24
Girolamo Maria Gotti	6
Luigi Oreglia de Santo Stefano	1
Alfonso Capecellatro	1
Guiseppe Prisco	1
Angelo Di Pietro	1

One cardinal wrote the word *nemini* on his ballot, a vote for no one.

The erosion of Rampolla's support was now well underway, but sufficient confusion had been engendered to promote the emergence of another minor candidate in Prisco. One cardinal simply could not make up his mind about what to do, so he simply dropped a blank ballot into the chalice.

As the tally was being made, Sarto kept saying that he wished only to return to his beloved Venetians and appeared on the verge of a complete nervous collapse. At the conclusion of the count, he rushed from the chapel and disappeared.

All were aware that either Sarto had to be persuaded to accept or that some other candidate had to be found quickly, lest the conclave degenerate into one of the months-long affairs that had characterized papal elections in the seventeenth and eighteenth centuries.

Oreglia, whose plot to spring Ferrata on the College depended on Sarto's refusal, conferred with Monsignor Merry del Val and charged the latter with finding the patriarch and obtaining from him a declaration of whether he intended to refuse the election. If so, stated Oreglia, he wished to make a public declaration of that fact before the afternoon voting to allow the cardinals an opportunity to test the chances of another candidate. The French cardinals conferred once again, and all but Perraud agreed that the time had come to abandon Rampolla—yet they were still unsure of supporting Sarto. Rampolla himself briefly considered urging his followers to vote for Sarto, but he gave up this intention before many had heard of it. At the same time Satolli, who genuinely feared a firm decline by Sarto, consulted Gibbons on the best way to persuade Sarto to accept. The American suggested thrusting the idea of duty and obligation directly at the candidate.

Meanwhile, Merry del Val found the object of his search lying face down before the altar in the darkened Pauline Chapel and exhorted him to accept the election. After a brief conversation, in which the Venetian wept again, Merry del Val left, uncertain of what effect he had had on the cardinal. Shortly afterward, Sarto left his prayers, for he was stopped in one of the corridors by Andrea Ferrari of Milan, who told him bluntly, "Return to Venice if you wish, but you will go with your soul torn with remorse, persecuting you to the end of your life." Sarto replied, again, "The responsibility of the papacy is too formidable," to which Ferrari continued, "Consider how formidable is your responsibility if you refuse." "I'm too old, I'll die soon," wailed Sarto; "Apply to yourself the phrase of Caiaphas," concluded the Milanese, "it is better that one die for the good of all.'" Not long after this Satolli, acting under Gibbons' prompting, had his turn at the reluctant candidate. He literally shouted at Sarto, "Accept, accept, God wills it, the supreme senate of the Church demands it, will Your Eminence oppose the will of God?" Sarto was now simply too distraught to carry on anymore and told his haranguer that he would bow to God's will.

Satolli had just time enough to return to the Sistine before the beginning of the afternoon vote to inform the others that their cumulative browbeating had been successful.

Sarto's following grew:

Guiseppe Melchiore Sarto	35
Mariano Rampolla del Tindaro	16
Girolamo Maria Gotti	7
Luigi Oreglia di Santo Stefano	2
Alfonso Capecellatro	1

And, as before, one vote for "no one."

The cardinal took considerable time with this voting procedure, because not only Herrero but also Lecot and Langenieux announced themselves too ill to attend, and the *infirmarii* had to make three calls instead of one. Perhaps the two Frenchmen were overcome with the excitement of Rampolla's collapse or, again, perhaps they could not bear to watch the face of the Sicilian as his most fervent supporters abandoned him. The result, for Sarto's adherents, was, however, well worth the wait. Their favorite was now only seven votes short of election. Six of the French—Perraud was the exception—now agreed among themselves to drop Rampolla completely and to vote for Sarto in the morning. Matthieu, already aware of the decision which virtually assured Sarto's elevation on the next ballot, called on him at seven in the evening to offer his personal assurance of loyalty as the only French-born Vatican cardinal, but he did not reveal what his countrymen had decided.

On Tuesday morning, August 4, after the usual preliminaries were over, Langenieux, an ailing seventy-eight years old, walked with difficulty to see Sarto about fifteen minutes before the beginning of the seventh ballot. He informed the patriarch that the French were going to vote for him *en bloc*.

When the drawing for the scrutators was made, Sebastiano Martinelli, Matthieu, and Cassetta found themselves chosen to preside. The voting procedure, which went smoothly for the first time since the opening day, produced the fully expected result:

Guiseppe Melchiore Sarto	50
Mariano Rampolla del Tindaro	10
Girolamo Maria Gotti	2

Before the certification of the result, a board of three cardinals, called revisers, consisting of François Marie Benjamin Richard, Achille Manara, and Franceso Salesio della Volpe, searched out Sarto's ballot and determined that he had not voted for himself. His own vote symbolized the temper and tone of his reign before it had begun—his had been one of the two votes for Gotti.

At the moment that the revisers announced the results of their search, the result became official. Oreglia, grim visaged as ever, moved to confront Sarto, asking him whether or not he accepted the election. Sarto quoted the words of Jesus in the garden of Gethsemane: "If this cup may not pass away from me, Thy will be done." The dean and chamberlain did not feel that a quotation of Jesus Christ met the constitutional requirements mandated by canon law, and asked again, bluntly and brusquely, "Do you accept?" and Sarto, barely audible, murmured, "I accept." At that moment, the other cardinals reached for the cords at the sides of their thrones so that only the one above number twenty-one remained elevated. Oreglia continued, "By what name will he be called," and Sarto replied, "In memory of the holy popes whose protection I need, and especially in memory of those who, in these latter times, have strenuously endured the persecutions against the Church themselves, I will be called Pius."

There was none of the outbreak of cheers and applause from the cardinals which had greeted the elevation of Leo XIII a quarter of a century before; the oppressive quality of the moment—Sarto's sadness, Oreglia's rudeness—prevented any of that. The cardinals simply went, one by one, to make their first obeisance to the new pope while the chapel doors were opened to admit the masters of ceremonies for the purpose of drawing up the document that ratified the election officially and burning the ballots. It was 11:45 A.M. When the doors opened, Langenieux left the chapel to go the his cell for rest, and it was he who told the cluster of conclavists outside the chapel the results of the election.

The cardinal archdeacon, Luigi Macchi, then made his way to the great balcony over the center doors of St. Peter's. The windows there, which had not been unsealed since the election of Leo, were thrown open. A large crowd had gathered, its numbers growing every minute as word spread from those who had seen the white smoke engendered by the burning of the ballots without wet straw, which announced the conclusion of the conclave.

During the entire course of the electoral meeting, the crowd had noticed from time to time that conclavists and servants alike had found openings above or to the sides of the window shields by which they could watch the comings and goings of the populace below. Now the people in St. Peter's Square saw hands appearing at one of the apertures making vigorous cutting motions. Some cried out at once that Sarto had been chosen, since the "scissors" motion seemed to indicate a tailor, which, in Italian, is "sarto." When Macchi stepped forward onto the balcony he found the crowd so excited that he drastically abbreviated the ancient formula for announcing a papal election so as to release the enthusiasm of the populace at once. After this scene, the most well-known part of every conclave, the people streamed into St. Peter's to receive the first blessing of the new pope from the inner balcony.

Once Pius X had imparted his first benediction, he went at once to the cell of Cardinal Herrero to wish him a speedy recovery. Then he returned to his cell for a few minutes rest before going once again to the Sistine for another obeisance by his former colleagues. Prince Mario Chigi and his sons, Luigi and Francesco, also were admitted to this ceremony, through a small door into the conclave area that was unsealed for the occasion. At six o'clock, the main gates of the conclave were opened, and the cardinals began to disperse through the city with their servants and their baggage.

The epilogue to the election of 1903 saw the rise of Merry del Val to the position of cardinal-secretary of state, an office that he retained for the entire reign. On January 20, 1904, Pius promulgated the constitution *Commissum nobis,* which specifically abolished forever the "right of exclusion." For all that Pius X occupies a special place in the history of the modern Church by reason of his great piety—he was canonized in 1954—the eleven year reign was itself perhaps the least distinguished of any in the past century. The Romans themselves, almost at once, began to call their bishop "Pio Non Decimo" (Pius the Ninth the Tenth)—and the label got right to the heart of the matter. Pius X, like Pius IX before him, was simply incapable of dealing with the political, social, and intellectual problems of the Church in the modern world. He alienated diplomats, scholars, and governments alike with a conservative intransigence which began at once to reverse the extraordinary good will developed by Leo XIII.

The conclave of 1903 left no one happy, Sarto least of all, for of all the modern popes he least desired the throne and was acutely conscious of his own shortcomings. The progressives saw much of Leo's work compromised, especially in France; and the conservatives felt somewhat betrayed by Pius's silent acquiescence to an accommodation with the realities of life in twentieth-century Italy. The brilliant Rampolla was consigned to oblivion. Only Oreglia, no friend to Pius as he had been no friend to Leo, hung on grimly to his power and his privileges until his death in December, 1913, only a few months before Pius's own passing. His cardinalate of but a few days short of forty of his eighty-five years was one of the half dozen longest and certainly one of the most malignant in the history of the Church.

IV
CONCLAVE IN WAR

THE END of Pius X's life came suddenly and as a direct result of the outbreak of World War I. Pius, like a number of well-informed and prescient men in Europe, had foreseen the outbreak of a major war for several years. As early as 1911, he would often greet his secretary of state, Cardinal Raffaele Merry del Val, with the phrase, "Things are going badly, we shall not get through 1914." At the close of May, 1913, he received the retiring Brazilian ambassador, Dr. Bruno Chaves, and remarked to him, "You are fortunate in returning to your home in Brazil, so you will not be here for the world war." Together with his deep fears of war, Pius had a number of other physical and emotional trials during the last year and a half of his life. Among them, on February 11, 1913, his sister Rosa died, the first of his generation of Sarti to go; and in the following spring he suffered a severe attack of influenza. Even though his hardy peasant background helped him overcome the illness, it certainly left its mark on a man of seventy-seven.

When 1914 arrived, the pope felt the time of crisis approaching. On May 25, he held his final consistory, at which he created thirteen new cardinals. In his speech from the throne on that occasion, Pius once again spoke of the trend of the European powers toward war. On the afternoon of June 28, when news arrived of the assassination of the heir to the Austrian throne, Franz Ferdinand, and his wife, Sophie Chotek, at Sarajevo, the pope realized that the time had come. He went to his chapel immediately and remained in deep prayer, not just for the dead archduke and his wife, but for peace.

During the following month, he exhorted everywhere for restraint, but in vain. On August 2, the day after hostilities began, he made a universal appeal for peace, which had as little effect as his other efforts. Shortly afterward, the Austrian ambassador called with a request for a papal blessing for the Austrian army. Exasperated, the pope told him sharply, "I do not bless war, I bless peace."

In spite of his deep grief at the outbreak of the war, Pius kept on with his full schedule of work and public appearances. Fresh reminders of the situation, such as the farewell reception he gave for the seminarians of all nations who had been ordered home for military service, only made his melancholia more profound.

On the afternoon of Saturday, August 15, Pius had the first symptoms of a sore throat and decided to retire early. Members of the household sent for his two principal physicians, Ettore Marchiafava and Diomede Amici, but, after a brief examination, they concluded that the pope was not gravely ill and they expected his full recovery within a day or two. Pius continued to be ill during Sunday and Monday, however, though he did go to his study table in his bedroom from time to time to continue business.

On Tuesday the eighteenth, Cardinal Merry del Val was not feeling well himself and sent the urgent business of the secretariat of state to the pope in the hands of his principal assistant, Monsignor Nicola Canali. When Canali arrived in the pope's bedroom, Pius said to him, "Tell the cardinal to get well, for when he is ill, I am ill too." During the course of Tuesday, the pope occasionally seemed on the point of complete recovery and little fear existed when he retired for the night. His chaplain, Monsignor Bressan, who had been with him since his days as patriarch of Venice, closed the door to his bedroom and slept, as usual, in a little alcove nearby. When Pius did not call for him at the usual hour on the morning of the nineteenth, Bressan became worried and entered the bedroom on his own initiative. He found Pius in very great pain with a high fever. The doctors were immediately called and arrived to find the pope's lungs greatly congested. By eight o'clock, Merry del Val had been sent for. When he came, the doctors told him that Pius's condition was very grave indeed. At ten o'clock, Pius had a sudden crisis, and when Merry del Val rushed to the bed, the pope could only grasp his hands and, gasping, cry out, "Eminence . . . Eminence. . . ." The cardinal turned and ordered that Pius be given the sacraments of the dying at once. The pope, realizing his condition, whispered, "I resign myself completely." These were the last coherent words he spoke. So suddenly had the crisis come that the cardinals who usually officiated at the bedside of a dying pope were all unavailable, so Monsignor Zampini, the pope's sacristan, administered the last rites with a simplicity in keeping with Pius's background and sympathies. At this time, his doctors gave him several injections which eased the pain and brought a quiet state without robbing him of full consciousness. For the rest of the day, Pius remained in bed propped up on pillows, unable to speak.

Throughout the afternoon a hot, dry wind swept over Rome, and the Vatican was plunged into frantic activity under the direction of Cardinal Merry del Val. Messengers were sent to find the few cardinals still in Rome during the height of the summer's heat, and telegrams were dispatched to the other members of the College of Cardinals announcing the imminent death of the sovereign pontiff and ordering them to Rome with all possible speed. The message was especially critical in the case of the archdeacon of the College, Francesco Salesio della Volpe, who, as chamberlain of the Church, would be in administrative charge during the coming vacancy of the Holy See.

Early in the afternoon, the cardinals who were nearby began to arrive at the Vatican—the first was Gaetano Bisleti, the fifty-eight year old cardinal-grand prior of the Order of Saint John of Jerusalem. By early evening, the antechamber of the papal bedroom was crowded with prelates, the doctors in attendance, and members of the pope's family—his sisters, Anna and Maria, and his nephew, Monsignor Giovanni Battista Parolin, as well as the latter's sister, the pope's niece, Gilda. They remained outside the bedroom, to provide Pius with as much fresh air as possible during the worst season of the Roman year, but the connecting door was left open so that they could see the pontiff. From time to time, Pius made the sign of the cross in the direction of those nearby. In the evening, Cardinal Diomede Falconio, former apostolic delegate to the United States, arrived to find the gates of the Vatican locked. His clamor eventually roused the guard and he hurried to the papal apartments.

Toward eleven o'clock, Merry del Val entered the bedchamber, being careful to approach the pope on the opposite side from the direction in which Pius was reclining so as not to disturb him. Pius turned and fixed his cardinal-secretary of state with a penetrating gaze which followed Merry del Val around the foot of the bed. The pope raised his arm in a gesture of embrace and, as the cardinal sat beside him, Pius vigorously grasped his hand and held him, gazing into his eyes, unable to speak, for almost forty minutes. After this farewell, which deeply moved everyone who witnessed it, Pius closed his eyes and let his head sink back on his pillows. Dr. Marchiafava then gestured for the Cardinal to come back into the adjacent room. The physician said that he wanted advice in preparing the latest medical statement on the pope's condition. Merry del Val was nonplussed. He asked how he could be of use in a matter in which he was obviously incompetent. The doctor replied that he needed no assistance with technical matters, but rather he needed a word to describe the extraordinary serenity of the pope in the face of death.

Merry del Val wished to stay near Pius but was pursuaded to get some sleep, on the grounds that there was no immediate danger of death. He left around midnight. Little more than an hour later, at 1:15 on the morning of the twentieth of August, the reign came to an end as Pius quietly passed from sleep to death, surrounded by his family.

At seven on the following morning, della Volpe arrived from his vacation at Imola to take charge of the arrangements for both funeral and conclave. His first act was to invite Merry del Val to retain his apartments in the Vatican until the election of a new pope, even though the office of secretary of state had ceased at the moment of Pius's end.

At five o'clock in the afternoon, the body of Pius X was taken to the Throne Room to lie in state through the night, then, at 10:00 A.M. on the following morning, the remains were taken to the Blessed Sacrament Chapel in Saint Peter's to receive the last tribute of the Roman people. Della Volpe had to order special precautions because of the crush of people who pressed forward toward Pius's body—he was already being hailed as a saint by many. The order of service for the dead pope was set forth by Cardinal Basilio Pompilj, in his capacity as cardinal-vicar of Rome.

At the moment of Pius's death, the College of Cardinals had sixty-five members, twenty-one of whom had been elevated by Leo XIII and the remainder by Pius X. The circumstances facing the College were among the most difficult ever encountered. No one had any idea how, or if, all the cardinals could come to Rome for a papal election in the state of war, even though Italy was still neutral. The worry became more acute when it was learned that the train on which the dean of the College, eighty-two-year-old Serafino Vannutelli, was returning to Rome was bombed by terrorists. Nine people were injured, but the first-class carriage on which Vannutelli was riding was undamaged.

While in 1878 and 1903 there had been ample time for the cardinals to test the waters regarding preferences for the throne, such was not the case in 1914. Many of those created earlier in the same year had not yet come to Rome to receive their red hats, and some were completely unknown in the curia. The College was completely unprepared to face a conclave in the opening days of the most devastating war thus far in history. Many of the progressives had hoped, throughout Pius's reign, eventually to enthrone Rampolla, their defeated candidate in the election of 1903. They were now completely disorganized, since Rampolla had died on December 16, 1913—too early for the papacy and too late for those who supported his cause to fix their attentions on another. Moreover, the war overshadowed every other consideration, from the difficulty of English and French cardinals being shut up with their Austrian and German colleagues, to the weighty thoughts that each cardinal gave to the prospect that his country's enemies might triumph in electing a partisan as the next pontiff.

In Rome, the final orders for Pius's funeral were issued by the three chiefs of order, della Volpe as archdeacon as well as chamberlain, Serafino Vannutelli, and Angelo Di Pietro, the third ranking cardinal-priest, who acted in the absence of his two senior colleagues, Jose Sebastião Netto of Lisbon and James Gibbons of Baltimore.

At half past four on Sunday the twenty-third, Saint Peter's was closed to the public, and the whole staff of the curia entered for the performance of the burial rites. Pius's body was taken to the Cappella Giulia, where Merry del Val, as archpriest of Saint Peter's, supervised the placement of the corpse into its set of three coffins. Pius was interred in the Vatican crypts beneath a simple masonry construction, on a site he had chosen himself a few years before. Then the basilica was closed. Merry del Val was the last to leave.

Cardinal Antonio Agliardi presided, as sub-dean, over the first general congregation of cardinals, which met on the morning of the twenty-first. Serafino Vannutelli was present, but he was too infirm to chair the proceedings. At this time, Monsignor Tommaso Pio Boggiani, an assessor of the Consistorial Congregation, was appointed secretary of the conclave. For his able administration of this papal election, Boggiani was rewarded with the cardinalate himself in 1916—his was the same office from which Merry del Val had begun his meteoric rise to power in 1903. The business of the shattering of the Fisherman's Ring, Pius's pontifical signet, was the next order of business. Della Volpe had ordered that all those who were not cardinals were to be excluded from the general congregation, and now it was found that none of the prelates present had the strength to do the job, so the surface of the ring was scratched and the rite deemed complete. The congregation then gave formal orders to begin the construction of the conclave area itself. Twenty-three cardinals were present at this first meeting; two others, Angelo Di Pietro, who, at eighty-six, was the oldest member of the College, and Sebastiano Martinelli, were in Rome, but were too ill to attend.

Squads of workmen began to construct the conclave's cells at once. Soon they discovered that, while all the equipment for the actual balloting in the Sistine could be recovered from storage easily, the furnishings of the cells used in 1903 had been given away to the Roman poor. Della Volpe solved the problem by renting furniture for the cells from a Roman hotel.

The second general congregation, on the twenty-second, over which della Volpe presided, was concerned almost exclusively with the date on which the conclave was to start. Several cardinals believed that some delay ought to be arranged, to give the cardinals from the Americas time to arrive. The majority opinion which prevailed, however, was that the election should begin on the earliest possible date, given the international situation. After some debate, the cardinals agreed on August 31.

In the third meeting, on the twenty-third, which the cardinals held before attending the burial of Pius, Antonio Agliardi made an impassioned speech urging the College to appeal officially as a body to the belligerents to halt the war. Many of the cardinals were moved visibly by the address, but the congregation decided to take no action during a time which was most delicate for the papacy itself.

The meeting of August 26, with thirty-two cardinals in attendance, was presided over by Serafino Vannutelli in person, in spite of his deteriorated health. In respect for his diminished physical faculties, however, the other cardinals stayed strictly within the bounds of parliamentary formality. This attitude, which carried over to other meetings as well as to the conclave itself, set a tone of transnationalism in which the rancors of the day played no part.

Cardinal Gustav Friedrich Piffl, the archbishop of Vienna, reveals in his conclave diary that the recently-arrived foreign cardinals as yet had no knowledge of the term "integrist," or its significance. They soon would. The integrists were the party of cardinals, mostly from the curia, who favored the conservative policies of Pius X and Merry del Val, and admitted no compromise on any matter with the secular world. Their greatest object was to banish forever the enlightened social and intellectual policies begun by Leo XIII. They were, in fact, the lineal successors of those who had cheerfully welcomed the devastation of Rampolla's candidacy for the tiara in 1903. In 1914, their leaders were Merry del Val; Gaetano de Laï, the most senior cardinal-bishop created by Pius X and secretary of the Consistorial Congregation of the curia; and the Benedictine Domenico Serafini, newly a cardinal, but a powerful member of the Supreme Congregation of the Holy Office, the successor to the Inquisition.

The progressive cardinals, the friends and sympathizers of Rampolla, grouped themselves around Cardinal Pietro Maffi, archbishop of Pisa, and Domenico Ferrata, a cardinal elevated by Leo XIII who had served for many years as nuncio in Paris. To this latter group belonged the cardinal-bishop and sub-dean Agliardi, who voiced the opinion that the new pope should allow bishops more authority in their own dioceses, thus placing himself squarely in opposition to the integrists.

While the cardinals in Rome were consulting among themselves about potential candidates for the throne, the members of the diplomatic corps in the Eternal City were busy sending dossiers on prominent cardinals back to their capitals and receiving, in turn, instructions from their governments, to be passed on to their national cardinals, on which members of the College were to be considered *papabili*. Late in the afternoon of the twenty-sixth, Prince Schönburg, the Austrian ambassador, called on Piffl with a list of nine names which he was about to forward to Vienna. This "short list" drawn up by the ambassador contained the names of all those he thought might reach the throne. At the head of the list stood Domenico Ferrata, followed by Cardinal Giacomo Della Chiesa, the archbishop of Bologna. This prelate, who sprang from the Genoese nobility, had served Rampolla for many years in the capacity of under-secretary. When Rampolla was replaced as secretary of state by Merry del Val, the younger disciple tried to carry on quietly some of Rampolla's more enlightened policies. For this bit of cheek, Della Chiesa was "exiled" in 1907 by being made archbishop of Bologna. The bitter pill was made all the more distressful for him, because, just a few days before his assignment to Bologna, it was announced that he was to be nuncio to Spain, a position he had desired for years. But within a few days, the promotion to Spain was cancelled. A consolation in the appointment to Bologna was the knowledge that elevation to the College of Cardinals would come in the next creation. This, however, was not to be the case. Ignoring the tradition that Bologna's archbishop was always a cardinal, Pius X waited seven years before finally conferring the red hat on Della Chiesa, in the consistory of May 25, 1914. Also on Schönburg's list were Merry del Val; Agliardi; Serafini; Vincenzo Vannutelli, a cardinal-bishop and the younger brother of the dean; Willem Marinus van Rossum, the cardinal-prefect of Propaganda Fide; Basilio Pompilj, the cardinal-bishop of Velletri; and Filippo Giustini, the cardinal-prefect of the Congregation for the Discipline of the Sacraments. The presence of Merry del Val on the list shows the level of power and prestige he had achieved under Pius X. For, at fifty, he was still the youngest member of the College and, moreover, he was Anglo-Spanish rather than Italian. These two factors alone would have been enough to exclude him from the list of *papabili* at any other conclave.

Also on the afternoon of the twenty-sixth, two more of the German members of the College arrived in Rome, Franz von Bettinger, archbishop of Munich, and Felix von Hartmann, archbishop of Cologne. Like Della Chiesa and Piffl, they had just been made cardinals and had not yet received the red hat.

The general congregation of cardinals that met on the morning of August 27 saw the number in attendance rise to forty-two, ten more than on the day before, including the two Germans. By now the actual number of electors who would be present when the conclave met began to be clear. It seemed certain that three of the cardinals from the New World were not going to arrive in time. William O'Connell of Boston and James Gibbons of Baltimore were on board the White Star liner *Canopic*, which was not expected to dock at Naples before September 1; while the Canadian cardinal, Louis Nazaire Begin of Quebec, was following on a vessel which was due even later. Sebastiano Martinelli, the prefect of the Congregation of Rites, was in Rome, but the state of his health was so bad that he could not be immured inside a hot and steamy Vatican in close quarters with so many others. Klaudius Vaszary, the eighty-two-year-old primate of Hungary, was simply too aged to travel. Ill health also forced the absence of Giuseppe Prisco, the archbishop of Naples; Franz Bauer, archbishop of Olmutz; and François Virgile Dubillard, the archbishop of Chambery, who died on the following December 1. These absences left the number of electors at fifty-seven.

During the afternoon of the twenty-seventh, the five Austro-German cardinals in Rome met informally for a walk on the Pincio. Besides the three already mentioned, Leo de Skrbensky-Hriste, archbishop of Prague, and Johann Csernoch, archbishop of Gran, marched with their colleagues. Though they did not decide in concert to whom to give their votes, their conversation indicated that they all leaned toward an anti-integrist candidate—indeed, von Bettinger had inveighed loudly against the integrists publicly at a luncheon only a few hours before. They did decide not to vote for Maffi, whom they regarded as too "modernist" in his feelings, and Ferrata they excluded because of an unknown personal animosity on the part of one of them—perhaps because he had been nuncio in Paris for so long, so they feared that his papal policy might prove to be pro-French. They finally narrowed their list of acceptable candidates to Della Chiesa and Pietro Gasparri, a cardinal of liberal views who had once taught at the University of

Paris and was now attached to the Holy Office. Gasparri was decidedly an anti-integrist.

At 8:45 on the morning of August 28, all the cardinals in Rome who were able to attend went to the first of the series of requiems for Pius X in the Sistine Chapel, at which Cardinal Vincenzo Vannutelli officiated. The four absolutions at the Mass were given by Agliardi, de Laï, Francesco di Paola Cassetta, and Diomede Falconio. Thus, the ceremony was the tribute of the cardinal-bishops to the memory of Pius, since all those of that rank were functionaries, except the dean, Serafino Vannutelli, who was too infirm.

At the end of the requiem, about 11:30, there was another general congregation of cardinals. At this meeting, Serafino Vannutelli expressed the wish to have a prelate of the pontifical household as one of his two conclavists, contrary to the terms of the election constitution of Pius X, *Vacante Apostolic Sedis* of December 25, 1904. This request was rejected promptly by the other cardinals. Their respect for Vannutelli was immense, but they could permit no deviation from the slightest requirement of the current constitution on elections in so tense a time. Since there was no other formal business on the agenda, the cardinals adjourned early.

By the end of the day, the French contingent of cardinal-electors had been made complete. It consisted of four archbishops, Louis Henri Luçon of Reims, Paulin Pierre Andrieu of Bordeaux, Leon Adolphe Amette of Paris, and Hector Irene Sevin of Lyon; together with the aristocratic François Marie Anatole de Roverie de Cabrieres, bishop of Montpelier, who, at eighty-four, was the second oldest cardinal present; and Louis Billot, a Jesuit curial cardinal. Billot was a major integrist who became, in 1927, the only cardinal in nearly two centuries to resign the red hat, in a personal dispute with Pius XI. The French leaned somewhat more toward the progressives, as a whole, because of the great deterioration in relations between the papacy and France under Pius X, a state of affairs which had culminated in the breaking of diplomatic relations. This last event left the French government entirely without representation at the Vatican, so the French cardinals were unable to sound out their government or receive suggestions from it concerning the *papabili* as readily as the electors from the central European powers—a decided disadvantage for the interests of France at the moment of embarking on a great war.

During the last days of August, which were dismal and rainy in Rome, other members of the College who resided outside the Eternal City arrived for the conclave. These included Michael Logue, the Irish national cardinal; Jose Sebastião Netto and Antonio Mendes Bello, the former and present patriarchs of Lisbon; Francis Bourne of Westminster, who had travelled with his curial colleague, the famous Benedictine scholar and librarian Aidan Gasquet, to represent England; Désiré Mercier of Belgium, the hero-cardinal of the war; Joachim Arcoverde de Albuquerque Cavalcanti, archbishop of Rio de Janeiro and the only Latin-American in the College; and John Mary Farley, the archbishop of New York and the only American present. Farley was vacationing with friends near Lausanne, after attending the Eucharistic Congress at Lourdes, when he received news of the death of Pius.

To this group of non-Italians must be added the four Spanish archbishops: José María Martín Herrera y de la Iglesia of Santiago de Compostella; José Maria Cos y Macho of Valladolid, Enrique Almaraz y Santos of Seville, and Victoriano Guisasola y Menendez of Toledo. The arrival of Karl von Hornig, archbishop of Veszprem in Hungary, on the evening of the twenty-ninth raised the number of Austro-Germans to six, and the number of non-Italian electors to twenty-five, including the Anglo-Spanish Merry del Val.

The great majority of the "foreigners" decidedly were anti-integrist, in spite of the fact that all of them except Netto, Logue, Herrera, and Skrbensky had been elevated to the College by Pius X. Generally, this was because of the worsening relationships the Vatican had with the various governments of the countries from which these cardinals came. If the integrists were to elect their candidate for the tiara, they would have to overcome the great desire of most of the non-Italians for a diplomatically more sympathetic pope—a desire which was strong enough to bridge the animosities of the cardinals from the belligerent powers.

At 9:30 on the morning of August 29, Saturday, the next requiem was chanted for Pius in the Sistine, attended by fifty-two cardinals. The celebrant was Gaetano de Laï, and the four absolutions were given by Girolamo Maria Gotti, the original candidate of the conservatives for the throne in 1903, Ferrata, Merry del Val, and Antonio Vico, the cardinal-prefect of the Congregation of Rites. After the Mass, the usual daily congregation of cardinals met, this time for the purpose of drawing lots for the cells in the conclave. A slight sensation was caused when Della Chiesa, known to be a possible candidate of the progressives, drew cell fifty-seven, the same number as that drawn by Pius X in the conclave of 1903.

By now, however, the daily activities of the cardinals were being crowded from the front page news, even in Rome, by the progress of the war. On the Western Front, spectacular German advances had forced an Anglo-French retreat after the battle of Mons on August 23. Now there were rumors that the French government would evacuate Paris, which it did on September 5. In the east, the first news from the Central Powers was not a comfort to the cardinals from that region. Early Austrian successes in Galicia were negated quickly by the overwhelming numbers of the Russians, who began to push southwestward. Elsewhere, however, the news was brighter. After the initial defeat of the German eighth army under General Friedrich von Prittwitz, the Russian first army began a push toward the Vistula. Prittwitz was dismissed immediately and replaced by Hindenburg, with Ludendorf as his chief of staff. By August 23, the two new German leaders had arrived at Marienburg. Three days later, after the two new commanders decided that General Aleksandr Samsonov's second Russian army was their best target, they began the brilliant engagement of Tannenberg. The four days of fighting saw the complete destruction of two Russian corps and the reduction and demoralization of three others, encompassing more than 10,000 dead and over 100,000 prisoners. In Rome, the latest news that the cardinals heard before entering the conclave was that the German triumph on both fronts was virtually complete, and that Samsonov had shot himself in the early hours of the morning of the thirtieth.

With the war uppermost in everyone's mind, the cardinals attended the third requiem on Sunday morning the thirtieth, after which the general congregation had most of the election constitution of Leo XIII, *Prædecessores nostri* of May 24, 1882, read to them. After this, the cardinals dispersed through Rome to see to the collection of their luggage and to enjoy a final supper and sleep before the ceremonies of the next day, which would culminate in their immural in the conclave.

Several groups of cardinals used the opportunity to meet together to determine their strategies for voting in the opening ballots. At four, perhaps the most important of these meetings took place when the six Austro-Germans: von Bettinger, von Hornig, Csernoch, von Hartmann, Piffl, and Skrbensky, bound themselves to vote as a bloc for Della Chiesa on the first ballot. Together, they reserved a reconsideration of their position for subsequent scrutinies, depending on the progress of the election. Their decision had wide ranging implications, since the tremendous military strides made by the Central Powers could only increase the prestige of their national cardinals in the conclave. Their espousal of the case of Della Chiesa placed all six of them firmly in the ranks of the anti-integrists.

The morning of Monday, August 31, saw the formal beginning of the conclave. At 9:30, the Mass of the Holy Spirit was celebrated in the Pauline Chapel by Domenico Ferrata. This was followed immediately by the *monitio*, the formal address to the cardinals, delivered by the functionary charged traditionally with that task, the papal secretary of Latin Briefs to Princes; at this time it was Monsignor Aurelio Galli. He warned the cardinals that the essential quality of the new pope must be great charity, and, if that virtue were not present, then the electors must pass a candidate by, no matter what his other qualifications were. At the end of Galli's address, the cardinals adjourned for their last general congregation before entering the walled area. At this meeting, the remainder of Leo XIII's constitution was read. Many of the cardinals found themselves distracted. They wished to have more details of the doings at the battlefront rather than to listen to a droning prelate course over a document which they had all studied carefully during the preceding days.

At five o'clock, after a short rest, the cardinals reassembled in the Pauline Chapel. The *Veni Sancte Spiritus* was chanted and the cardinals began to process to the Sistina, two by two. When the electors arrived, they found the chapel fully prepared for the conclave, ringed by sixty-five thrones with canopies, one for each member of the College, even though eight were absent. The prayers in the Sistina were recited by Antonio Agliardi, because again Serafino Vannutelli was too exhausted by the events of the day to fulfill his traditional rôle. At the conclusion of the prayers, a lector read that portion of the constitution of Pius X which dealt with the conduct of the conclave, and each cardinal took an oath on the Gospels to uphold its provisions. At this time, a similar oath was administered to the prince-marshal of the conclave, Ludovico Chigi-Albani, the son of the man who filled the same office in 1878 and 1903. Chigi then left the area and began to inspect the exterior of the conclave's precincts to ensure that there would be no breach of security. The cardinals, now locked in, were served supper at 8:30, after which they retired to their cells for the night.

At seven o'clock on the morning of September 1, the cardinals together attended a low Mass, said by Vincenzo Vannutelli, at which all of them received the Eucharist, except Cardinal Benedetto Lorenzelli, archbishop of Lucca, who was gravely ill and kept to his bed. At the end of the Mass, the *Veni Sancte Spiritus* was once more intoned. Then the cardinals drew lots for the names of the nine officials from among themselves who would preside over the first two ballots.

The three scrutators chosen were Luçon, Merry del Val, and della Volpe; the three infirmarians, who would go to Lorenzelli's cell to collect his vote, were Hornig, Netto, and Bartolomeo Bacilieri, the bishop of Verona; and the tellers who would announce the counting of the vote were Arcoverde of Rio de Janeiro; Andrea Ferrari, archbishop of Milan; and Scipione Tecchi, the assessor of the Consistorial Congregation.

At 9:27 A.M., precisely, the actual voting began. Each cardinal, in order of seniority, swore publicly that he had voted for the man he believed best capable of the papacy, then marched to the altar, solemnly deposited his ballot on a paten, and tipped it into the large chalice on the altar. At the end of the voting, the infirmarians brought Lorenzelli's ballot and did for it what had been done for the others. The chalice was then shaken, and the ballots poured into a ciborium. The act now was repeated in reverse, and then the ballots were counted ceremonially, as they were returned to the first vessel. The tellers then began to open the papers and call out the names of those who had received votes, one by one. At the conclusion of this procedure, the tally was:

Pietro Maffi of Pisa	12
Giacomo Della Chiesa of Bologna	12
Basilio Pompilj	9
Raffaele Merry del Val	7
Domenico Serafini	4
Alessandro Lualdi of Palermo	3
Domenico Ferrata	2
Bartolomeo Bacilieri of Verona	2
Pietro Gasparri	1
Antonio Agliardi	1
Diomede Falconio	1
Andrea Ferrari of Milan	1
Girolamo Maria Gotti	1
Gaetano de Laï	1

The result was a decided setback for the integrists at the very opening of the conclave, for no fewer than thirty-two votes out of the fifty-seven cast were for progressive cardinals: Maffi, Della Chiesa, Lualdi, Ferrata, Agliardi, Gasparri, and Ferrari. But the spread of the votes over such a large field, however, certainly aroused fear among the progressives that such diffusion might allow the integrists to rally behind one of their own and bring about a surprise election. Motivated by that fear, Agliardi addressed the College. He urged them to cancel the second ballot of the morning. Such a move, which would have given space to both sides for conference, was rejected overwhelmingly.

The first ballot of every conclave is a dress rehearsal. Each cardinal pays special attention to his rôle and his attitude, so as not to embarrass himself or invalidate the voting. Thereafter, with familiarity, the pace proceeds more swiftly. In 1914, the electors found their stride with great celerity. The second ballot, which began at 10:42, lasted only thirteen minutes. It went so smoothly, in fact, that a delay of five minutes had to be imposed, to allow time for the infirmarians to collect Lorenzelli's ballot. When the results were announced and tallied, the progressives could begin to feel somewhat easier in mind, as their favorites began to build up a substantial block of votes:

Pietro Maffi	16
Giacomo Della Chiesa	16
Basilio Pompilj	10
Raffaele Merry del Val	7
Domenico Serafini	2
Alessandro Lualdi	2
Domenico Ferrata	2
Bartolomeo Bacilieri	1
Agostino Richelmy of Turin	1

In the first ballot, thirty-two votes had been given to candidates who clearly were anti-integrist in their thinking. In the second, that number had risen to thirty-six. The progressives were cheered, not only by the narrowing of the field of candidates but also by the increased support their cause was marshalling. The conservatives, meanwhile, could still count on enough votes to bar anyone from the throne who was not of their number, for the twenty votes given to Pompilj, Merry del Val, Serafini, and Richelmy were one more than the one-third necessary to prevent the election of a progressive.

The ballots and tally sheets from both the morning scrutinies were bundled together and burned. At 11:37, the crowd in Saint Peter's Square saw the black smoke which told them that the cardinals had made no choice.

Inside, the electors agreed to take the first scrutiny of the afternoon at five o'clock, which allowed them substantial time for internal politicking; then they adjourned for lunch.

Unlike the 1878 election, when conclavists carried on much of the inter-scrutiny campaigning, by carrying messages back and forth for their masters, the cardinals in 1914 kept every aspect of their political discussions in their own hands. The war raging outside and the constitution of Pius X ruling inside combined to make each elector much more cautious about revealing his convictions or intentions.

During the long, warm Roman afternoon, several cardinals busied themselves by visiting colleagues for the purpose of swaying votes. The most important of these calls was Agliardi's visit to the junior German cardinal, von Bettinger, who could be relied upon to communicate fully with his colleagues from the Central Powers whatever he learned from other members of the College.

It was apparently common knowledge that six of the votes Della Chiesa had received in each scrutiny had been cast by the Austro-Germans, and Agliardi now tried to enlist von Bettinger in persuading his colleagues to switch their votes to Maffi. The archbishop of Pisa, Agliardi explained, was the progressive cardinal who was endowed with the most comprehensive intelligence, and was the most fit to lead the Church in a time of world crisis. Della Chiesa, by contrast, was only a good bureaucrat, a *mediocris homo*. Von Bettinger duly carried these comments to his fellow northerners but, after some discussion, the Austro-Germans decided to continue to vote for Della Chiesa as before. Meanwhile, Amette and the other non-German progressives resolved to continue their efforts for Maffi. Though the Pisan cardinal's supporters did not realize it yet, the rejection of their advances by the Austro-Germans meant that the high tide of favor for their candidate had passed. The six central European votes were essential to the ultimate success of any anti-integrist candidate, so, if the Germans would not bend, then perforce the others must rally to them, or face one of two unacceptable outcomes: an integrist pope or a lengthy, divisive conclave. In addition, some of Maffi's supporters realized that several progressive Italians were splitting the liberal vote by supporting Della Chiesa: Ferrata surely, and probably Lualdi, Gasparri, and Maffi himself. If these cardinals, who were receiving the Anglo-French votes, as well as many of the Italian progressive ones, were themselves supporting Della Chiesa, what other result could there possibly be?

When the cardinals reassembled in the Sistine at five o'clock, there was an anxious quality to the meeting that was absent in the morning. Each cardinal surely wondered how the campaigning of the afternoon had affected the chances of the candidate he supported, or of his own opportunity.

The first order of business was the usual drawing to determine the scrutators, infirmarians, and tellers. The infirmarians would be only ceremonial on this occasion, since Lorenzelli had struggled into the chapel to take part in the balloting with his healthier colleagues. The scrutators were Almaraz y Santos of Seville, Bourne of England, and Ottavio Caggiano de Azevedo, the chancellor of the Church. The infirmarians were de Cabrieres of Montpelier, Farley of New York, and Lualdi of Palermo. The tellers were von Bettinger of Munich, Gasparri, and—Della Chiesa of Bologna. This whole proceeding took only ten minutes, and then the cardinals held the third scrutiny. During the tally, several cardinals remarked on Della Chiesa's demeanor as he called out his own name time after time. "His rather high-pitched voice read the name of each candidate. . . slowly, calmly, and distinctly as though it were his task to read a bulletin which had reference to some person who concerned him only very remotely." When the results were complete the count was:

Giacomo Della Chiesa	18
Pietro Maffi	16
Basilio Pompilj	9
Raffaele Merry del Val	7
Domenico Serafini	2
Alessandro Lualdi	2
Agostino Richelmy	2
Domenico Ferrata	1

Only a little had changed since the morning vote, but that little had great significance. Maffi had retained his sixteen votes but had added none. Lualdi and Serafini each retained their two, and Merry del Val had kept his seven curial stalwarts. But Pompilj, the leading integrist, had lost one of his valued ten to Richelmy, which began the erosion of the former's position. And Della Chiesa had gained two: one from Ferrata, which in itself was not too surprising, but apparently also the vote which had gone to Bacilieri during the morning, a vote which had appeared to be neutral in the progressive-integrist controversy—Bacilieri's position.

The fourth scrutiny began at 5:45, after only a brief pause. When the results were tallied by Della Chiesa, von Bettinger, and Gasparri, they were:

Giacomo Della Chiesa	21
Pietro Maffi	14
Basilio Pompilj	9
Raffaele Merry del Val	6
Domenico Serafini	2
Alessandro Lualdi	2
Girolamo Maria Gotti	1
Agostino Richelmy	1
Domenico Ferrata	1

The trend in the election was now apparent, for Maffi had lost two of his votes to Della Chiesa, who had also picked up another vote, possibly the one which had gone to Richelmy in the third scrutiny. If that were so, and many cardinals believed it, it marked the first conservative vote which was detached from the integrist bloc in favor of Della Chiesa. Moreover, the voters saw a further breakdown in the conservative ranks, as Merry del Val lost one of his seven to Girolamo Maria Gotti, the aging "Marble Cardinal" whose time had passed in 1903.

The ballots and tallies were once more bundled together and burned. The black smoke became visible to the crowd outside at 6:30.

Through the evening after supper, and on into the night, various partisans made efforts on behalf of all the major candidates. The thought uppermost in the minds of the integrists was to defeat the candidacy of Della Chiesa, no matter what they had to undergo, since the archbishop of Bologna was the one cardinal in the College who represented most thoroughly the views and policies of Leo XIII and Rampolla—not only had he been the latter's able under-secretary for many years, but he made no secret of his admiration for his former mater.

A part of the conservative maneuvering saw Gaetano Bisleti seek out another of the Germans, von Hartmann this time, to urge from the other side that the central European cardinals give up their support for Della Chiesa. Bisleti sought to convince von Hartmann that a vote for the Bolognese archbishop was simply an affront to the memory of Pius X, because the late pope had "exiled" Della Chiesa to Bologna as mark of disapproval, rather than giving him the valued nunciature at Madrid. Everyone knew, continued Bisleti, that every pope elevated a new archbishop of Bologna to the cardinalate at the earliest possible time after his archiepiscopal appointment, but Pius X had made Della Chiesa wait seven years for that honor. And all this was done, so he said, because Della Chiesa had continued to espouse the views of Rampolla after the latter had been dismissed as secretary of state. Bisleti offered von Hartmann two other thoughts—that Della Chiesa was hot-tempered, and therefore unfit, and that he did not truly represent the views of a majority of the College.

Von Hartmann conveyed these opinions into the conversation of the Austro-Germans that evening, but Bisleti's efforts were a failure, since all six decided to continue to back Della Chiesa in the morning, and only then to reassess their position, if the relative positions of the candidates were to change.

Meanwhile, the conservatives found themselves under the immediate necessity of uniting behind one candidate if they were to have any chance at all. Under Pius X, Gaetano de Laï had exercised almost as much influence over internal affairs as Merry del Val had over external affairs. De Laï now moved strongly to have the conservatives unite to raise his candidate for the throne, Domenico Serafini. Most of the electors knew that Serafini was not a strong-willed man and, if elected, would be so obligated to de Laï as to make the latter a complete power behind the throne. Yet they also realized that de Laï was, if anything, even more reactionary, and more hated by the progressives, than Merry del Val himself, so he stood no chance of election in his own right. During these discussions, de Laï managed to woo eight of the integrists away from the side of Pompilj and Merry del Val. It was a desperate attempt, obvious in nature, but with a slight possibility of success.

By about eleven o'clock, most of the cardinals had retired for the night, anticipating early Mass in the morning. The overtures during the evening had come almost exclusively from the integrists, and only the following day's vote would show whether or not they had made any inroads into the growing party for Della Chiesa.

On the morning of Wednesday, September 2, the cardinals attended a low Mass celebrated by the sacristan of the conclave and then went to the Sistine for the fifth scrutiny, which began at 9:30.

Conclave in War

The three *scrutatores* were Ferrata, Billot, and Giulio Boschi, the archbishop of Ferrara; the three *infirmarii* were Filippo Giustini, the cardinal-prefect of the Congregation for the Sacraments; Aristide Rinaldini, a curial cardinal attached to the Congregation for Extraordinary Ecclesiastical Affairs; and Almaraz y Santos, who had acted as a scrutator on the previous evening; the *recognitores* were Guisasola y Menendez, Netto, and Luçon.

Within half an hour, the scrutiny was over, and the tally now read:

Giacomo Della Chiesa	20
Pietro Maffi	13
Domenico Serafini	10
Basilio Pompilj	6
Raffaele Merry del Val	2
Alessandro Lualdi	2
Agostino Richelmy	1
Bartolomeo Bacilieri	1
Giuseppe Francica-Nava di Bontifé	1
Willem van Rossum	1

Subtly, the integrist surge was having an effect. Della Chiesa did not seem to have been damaged too much, yet he had lost one vote, which probably had reverted to Bacilieri. But Maffi had sustained yet another loss, while Pompilj and Merry del Val could watch almost cheerfully as their candidacies declined, since ten conservative votes rallied behind Serafini, thanks to the campaigning of de Laï. The trend was further revealed in the vote for Francica-Nava and that for van Rossum. The latter, one of the few non-Italian integrists, was possessed of great dignity and poise. Piffl remarked that he, at least, looked like a pope, especially when compared to Della Chiesa, who had a birth defect which left him with a decided limp and a lopsided expression in addition to his very short stature.

Suddenly, there was no time for campaigning. The forthcoming sixth scrutiny required the electors to make crucial decisions in a few moments, without consultation. What if the sudden boomlet for Serafini turned into a tide that swept him to the throne? What if there should be a sudden surge by a large number of cardinals in favor of an unknown quantity, like Francica-Nava? This was the critical moment. However, the votes turned on the sixth ballot would determine the tempo for the next series of scrutinies, and might well lead to an election.

At 10:15, the cardinals began again, acutely aware of the moment. Within a few minutes, all fifty-seven ballots were in the chalice waiting to be counted. When the results were tallied, it was clear that the first stage of the final battle between the progressives and the integrists had been joined:

Giacomo Della Chiesa	27
Domenico Serafini	17
Pietro Maffi	7
Giuseppe Francica-Nava di Bontifé	1
Alessandro Lualdi	2
Basilio Pompilj	2
Agostino Richelmy	1

In a sudden realization that their cause might be lost were they to divide further, six of Maffi's supporters moved to Della Chiesa. And when they sensed that they must support Serafini now or the integrist cause would sink forever, four of Pompilj's six backers and both of Merry del Val's remaining votes went to Serafini, who gained still another vote, probably that which had gone to van Rossum a few minutes before. Bacilieri's supporter also abandoned him, probably in favor of Della Chiesa.

The cardinals burned the morning papers—the crowd outside saw the black smoke at eleven o'clock—and then they adjourned until five o'clock. During the afternoon, the conversations between cardinals were quite straightforward. If you are a conservative and wish a continuation of the policies of the late reign, then you must vote for Serafini. If you long to return to the urbanity of Leo XIII and desire to mend the diplomatic fences so badly damaged in the preceding decade, then you must vote for Della Chiesa. The time for the most intensive examination of conscience and purpose was at hand. A "religious" pope—Serafini, or a "diplomatic" one—Della Chiesa. For the aged, senior cardinals, it was their last chance to influence the course of the Catholic Church. For the younger electors, it was their opportunity to determine how the Church would be administered during a great war, one that would see half of Europe humbled at its end and the victorious half ruined.

At five o'clock, the Sistine heard once again the names of the nine officials who would preside over the next two scrutinies. Logue, Skrbensky, and Cos y Macho, would be the scrutators; Ferrata, Arcoverde, and von Hartmann, the infirmarians; Andrieu, Caggiano de Azevedo, and van Rossum, the tellers. Quickly the vote was taken and tallied:

Giacomo Della Chiesa	31
Domenico Serafini	21
Pietro Maffi	2
Agostino Richelmy	1
Giuseppe Francica-Nava di Bontifé	1
Basilio Pompilj	1

The battle-lines drawn on the sixth vote were becoming clearer. Two liberals still held out for Maffi and one conservative remained with Pompilj, while the cardinal who had been inspired by Francica-Nava quixotically held to his late conversion, and Richelmy kept the vote he had held from the second ballot forward—which later was revealed to be that of Serafini himself, who could not bring himself to vote for Della Chiesa and was ineligible to vote for himself. Ninety per cent of the College now had coalesced into a firm party position.

The electors immediately moved to the eighth ballot, the last of the day. Grimly or hopefully, they made their choices:

Giacomo Della Chiesa	32
Domenico Serafini	24
Agostino Richelmy	1

Della Chiesa had gained one of Maffi's last two votes, and lost the other; while Serafini had swept all the remaining waverers, giving his own vote to Richelmy. The conclave was now deadlocked!

The agitation in the Sistine became apparent to those outside, when they saw the smoke from the burning ballots. At 6:46, white smoke issued from the chimney, and the crowd, nearly a hundred thousand strong, became more excited as it reacted to the presumed election of a new pope. Inside, the cardinals simply had failed to add the wet straw to cause black smoke. Realizing their mistake, they did so, and the smoke quickly turned gray, then black. The ardor in the square dampened, and the crowd dispersed.

As they left the Sistine for supper, the electors knew that they were facing some of the most dangerous moments in the history of the modern Church. Della Chiesa could not attain the thirty-eight votes he needed for election without the support of a few conservatives. The twenty-four supporters of Serafini likewise knew that, if they stood fast with him, they could block the election of any progressive—Della Chiesa or another. If both sides were unaltered in the morning, the fate of the conclave would be clear—either a complete dismantling of the current electoral coalitions followed by a new search for a compromise pope; or a long, bitter conclave which would only grow more polarized inside while Europe was being destroyed outside. In this frame of mind, each cardinal retired to his cell to consider his morning vote.

By nine on the morning of the third of September, all the electors were at their thrones in the Sistine for the ninth ballot. They had heard a low Mass and had breakfasted speedily in order to begin the proceedings thirty minutes earlier than they had on Wednesday.

Caggiano de Azevedo, Merry del Val, and Bacilieri were the scrutators; Luçon, Logue, and Tecchi were the infirmarians; and Falconio, Andrieu, and de Laï were the tellers. Again, the cardinals did their voting with haste—each desired to know if one of the opposing walls would crack. When the results were announced, the rift, small but critical, plainly was in view:

Giacomo Della Chiesa	34
Domenico Serafini	22
Agostino Richelmy	1

It seemed that it was the conservatives who were giving way, but would the erosion continue? The cardinals balloted a second time, at 10:21. Now their speed was feverish—the progressives hoped for a quick victory, while the die-hard integrists hoped to stall one more time to give them the opportunity for a last ditch campaign before the evening scrutinies. In nine minutes it was over. De Laï, in a controlled voice, read the name Della Chiesa over and over again, each time a stroke in the knell that was bringing his years as a Vatican power to a close:

Giacomo Della Chiesa	38
Domenico Serafini	18
Agostino Richelmy	1

The archbishop of Bologna had obtained a majority of just two-thirds. The cardinals turned, to untwist the cords which controlled the canopies over their heads and lower them in the presence of the new supreme pontiff. But the agony was not quite over. A die-hard integrist, unknown today, demanded that the ballots be opened until the tellers verified that Della Chiesa had not voted for himself, which would have invalidated the scrutiny. Della Chiesa made no protest. He sat, cold and tight-lipped, on his throne while the tellers carried out the examination—the last insult he would ever endure publicly in his career. Falconio, Andrieu, and de Laï opened the ballots, one by one, until they found the new pope's—he had voted for Serafini.

Conclaves are not as secret as they are supposed to be. Outside, in Saint Peter's Square, someone had passed the word to the throng that the election was over, yet there was no smoke at all. Rumors and murmurs began to mount as certainty grew.

Inside, Serafino Vannutelli performed his most solemn act as dean of the College of Cardinals. He stepped slowly before Della Chiesa, whose throne was the seventeenth from the altar on the right side. Firmly, he put the age-old question, and Della Chiesa replied that he accepted the election. The dean then asked by what name he would be known. Every new pope for a century and more had taken the time to briefly explain his reasons for choosing the name he did, but this time the reply was abrupt, "Benedictus"—

Benedict the Fifteenth. The pope never did explain his choice, but many thought that he chose the name Benedict in honor of Benedict XIV, the last archbishop of Bologna before him to be elected pope. It was now a few minutes before 11:30 A.M. Della Volpe, as chamberlain, now came forward and slipped the Fisherman's Ring onto Benedict's hand, and then the ballots and tallies were burned, finally confirming the rumors outside. A procession was formed to conduct della Volpe, as archdeacon of the College, to the central loggia of Saint Peter's for the formal announcement of the election to the people. The great windows were swung wide and a tapestry was unfurled over the rail. The Romans knew at once that there had been a sudden break with the customs of the past because, contrary to tradition, the coat-of-arms on the tapestry was not that of Pius X. Della Volpe appeared and announced the elected in a somewhat abbreviated version of old formula, "Annuntio vobis, gaudium magnum, habemus papam. Eminentissimum et Reverendissimum Cardinalem Iacobum Della Chiesa, qui sibi nomen imposuit Benedictum decimum quintum." After a few moments of thundering cheers, 50,000 of those outside streamed into Saint Peter's to receive the first blessing of the new pope from the interior loggia, in keeping with the custom begun by Leo XIII and continued by Pius X.

Meanwhile, in the Sistine Chapel, Benedict had been conducted to the sacristy to be fitted into one of the three sets of robes which had been prepared for the new pontiff. Even the smallest of them, though, proved far too large for his tiny frame. His finger-tips barely escaped the cuffs and the cape utterly engulfed his small, uneven shoulders. While robing him, his principal conclavist, Monsignor Giuseppe Migone, was suddenly overcome with the fact that his master was now the pope and he began to weep; tears blurred his vision and he fumbled and dropped pins all over the place. Characteristically, the reserved Benedict chided him, "Come now, come, one would think you had been elected pope and not I."

As soon as the robing was complete, the cardinals came forward one by one for the first informal obedience, kissing first his feet, then his ring, and then both cheeks. When it came the turn of Merry del Val to offer his submission, the cardinal took a few seconds to ask two favors of the new pope: that Pius X's nephew,

Monsignor Parolin, be made a canon of Saint Peter's, and that the small pension that Pius X paid to his sisters be continued. Benedict immediately complied with both requests, and indeed quintupled the amount of the pension. The Vatican's newspaper, *Osservatore Romano*, carried two announcements in its issue for September 3, one of the new pope's election and the other of Parolin's appointment.

When the first act of obedience was complete, Benedict went immediately to the inner loggia and imparted his blessing; then to the apartments of Pius X, where the doors were unsealed and Benedict began at once to go through the state papers of business left incomplete at Pius's death, "just as if he had been pope for years." No tears, no lamentations by Benedict, as Leo and Pius had wept—just duty.

The vantage of most of a century makes it possible to assess the conclave of 1914 somewhat better than many of its participants did. The six Austro-German cardinals were viewed collectively as the grand electors in the assembly, and so regarded themselves. Piffl noted in his diary: "Thus, thanks to our perseverance, we Austrians and Germans have succeeded in getting our candidate elected." But if Piffl thought that the efforts of the central European cardinals were to be rewarded with favoritism, he was mistaken. Benedict immediately replaced Merry del Val as secretary of state with Domenico Ferrata, the former nuncio in Paris, and when that cardinal died after only a month in office, Gasparri was chosen in turn. Thus, the new pope displayed, from the very outset of the reign, a sympathy for France, which belied the Germanophile feelings many French thought he had during the course of World War I. Benedict tried to steer an even, neutral course among the powers, even after Italy entered the war on the side of the Allies. Perhaps his greatest public achievement was his seven point proposal for peace, issued on August 1, 1917. The ultimate failure of this proposal was engendered by the firm rejection of the United States, yet the most salient of Wilson's fourteen points derived from Benedict's document.

Benedict's reign saw a substantial diminution of integrist power in the Vatican. Benedict replaced not only Merry del Val but also Nicola Canali and several other conservative members of the secretariat of state, and he began the difficult labor of winning back good diplomatic relations with many governments whose dealings with Pius and Merry del Val had been anything but cordial. Success followed these effects, and, by the end of the reign, the number of countries represented at the Vatican had risen from fourteen to twenty-six, including France.

Since Benedict was only fifty-nine when he came to the throne—one of the six youngest popes in the last two hundred fifty years—his contemporaries predicted a relatively long reign. Indeed, his three modern predecessors who were under sixty when they were elected, Pius VI, Pius VII, and Pius IX, had each reigned for more than twenty years. Such was not the case for Benedict, however. The trouble of his birth and his natural inclination to frailty endowed him with a delicate constitution, even though he always was healthy in adulthood. The essential strength of his constitution was sapped by anxiety and frustration caused by the war. Ultimately, Benedict XV, as well as Pius X, can be considered its casualty.

V
THE "ROMAN QUESTION"

UNLIKE ANY of the three past reigns, the end of the pontificate of Benedict XV was heralded by several warnings; but no one, except perhaps the pope himself, appeared to notice. The first occurred late in November, 1921, when Benedict was asked by the Sisters of the Hospice of Saint Martha to say Mass for them on the final day of their spiritual retreat, a request the pope granted willingly. In order to reach the sisters's chapel, it was necessary to traverse a number of Vatican corridors and cross through Saint Peter's. Early on the appointed morning, Benedict made his way on this route, only to find one of the doors on his way locked. At that time, no portion of the Vatican was equipped with central heating, and the pope was forced to stand for more than half an hour in a cold and damp passage until a functionary could be found with the correct key to unlock the door. Within a day the pope had contracted a cold which it seemed impossible for him to shake. Throughout the festivities for Christmas and the New Year, the illness persisted, gradually weakening his health. By the time the pope gave the annual reception for Roman patricians, on Thursday, January 5, 1922, he was suffering from a wracking cough. When he left this reception, Benedict was overheard to remark, "A cough is the drum of death." One week later, at 6:30 on the morning of January 12, the pope said Mass in the Cappella Matilde for the students of the College of the Propaganda. Those who took communion from Benedict's hands noticed that they were hot and feverish. The address that the pope gave to the students was punctuated by seizures of violent coughing.

Throughout this six-week period the pontiff had not varied his usual schedule. He arose at five o'clock and retired at ten at night. During the week following the Mass for the students, he continued with a heavy schedule of private audiences, as well. On Sunday, the fifteenth, he received seven persons in separate private sessions; on Monday, five; and on Tuesday, seven more. During the course of Monday, the pope was examined by his regular physician, Dr. Raffaele Battistini, who persuaded the pope to retire at eight o'clock that evening instead of the usual ten.

Tuesday's round of visitors included Cardinal Teodoro Valfré di Bonzo, an old friend who was nearly the same age as the pope and who also was in the last year of his life. Following this audience, Benedict received the new Apostolic delegate to the Ukraine, Father Gennochi. These men, and others, could not but notice the pontiff's deteriorated condition, yet apparently no one felt it necessary to impress upon the pope the need for rest. By six o'clock on Tuesday evening, the pope was near exhaustion and finally was persuaded to go to bed before the usual hour.

On the next morning, January 18, the pope was unable to rise. Dr. Battistini was summoned at a very early hour. After he examined his patient, he released a medical bulletin which stated that the pope had remained in bed with a feverish cold—something of a serious understatement. Later in the morning, Benedict received the cardinal-secretary of state, Pietro Gasparri, for a long diplomatic briefing. Meanwhile, Dr. Battistini asked Dr. Amico Bignami, a specialist in respiratory diseases, to join him on the case. Dr. Ettore Marchiafava, a close colleague of Bignami and one of the physicians who had treated Pius X in his last illness, also was called to the medical team. Shortly after two o'clock in the afternoon, Benedict once again was examined by Dr. Battistini, who pronounced himself satisfied with the pope's condition. The pontiff spent the remainder of the day resting, and was seen by both Battistini and Bignami again in the evening. The night passed easily for Benedict and, at 5:30 A.M. on Thursday, January 19, he received yet another visit from his physicians, who spent an hour and a half with him. At the close of this examination, the medical team emerged from the papal bedchamber with an optimistic report. Bignami stated that "a few days in bed would completely restore the pope's health."

After this medical introduction to the day, Benedict attended Mass from his bed. A small portable altar was set up outside his door, but within his vision, at which Monsignor Giuseppe Migone, his aide since his years as archbishop of Bologna, officiated. At eight o'clock, after a brief conversation with Cardinal Gasparri, both doctors left the Vatican, Battistini saying that he would return at two in the afternoon.

Later in the day, Benedict had a long briefing from Gasparri which continued into a personal conversation. The pope confided to his favorite cardinal that, up to that time, his entire expenditure for medical care in adulthood had amounted to only two and a half lire. At one point, the pope asked Gasparri to get some papers for him from the work desk in the bedroom. Benedict was amused as he watched the cardinal rummage fruitlessly through his personal possessions; "Please bring me the whole drawer," he finally said, "I should have known that you couldn't see with my eyes."

After Gasparri's departure, Migone and the others near the pope made every effort to see that he remained as quiet and undisturbed as possible. Members of the diplomatic corps, many of whom were personal friends of the pope, were turned away from the papal apartments as they came to inquire about the pope's condition. The papal servants apparently kept the curial staff at a distance as well, so that the pontiff was allowed to be alone during nearly all the rest of Thursday.

When he finally fell asleep that night, there was every expectation that the improvement in his condition predicted by the doctors would occur and that soon the full pontifical schedule would be met again. Like his predecessor, Pius X, Benedict's end was signalled by a crisis at night while he was alone, for when he awakened on Friday morning he had taken a dramatic turn for the worse; his gasping breath was audible to everyone who came near his door. Dr. Lorenzo Cherubini, another respiratory specialist like Bignami and Marchiafava, already had been called to the Vatican, and now he was ushered into the bedroom in great haste. He immediately administered both sedatives and expectorants in the hope that the pope would gain some relief by expelling some of the congestion which caused his breathing to be so labored. A Vatican car was sent to bring Bignami from his Roman residence, and by 5:00 A.M. he was at the pope's bedside. After a brief examination, Bignami left to consult with Marchiafava, who then returned to the Vatican with him. By seven o'clock they were joined by Battistini. This team of four would watch and care for Benedict throughout the final hours. At eight o'clock, they issued a medical bulletin which stated that the pope's right lung was fully congested and that his respiration had become labored, though Benedict's temperature was only slightly more than a hundred degrees.

After this, the pope once again heard Mass from his bed, celebrated by Monsignor Migone, who gave communion to his master of many years. Then Benedict's doctors gave him oxygen in the hope that his breathing would ease. At the conclusion of the Mass, the pontiff expressed a strong desire to receive the last rites, and someone sent Agostino Zampini, the Augustinian titular bishop of Porfireone, the sacristan of the palace, to perform this office—just as he had for Pius X, seven and a half years before. Benedict also had asked for solitude to prepare himself for the final rite of the Church to which he had given his life. Those about him gave him these few minutes of peace, but Bishop Zampini did not have the opportunity of quietly doing his office as he had for Pius X, because by the time his little procession had reached the door of the bedchamber it had been joined by twenty cardinals. At the same time, the little antechamber next to the bedroom had filled with virtually every member of the diplomatic corps then in Rome. Cardinal Oreste Giorgi, the major penitentiary, began the final rites at 11:30. He began to read the profession of faith of the Council of Trent and then that of the First Vatican Council while the pope was being vested, over his night clothes, in rochet, pectoral cross, and stole. By this time, Benedict was too weak to sit up in bed and read the formula, so the profession was repeated, a few words at a time, and the pope thus had time to collect himself sufficiently to answer. After this, Giorgi pronounced a general absolution over his dying leader. As the bedchamber filled with cardinals, Benedict heard one of them say, "Holy Father, worry about nothing, but do just as your doctors tell you." Unable to identify the prelate who had spoken, Benedict, in a clear, firm voice, audible to all, replied, "If it pleases the Lord that I shall work again for his Church, I am ready; if he says, 'Enough,' let His will be done." He then turned to Cardinal Augusto Silj who, as Prefect of the Supreme Tribunal of the Apostolic Signature, was responsible for much of the daily office procedure at the Vatican in Benedict's time. To him the pope said, "I beg you to pray for me to the Virgin of Pompeii." Now the medical team came in for a brief check on how the pontiff was bearing up under the ceremonies of his death. Benedict was raised a little in bed, and his right hand laid upon a gilt-edged scarlet velvet cushion so that the cardinals could come forward singly and kiss his ring for the last time. Throughout the lengthy procession of cardinals, the pope seemed comatose, but when Merry del Val approached, he opened his eyes and said, "Alive or dead, pray for me."

After the members of the College had left, Gasparri returned and spent about twenty minutes in conversation with the pope. It was at this time that the cardinal-secretary of state took charge of the pope's will. Afterward, Gasparri ordered telegrams to be dispatched to all of the forty-one cardinals who were outside Rome directing them to prepare for their journey to take part in a conclave. Other messages that announced the pope's serious condition were sent to Vatican diplomats stationed around the world and to members of the Della Chiesa family in Genoa and Piacenza.

In the evening, Benedict received his nephews, Count Giovanni Persico, the son of his beloved elder sister, Giulia, and the Marchese Giuseppe Della Chiesa. He asked them for their prayers and was told in return that the whole world was praying for him. Later, Benedict overheard Dr. Battistini mutter, "Take me away, O Lord, but spare the pope." The pontiff turned toward him and said, "It is you who should go to bed. You are older than I. Go to bed." After another administration of oxygen and injections of camphor, the pope was able to rest somewhat more comfortably during the remainder of the evening of the twentieth, but at two o'clock on Saturday morning he was again awake, and requested viaticum once more. Bishop Zampini now performed the rite for which he had been sent on the preceding evening. After he received communion, Benedict seemed to regain some strength. But, after this short respite, the pope's condition worsened suddenly, and all visitors were dismissed. This crisis, shortly before dawn, left him gasping for breath and in intense pain. Dr. Battistini emerged from the sickroom at 5:15 to make an announcement that the pope's decline was now irreversible. Cardinal Gasparri and the pope's eldest nephew, Giuseppe Della Chiesa, were sent for.

Now the physicians held another consultation to determine if they should try any new measures to ease the pope's passing. At

7:00, Gasparri came out into the antechamber and said to those present that, in his opinion, death was near. About half an hour later, the sun began to rise over a grey Rome. Some of the attendants present in the antechamber moved over to a window, to look out on a large silent crowd which had gathered to pray for the pontiff, and one of them remarked, "Now it is dawn, it brings hope." An hour later, the four doctors issued another medical bulletin which stated that the pneumonia had advanced during the pope's agitated and sleepless night and that Benedict's fever was once again at 101 degrees.

Immediately after the medical consultation, however, the pope experienced a marked turn for the better. He asked to be turned on his side and, when this was done, he fell asleep almost at once. This development was so startling to the physicians that one of them voiced the thought that if Benedict would only remain at complete rest for even three or fours hours there might yet be some hope of saving his life. The pope's rest, however, lasted only about an hour. When he awoke, he felt sufficiently improved to ask for breakfast. In response to this request, he was given some soup, a serving of tapioca, and a small glass of wine.

January 21 is the feast of Saint Agnes, patroness of the Capranica College, where the pope had studied in his youth. Remembering this, Benedict asked that a small statue of the saint, which had been presented to him by students at the College, be brought in and placed so that he might see it. He then gave short audiences to several cardinals, including Vincenzo Vannutelli, the dean of the College; Raffaele Merry del Val; and Camillo Laurenti, the junior member of the College.

At eleven o'clock, he asked that the new archbishop of Bologna, Giovanni Battista Nasalli-Rocca di Corneliano, be brought to him. The pope and the archbishop had a fairly long, spirited conversation which turned on the reception the latter had received at his enthronement in Bologna a few weeks before. After a time, they were joined by Ersilio Manzani, bishop of Piacenza, for whom the pope also had asked.

Suddenly, a few minutes after noon, the pope suffered a complete relapse. The visitors were hastened away and their place taken by Benedict's doctors. As the pontiff sank into delirium, Battistini tried to listen to his heart rate, but Benedict strenuously resisted any further handling by the doctors—"I am tired, I am tired, leave me alone. I want rest, I want sleep." At 12:30, Prince Ludovico Chigi-Albani entered the papal apartments in expectation of the pope's end. It was his duty to seal the rooms Benedict had occupied immediately after the official pronouncement of death. At once the antechamber began to fill again with the cardinals resident or working at the Vatican—old adversaries, Gaetano de Laï, Willem van Rossum, Basilio Pompilj, Louis Billot, Antonio Vico, Ottavio Caggiano de Azevado; and his own creations, Tommaso Pio Boggiani, Donato Sbarretti, Teodoro Valfré di Bonzo, Andreas Franz Frühwirth, Vittorio Amadeo Ranuzzi de' Bianchi, Niccolo Marini, Giovanni Cagliero, and Francesco Ragonesi.

At two o'clock, Benedict suddenly threw back his covers and began to rise, announcing that he intended to resume work, that he had so much to do. Some force was necessary to persuade him to stay where he was. Shortly after this, his delirium became worse but, about four o'clock, he regained lucidity once more. At this time, Dr. Battistini told him directly that the coming hours would be his last. Benedict's reply was fully in keeping with his life's dedication, "Willingly do we offer our life for the peace of the world." He then sank down on his pillows, from the slight rise he had made while he addressed Battistini, and called for Fra Celidonio, his male nurse. He told the latter that Cardinal Antonio Vico would say the next Mass at the little portable altar, in place of the majordomo of the palace, Monsignor Riccardo Sanz de Samper, who was ill. Under no circumstances, continued the pope, was the majordomo to be awakened in the morning, for this would cause him to lose the rest he needed to regain his health.

Gradually, the pope's vital signs grew weaker. He drifted off into a fitful sleep. At 5:10 P.M., Cardinal Gasparri left Benedict's bedside and went into the antechamber to tell the members of the diplomatic corps gathered there that the end was now very near. His voice was choked with emotion.

During the course of the evening there was no sudden change in the pope's condition, but it was clear that his struggle was drawing to a close. At about eight o'clock, he awoke and turned to his nephew, Giuseppe, to ask if prayers were really being offered for him. "Not only in Rome, but in all the churches in Italy and the world," was the reply. Again the pope closed his eyes, but at eight thirty he spoke to Nasalli-Rocca, who was standing nearby, "It's too late for you, go to bed." About an hour later, he attempted to rise once more but was restrained gently. Unexpectedly, he then asked what time it was. When he was told that it was nine thirty, he replied, "Well, there is plenty of time before six o'clock." This response was ascribed to another attack of delirium at the time, but later it would achieve great significance for those who had heard it. At 11:15, Benedict made one final effort to rise and, when he sank back, he entered a motionless state which persisted, with one moment's exception, to the end.

Shortly after midnight, Monsignor Migone said another Mass in the antechamber, but this time Benedict paid no heed to the service. At about one in the morning, Dr. Battistini came in and, glancing at the pope, came out at once to tell those clustered about the door that the end had nearly come. At this, Cardinal Oreste Giorgi, in his capacity of major penitentiary, entered the death chamber so that he could grant a final absolution to the pope and preside over the last minutes of papal life. By two o'clock, Benedict's face had become waxen, his nose seemingly even more pointed; his mouth had dropped open and the death rattle could be plainly heard throughout the room. Giorgi stepped forward, and, shouting, so as to penetrate the closing curtain of life, cried, "Holiness, bless your relatives." A barely perceptible movement of the right hand could be seen. Again Giorgi shouted, "Holiness, now bless your household." And again there was a slight motion of the hand. Now Giorgi cried, "Holiness, bless the people who desire peace." With a sudden, convulsed jerk Benedict rose to a half seated position—eyes wide open—and, in a voice which contained the last of his strength, he cried out, "May the blessing of Almighty God, Father, Son, and Holy Spirit, descend on you now and remain forever," as he slowly and deliberately traced the sign of the cross in the air three times in a grand benediction. His whole constitution was now exhausted, and he collapsed backward in a completely moribund state, while the others in the room tried to regain their composure after this splendid moment.

In the room were gathered both of Benedict's nephews, the four doctors, Gasparri and several other cardinals, Nasalli-Rocca, Zampini, and the faithful Migone. They stood and watched the pope's breathing become shallower and more irregular until, at six o'clock, the very hour he had mentioned earlier, Benedict gave a great sigh. Dr. Bignami leaned forward and held a candle near the lips of the pontiff. The flame did not flicker.

A few moments later, Gasparri reëntered the bedroom clad in the purple robes of the chamberlain of the Church. While the other cardinals, robed in black, stood clustered around the bed, Gasparri raised the veil which had been placed over Benedict's face and, trembling, called out the dead pope's Christian name three times. He then turned and pronounced the pope truly dead. He slipped the Fisherman's Ring from the motionless finger and collected the papal seals that were kept in the bedroom desk. He turned and announced to the assembled members of the College a startling break with tradition—there was to be no prolonged lying in state for the people, because Benedict had commanded that his body not be embalmed. Moreover, tradition was shattered further when Gasparri broke the news that the first official notice of the pope's death had been sent to Premier Ivanoe Bonomi of Italy, thus ending forever the non-recognition of the Italian government by the Vatican. This gesture was in response to the official call made by the Italian minister of agriculture, Angelo Mauri, on the preceding day to inquire about the health of the pope.

For the remainder of the twenty-second, Benedict's corpse lay on the bed in which he had died, treated with only a few slight injections of formalin, receiving the homage of Vatican prelates, members of the diplomatic corps, and the representatives of Rome's old aristocratic families.

In the evening, the body was robed in full canonicals, with golden mitre, gloves, and ring, and taken to the throne room in the apartments just below the living quarters of the pope. On the morning of the twenty-third, a procession carried the body to the Chapel of the Blessed Sacrament in Saint Peter's for only one day's exposure to the veneration of the Roman populace. Gasparri had intended to have Benedict interred on the twenty-fourth, but the press of people to gain admittance to the basilica was so great that, embalmment or not, the pope's burial was postponed to the twenty-sixth. However, Gasparri did give strict orders that the pontiff's feet were not to be allowed to project through the grating to receive the kisses of the faithful, because of the advancing decay of the remains.

During this period, Gasparri began to put into motion steps leading to the holding of the conclave. In response to the telegrams and cables already dispatched, the cardinals who resided outside Rome were preparing quickly for their journeys to the Eternal City. The greatest difficulty was had, once again, by the cardinals from the New World. William O'Connell of Boston made the fastest preparation. By the afternoon of the twenty-third, he had flown to New York, possibly winning the distinction of being the first cardinal in the air, and, on the following day, he embarked on the Italian liner *Presidente Wilson*. The junior American cardinal, Denis Dougherty of Philadelphia, was enjoying a winter cruise to the West Indies when he received news of Benedict's impending death. When he chose to hasten back to Philadelphia first, to establish a long-term administration, he also chose a delay of several days. He did not leave New York until Saturday, the twenty-eighth, aboard the French line's *Lorraine*, in the company of Cardinal Louis Nazaire Begin of Quebec. They surely knew, as the Statue of Liberty slipped behind them, that they would be too late, unless some sudden crisis were to seize the conclave—modern elections happen quickly. Difficulties also beset the archbishop of Rio de Janeiro, Cardinal Joachim Arcoverde de Albuquerque Cavalcanti. In the end, none of these four would reach Rome in time to vote for a new pontiff. For the cardinals in Europe, the situation was not quite so severe. The Irish cardinal, Michael Logue, was ready to go to his third conclave on the twenty-third; while the three German cardinals, Adolf Bertram, prince-bishop of Breslau, Michael von Faulhaber of Munich, and Karl Josef Schulte of Cologne, left on the preceding day to join their German curial colleague, the Dominican Andreas Franz Frühwirth. Four of the French, Louis Henri Luçon of Reims, Paulin Pierre Andrieu of Bordeaux, Louis Ernest Dubois of Paris, and Louis Joseph Maurin of Lyon, likewise made speedy preparations and were on their way within a few days. The fifth Frenchman in the College, Louis Billot, already was in Rome as a member of the staff of the Holy Office.

The Spanish delegation to the conclave, however, underwent two sudden changes during the hours immediately following the pope's death. At that moment, the Sacred College consisted of sixty-one members, but, on the morning of the twenty-third, the archbishop of Toledo, Enrique Almaraz y Santos, died in his residence at the age of seventy-four, thus reducing the number of potential electors to sixty. Shortly afterward, the staff of the archbishop of Santiago de Compostella, José María Martín Herrera y de la Iglesia, at eighty-six the oldest cardinal, announced that their master was too infirm to make the journey to Rome. These events reduced the number of Spanish participants to Juan Soldevila y Romero of Saragossa, Juan Benlloch y Vivo of Burgos, and Francisco d'Asis Vidal y Barraquer of Tarragona.

Two British cardinals, Francis Bourne of Westminster and Aidan Gasquet of the curia, joined their Anglo-Spanish colleague, Merry del Val. Désiré Mercier of Belgium, Antonio Mendes Bello of Portugal, Willem van Rossum of the Netherlands, Gustav Friedrich Piffl of Austria, Johann Csernoch of Hungary, and two Poles, Edmond Dalbor and Alexander Kakowski, rounded out the non-Italians at twenty-three of the twenty-nine alive. The Czech cardinal, Leo de Skrbensky-Hriste, was prevented by illness from going to Rome.

Of the thirty-one Italians, only one, eighty-five-year-old Giuseppe Prisco of Naples, failed to attend. Besides the sixteen Italian curia cardinals in Rome when Benedict died, there were fourteen other electors: Giuseppe Francica-Nava di Bontifé of Catania, Agostino Richelmy of Turin, Bartolomeo Bacilieri of Verona, Pietro Maffi of Pisa, Alessandro Lualdi of Palermo, Alfonso Maria Mistrangelo of Florence, Pietro La Fontaine of Venice, Alessio Ascalesi of Benevento, and Achille Ratti of Milan, representing the residential dioceses; and Gennaro Granito Pignatelli di Belmonte, Raffaele Scapinelli di Leguigno, Giovanni Tacci, Gaetano Bisleti, and Michele Lega—all members of the curia but all absent from Rome during Benedict's last hours.

So quickly did the Italians respond to Gasparri's telegrams that when the general congregation of cardinals met for the first time, on the evening of the twenty-third, almost all of them were present. At this meeting, the cardinals voted to begin the conclave on Tuesday, February 2—a decision which all those present knew would bar the New World cardinals from attending the opening. The selection of a secretary of the conclave was the next order of business. For this office, the cardinals chose Monsignor Luigi Sincero of Vercelli. When he entered the assembly to receive the formal appointment to his new office, he was well aware that the cardinalate would surely be his from the hands of the next pope, if he did his job well, for near him were the men who had been conclave secretaries during the two preceding elections, Merry del Val and Boggiani.

While the cardinals were preparing for the election at the Vatican, elsewhere in Rome the Italian government was hastening to try to extend the new cordiality in relations with the Church by yet another gesture. Premier Bonomi issued a secret circular to the Italian prefects, urging them to handle the cardinals who passed through their territories on the way to Rome with tact and to make every effort to speed them comfortably on their journey. One of the travellers could be the next pope, after all, and might continue the policy of Gasparri, finally reaching an accommodation which would settle the vexing "Roman question" that had caused the government nothing but trouble since 1870.

Just how vexing the "Roman question" was on the Church's side may be seen from its rôle in the sudden outburst of animosity in the College following the death of Benedict. In spite of a large change in personnel in Benedict's seven years as pope, the battle lines of 1922 were still those of 1914—integrists against progressives. Of the fifty-three cardinals who would elect Benedict's successor, no fewer than twenty-seven had been made members of the College by the progressive Benedict; yet the integrists, still under the leadership of Merry del Val, numbered more than twenty and were opposed unalterably to any change in the policy toward the Italian government that had been maintained during the past three reigns. When Gasparri not only received an official Italian delegation during the last hours of Benedict XV, but also sent a formal notification of his death to the Italian premier, integrist spirits were enraged. Merry del Val and his partisans responded to Gasparri's hand of goodwill toward Italy by leaking to the press the fact that Leo XIII's election constitution, *Prædecessores nostri*, had invested the chamberlain with purely administrative powers during a vacancy of the throne and that, by initiating new policy, Gasparri had incurred excommunication automatically. When this "bombshell" had no effect whatever, Cardinal Boggiani was moved to raise the question in the general congregation, where it also was dismissed by a majority of those present. Nevertheless, the vehement opposition to Gasparri by a substantial number of the cardinals seriously compromised his ability to govern during the interim.

Every progressive churchman could only deplore the fact that no formal agreement to settle the differences between Church and State had been reached, more than a half-century after the occupation of Rome by the Italian army and the unification of the nation. Clearly, both the papacy and Italy stood to gain from a rapprochement which would put an end to the problem that had divided the people of the peninsula bitterly for two generations. Benedict XV, and the conservative Pius X for that matter, had taken small steps to ease the tension that had descended on the Eternal City during the closing years of Pius IX, but any compromise of the rights of the pope to be the administrative as well as the spiritual leader of the ancient imperial capital was resisted by the integrists with every force at their command. That this obstructionism was foolhardy, given the changed nature of politics in Europe, especially after World War I, hardly needs comment today, but the integrists still commanded a large and loyal following which vigorously supported their position at every level of the Church.

Gasparri continued to function as best he might without involving himself or his party in any visible counterblasts to Merry del Val. It was clear from the manoeuvres of both sides, however, that the central issue which would dominate this conclave would be the "Roman question"; whether the new pope would move further in the direction of accommodation with the Italians or whether he would retreat from the frontier achieved by Gasparri and retire into a dark fastness as the "Prisoner of the Vatican" once more.

While the cardinals were wrangling over this point, they received the alarming news that the Vatican was almost bankrupt and that there was serious doubt about whether the two million lire to fund the conclave could be raised. The general congregation decided to enforce severe economies in order to hold costs to a minimum. Furniture for the cells was culled from ecclesiastical schools and hospitals, rather than rented, as had been done in 1914. The Little Sisters of the Sacred Family were invited to take over the conclave's kitchens, thus becoming the first women to be immured in a conclave, when it was found that the expenditure for them would be less than for the squad of monks who usually did the office. And the number of rooms allotted to each cardinal was reduced from three to two, except in the case of the six cardinal-bishops. The actual standing interior walls of the Vatican, with doors that locked, would serve in place of the vast temporary internal construction which had characterized earlier papal elections. With these, and other lesser economies, a reduced budget could just be met. One luxury the cardinals did afford themselves, however, was an intra-conclave telephone system operated from a central switchboard. It had an extension in each cell, so that the electors could carry on their most secret negotiations from bedside to bedside without anyone, except the operator, being aware. The switchboard operator was doubtless chosen for his boundless rectitude. In spite of all these parings, however, wartime inflation had driven up the cost of holding a papal election by more than 1,200,000 lire since 1914.

Each day now saw the arrival of more cardinals in Rome. Bourne arrived on the twenty-fifth, while Mercier, Dubois, Luçon, Dalbor, Kakowski, and Piffl all departed from their dioceses on the same day.

At three o'clock on the afternoon of Thursday, the twenty-sixth, Benedict's funeral was held in Saint Peter's. The body was placed in a crypt tomb next to that of Pius X, and once again Merry del Val, as archpriest of the basilica, was the last to leave a cold and gloomy Saint Peter's.

On the twenty-seventh, the arrival of Schulte, Bertram, Faulhaber, and Piffl brought the number of non-Italian residential cardinals in Rome for the election up to nine—the four Frenchmen, Bourne, and Vidal y Barraquer had arrived already.

At ten o'clock on the twenty-eighth, the general congregation of cardinals met to receive the official condolences of the diplomatic corps and of the knights of Malta. After this brief meeting, the "foreign" cardinals began rounds of calls on their Roman friends to sound out the prospects of potential candidates. In these conversations, it became clear that many of the European moderates were still neutral on the "Roman question" and that some, notably the Spanish cardinals, favored the election of a non-Italian as a method for avoiding an impasse between the two Italian parties. However, the Spanish choice, van Rossum, would have done nothing to reduce tension, since he was among the most intransigent of the reactionaries. The German curial cardinal, Frühwirth, supported the candidacy of Ratti of Milan—something of a surprise, since Ratti, as nuncio to a newly-independent Poland, had offended many Germans simply by his presence in Warsaw. The Italian cardinals, meanwhile, were meeting among themselves to decide who would be the official candidates of the two contending parties. Both the integrists and the progressives decided to allow their leaders to try for the throne to test the reactions of less committed cardinals. By that evening, most of the electors in Rome felt a growing sense of excitement—Merry del Val and Gasparri would vie head to head for the tiara.

On the morning of Sunday, the twenty-ninth, the general congregation met at 9:30. Gasparri offered a proposal to delay the opening of the conclave for a few days in order to allow time for the trans-Atlantic cardinals to arrive. As had been the fate of a similar suggestion in 1914, the idea was rejected overwhelmingly.

This meeting was the first attended by the Belgian cardinal primate, Désiré Mercier, whose arrival in Rome on the day before had climaxed a triumphal progression from his homeland. As the Church's principal hero in World War I, his presence caused thousands to turn out for a glimpse of him, and his opinion carried great weight in the College. When he arrived, he held a press conference in which he responded to inquiries about his attitude to the "Roman question" with the quotation, "Forgive your enemies." There could now be no doubt that he was going to bring the full weight of his reputation behind a progressive candidate. Kakowski, Dalbor, and Csernoch arrived on the twenty-eighth, as well, so the congregation on the twenty-ninth included nearly all those who would participate in the election itself. The two Poles came prepared to support the candidacy of Ratti, who had gained their friendship and respect in his days as nuncio.

Monday, the thirtieth, at ten o'clock, saw the beginning of the final sequence of requiems for Benedict. The celebrant was Gaetano de Laï, and the absolutions were given by Basilio Pompilj, Giovanni Cagliero, and Gennaro Granito Pignatelli di Belmonte. Immediately after this rite, the cardinals assembled to draw lots for their cells. The sixty-year-old Francis Bourne was somewhat nonplussed at the thought that the luck of the draw might give him a cell on the uppermost floor of a palace which had an inoperable elevator. He turned to the dean of the College, Vincenzo Vannutelli, whose eighty-five years made him the oldest cardinal in attendance, and wryly said, "I hope young men like you are selected by fate to occupy the upper stories." Vannutelli smilingly replied, "The Lord will provide."

After the cells were allotted, the cardinals dispersed in small groups to continue their negotiations. Valfré di Bonzo expressed the view that Ratti was the best candidate, Scapinelli di Leguigno supported Bisleti, while van Rossum seemed ready to take anybody but Gasparri. In the evening, there was a quiet meeting of the Austro-Germans, similar to the caucus they had held in 1914. Piffl, Bertram, Schulte, Faulhaber, Frühwirth, and Csernoch agreed to support Gasparri and, if his candidacy were to fail, to switch to Laurenti.

January 31 was an uneventful day for most of the electors. The requiem, begun at ten o'clock, was celebrated by Antonio Vico, assisted by Francica-Nava, Merry del Val, Cagliero, and Maffi. The general congregation then had a short meeting and dispersed.

February 1 followed much the same pattern. The requiem was celebrated by Pignatelli and the absolutions were given by Gasparri, Lualdi, Mercier, and Luçon. The meeting of the general congregation was even shorter than the one held the day before, to allow the electors the maximum time to prepare themselves for the entrance into the conclave on the next day.

By seven in the morning of Tuesday, February 2, the crowd in Saint Peter's Square already was substantial, awaiting the procession of the cardinals. At 9:30, Vannutelli chanted the Mass of the Holy Spirit. After this, Monsignor Aurelio Galli, secretary of the

The "Roman Question"

Roman Rota, delivered the election allocution, just as he had done seven years before. This was followed by a short meeting of the general congregation, and then by lunch. At four in the afternoon, the cardinals assembled in the Cappella Paolina. All but one of the fifty-three cardinals in Rome attended—Niccolo Marini, still suffering from an attack of influenza, was assisted by his aides directly into the conclave's precincts and put to bed. The *Veni Sancte Spiritus* was intoned and the electors then marched to the Sistina to take the oath to preserve the inviolability of the conclave. The dean then gave a short address. At its conclusion, Prince Ludovico Chigi-Albani, the marshal of the conclave, was admitted and swore, in turn, to protect the cardinals and their secrecy during the coming days. Then the cardinals, each accompanied by a member of the pontifical noble guard with drawn sword, visited their cells and received a few last minute callers before the final closure.

Vannutelli and Gasparri stayed behind in the court of San Damaso to examine the credentials of the large staff who were to be immured with the electors, including Monsignor Sincero, the secretary; Dr. Battistini and two other physicians, five pharmacists, a sacristan and his assistant, eleven cooks, seven masters of ceremonies, nine janitors, an architect, three firemen, two night watchmen, a carpenter, a bricklayer, a blacksmith, a plasterer, an electrician, two plumbers, three barbers, nine waiters, over a hundred conclavists, and the telephone operator—more than four hundred persons in all. As soon as the senior master of ceremonies had begun the cry, "Extra omnes," everybody out, the masons began walling up the final doors into the area. All journalists and photographers had been barred from the interior, but one enterprising photographer had managed to slip in among the callers. His discovery and seizure by the conclave guards provided the only nonceremonial excitement of the afternoon. After the exit of the last visitors, Gasparri and Vannutelli closed the bolts on their side of the last door, and Prince Chigi-Albani did the same on the outside.

The cardinals then went to supper, where they were served a large collation of ham, soup, chicken with potatoes, cheese, and fruit—altogether better fare than their predecessors had enjoyed since the days when the cardinals had their food prepared in the kitchens of their palaces and brought to the conclave in long stately processions of liveried servants called *dapiferi*.

The Germans met for a final, brief session before they retired for the night. They decided to make La Fontaine their second choice, if Gasparri were to withdraw as a candidate, at least for the first two ballots. Then they followed the example of their colleagues and went to bed.

By six the next morning, the members of the College were awake and preparing for the day's events. They had their choice of saying Mass themselves or attending another service and receiving communion there. In 1914, nearly all the cardinals had attended the general Mass, but this time most of the electors said Masses in private. When Vannutelli celebrated at 8:30, only four cardinals, Ratti, Scapinelli, Pompilj, and Maffi, received communion.

After Vannutelli's service, the electors assembled in the Sistine for the first and second ballots of the election. Only fifty were present, since Marini was still abed with influenza and Pompilj and Bacilieri stayed away with colds. After the selection of the scrutators, infirmarians, and tellers, the cardinals cast their first vote, and once the infirmarians had collected the votes of their three ill colleagues, the ballots were counted—revealing that the division between the integrists and the progressives had grown no narrower during the pontificate of Benedict XV:

Raffaele Merry del Val	12
Pietro Maffi	10
Pietro Gasparri	8
Pietro La Fontaine	4
Achille Ratti	5
Willem van Rossum	4
Gaetano Bisleti	3
Gaetano de Laï	2
Basilio Pompilj	2
Désiré Mercier	1
Camillo Laurenti	2

The two principal conservative candidates, Merry del Val and La Fontaine, had gathered sixteen votes, while the two main liberals, Gasparri and Maffi, commanded eighteen; but the thirteen votes scattered among van Rossum, Bisleti, de Laï, Pompilj, and Laurenti also were integrist or leaning that way. Only six progressive votes, by contrast, had fallen outside the suffrage of the two main candidates, the five for Ratti and the single vote for Mercier. The two Polish cardinals were known to support Ratti, Valfré di Bonzo backed him, and circumstances would soon reveal that one of Ratti's other votes came from Gasparri himself.

The cardinals repeated their task, with the result:

Raffaele Merry del Val	11
Pietro Maffi	10
Pietro Gasparri	10
Pietro La Fontaine	9
Achille Ratti	5
Gaetano Bisleti	1
Gaetano de Laï	2
Basilio Pompilj	1
Camillo Laurenti	4

A few minor shifts had taken place. Van Rossum had lost all four of his votes, presumably to La Fontaine; while Gasparri had gained the vote that had gone to Mercier. Still the deadlock was looming—twenty solid progressives in the Gasparri-Maffi column and twenty equally solid integrists who supported Merry del Val and La Fontaine. At 12:30, it was over, and the papers burned.

Outside, in Saint Peter's Square, there was a sensation when someone started a rumor that Bisleti had been elected and had chosen the name Gregory XVII. Looking for confirmation or denial, the crowd began to push forward for a finer vantage if there were to be an announcement. Gazing up, many in the throng now noticed that conclavists and other attendants were looking out of the upper windows of the Vatican palace; windows which had not been boarded over because of the economies mentioned earlier. Surely, many in the crowd surmised, such a breach of discipline would not be tolerated unless an election had been held. Then, too, there had been no smoke from the chimney above the Sistine, and it was now well into the afternoon. Such a delay must mean that a decision had been reached. Just as the huge mass of people was on the verge of disorganization, black smoke began to issue from the chimney. When they saw it, the crowd began to leave quietly.

Inside, the cardinals adjourned for a midday meal, having agreed to reconvene at 3:30 for the third and fourth ballots. During this break, some speculated that La Fontaine might emerge quickly as a candidate acceptable to both parties, though he was an avowed integrist, so striking had been his rise from four to nine votes in the space of two ballots. Early in the afternoon, in order to destroy his chances for the throne, someone started a rumor that his family had a history of mental instability. The results of this ploy, reminiscent of the sixteenth century, would become visible in the third ballot. An integrist was not the only victim of rumor-mongering during this interim. Opponents of Gasparri whispered that he was a secret nepotist and that if he were elected hordes of grasping relatives would swarm to the Vatican. No one took this seriously, however, since the chamberlain had been a powerful figure in Church affairs for more than a decade and the fearsome throng had never yet put in an appearance. On the more straightforward side, van Rossum spent his time openly canvassing for Merry del Val.

The third ballot revealed the changes that had been wrought during the first pause in the voting:

Raffaele Merry del Val	14
Pietro Maffi	10
Pietro Gasparri	11
Pietro La Fontaine	2
Achille Ratti	6
Gaetano Bisleti	4
Gaetano de Laï	1
Basilio Pompilj	1
Camillo Laurenti	3
Michele Lega	1

It was clear that the slander of La Fontaine had cost him most of his support, but what alarmed the progressives was that Merry del Val had picked up three more votes, probably because of the efforts of van Rossum, while Gasparri had advanced by only one from his morning position. The fourth ballot now quickly followed:

Raffaele Merry del Val	17
Pietro Maffi	9
Pietro Gasparri	13
Pietro La Fontaine	1
Achille Ratti	5
Gaetano Bisleti	4
Basilio Pompilj	1
Camillo Laurenti	2
Michele Lega	1

The lines of conflict between the integrists and progressives were now growing clearer. Because Merry del Val was the leading conservative, several of that persuasion decided to switch their support to him. Pius X's secretary of state picked up one more vote at the expense of La Fontaine, whose candidacy now appeared finished; he got a vote away from Laurenti, and he picked up de Laï's last adherent. Gasparri, as the leading candidate among the liberals, gained votes from Maffi and Ratti on the same rationale. Behind the ebb and flow of cardinals searching for a candidate stood an important set of five votes, those going to Ratti. At the end of the first day, there were at least these few who remained firmly behind their minority candidate and refused to budge.

By five o'clock, the papers were ready to be burned. On the outside, another moment of excitement gripped the crowd. There was a sudden emission of greyish-white smoke from one of the palace's chimneys which caused thousands to react. A few knowledgeable persons pointed out that this smoke was coming from the wrong chimney, but their voices were drowned in another press of people toward the basilica. When, a few moments later, black smoke began to come from the stove in the Sistine, the crowd began to grow ominously restless with confusion. Monsignor Sanz de Samper, the papal majordomo, and Prince Chigi-Albani, finally clarified the situation by appearing on one of the balconies and waving negative signs down to the people.

The discussions among the cardinals during the evening are lost in detail but recoverable in substance. It was becoming obvious that a deadlock, similar to that in 1914, would soon be reached. So certain was this that Gasparri sent word that an additional 120,000 lire were to be raised from Church holdings to purchase more provisions for the conclave. Among the conservatives, the falsity of the rumor about La Fontaine's family was learned, and several of those who had abandoned his cause decided to return to his support once more. For the liberals, there was encouragement in the rising tide in favor of Gasparri, and Maffi's loyalists were pressed urgently to swing to the chamberlain's side, in the hope that a united front on the next ballot might bring the election their way, much as the united progressives had brought about the election of Della Chiesa in 1914.

At 9:30 on Saturday, Mass was held for the electors and was followed by the first ballot. The three cardinals who had been too ill to participate publicly on the day before were now at their thrones, so the rôle of the infirmarians became purely ceremonial. When the tellers had finished announcing the results of the voting, the products of the previous evening's campaigns were to be seen:

Raffaele Merry del Val	13
Pietro Maffi	1
Pietro Gasparri	21
Pietro La Fontaine	7
Achille Ratti	5
Gaetano Bisleti	2
Gaetano de Laï	1
Basilio Pompilj	1
Camillo Laurenti	2

All but six of the convinced progressives had now fallen into line behind Gasparri. Five liberals still held with Ratti and one with Maffi. Gasparri's own vote now stood revealed in spite of the official secrecy. He had voted for Ratti, since a vote for himself might have invalidated the scrutiny and he was known not to favor Maffi. The integrists displayed considerable confusion in their ranks, perhaps because of the slander of La Fontaine. The latter was making a comeback, but de Laï had regained his vote from the day before, and there were still holdouts for Bisleti, Pompilj, and Laurenti. Trying to find a candidate behind whom the conservatives could unite, Merry del Val passed the word that his candidacy was over. He urged his followers to support La Fontaine. When the results of the sixth scrutiny were tallied, they showed the consequences of his decision:

Raffaele Merry del Val	7
Pietro Gasparri	24
Pietro La Fontaine	13
Achille Ratti	4
Gaetano Bisleti	2
Gaetano de Laï	1
Camillo Laurenti	2

Gasparri had now gained the last of Maffi's adherents and had managed even to detach one of Ratti's group while also picking up the vote that had gone to Pompilj, of all people. The liberals were beginning to run a strong tide. The positions of Merry del Val and La Fontaine were exactly reversed from their standing at the end of the fifth ballot; Merry del Val's message had managed to reach just half his party. But the essential division in the College was not changed—twenty-eight liberal votes split between Gasparri and Ratti and twenty-five conservative votes, eighty per cent of which were held between Merry del Val and La Fontaine.

Shortly before noon, an unmistakable emission of black smoke was seen outside. Yet still some held that an election had taken place, and there was another rush toward the doors of the basilica; once again members of the papal court had to appear on balconies and wave the people away.

During the luncheon recess, Merry del Val succeeded at last in notifying all his integrists that La Fontaine was now the official candidate of the Party. Under this ægis, the conservatives now campaigned vigorously to achieve at least as united a front as the liberals were holding for Gasparri. The progressives, meanwhile, had done all they could for their chosen leader, for Ratti's four could not be dissuaded from their cause. When the cardinals reconvened at 3:30 for the seventh ballot, the deadlock had been reached. The tally was:

Raffaele Merry del Val	1
Pietro Gasparri	24
Pietro La Fontaine	22
Achille Ratti	4
Gaetano Bisleti	1
Camillo Laurenti	1

The orientation of twenty-eight liberals to twenty-five conservatives was maintained, but La Fontaine had emerged definitely as the unifying integrist candidate. Gasparri's support had peaked. At the worst, a few of the integrists had thought he might get Ratti's votes at last, but this had not happened. Grimly, the cardinals moved to conduct the eighth scrutiny, the last of the day. The results contained a small but sharp surprise:

Pietro Gasparri	24
Pietro La Fontaine	21
Achille Ratti	5
Gaetano Bisleti	1
Basilio Pompilj	1
Camillo Laurenti	1

Merry del Val's last holdout had moved to the column of another archconservative, Pompilj. Otherwise, the results seemed the same—except that Ratti had gained a vote at the expense of La Fontaine, at a moment when minority candidates were supposed to fade! This almost imperceptible gain gave several of the cardinals considerable room for thought during the following evening and night.

After all, wasn't Ratti, well, rather harmless? He had been a librarian for years, first at the Ambrosiana in Milan and then at the Vatican, before Benedict had chosen him suddenly to be the envoy to Poland; and his job there had been rather successful without raising too many hackles, though his nunciature had ended under something of a cloud, because of internal Polish passions. Benedict had extricated him neatly from an impasse by making him a cardinal on June 13, 1921, and giving him Milan as an archiepiscopal seat. Ratti was thought to be somewhat progressive, but then who knew much about his views at all, at least in detail? He might make the ideal candidate, though he was the junior cardinal-priest in the College. Then, also, some liberals may have considered, he is the candidate who receives Gasparri's vote and, therefore, he must be quite acceptable to the chamberlain. Ratti was perhaps the man to prevent the election of 1922 from strangling on its own politics.

The fruits of these thoughts showed themselves in the ninth ballot, the first held on the fifth of February:

Pietro Gasparri	19
Pietro La Fontaine	18
Achille Ratti	11
Basilio Pompilj	1
Camillo Laurenti	3
Oreste Giorgi	1

The integrists sensed at once the trend in the voting. Some, perhaps better acquainted with Ratti's liberal views and knowing that La Fontaine could not now be elected, decided to start an effort to switch the conservative vote in the direction of the seventy-year-old Pignatelli. That movement managed to gather eight votes in the few minutes before the tenth scrutiny; but the boomlet was to fade as quickly as it began. The results of the next ballot showed the liberals moving firmly to Ratti:

Pietro Gasparri	16
Pietro La Fontaine	8
Achille Ratti	14
Camillo Laurenti	5
Oreste Giorgi	1
Gennaro Pignatelli	8
Donato Sbarretti	1

La Fontaine's sun seemed to be setting and Ratti's rising as the cardinals watched the morning's ballots and tallies being burned.

To Gasparri, who well knew Ratti's views, the result was quite satisfactory even though his own candidacy was foundering.

During the recess, Gasparri worked actively but quietly in Ratti's favor, becoming, in the process, the grand elector of 1922. By the next vote, at 3:30, the French had joined the Poles in their support for the Milanese archbishop, and several others from among the chamberlain's adherents were ready to switch, though four were said to favor La Fontaine now. The scrutators chosen for this session were Logue, Piffl, and Valfré di Bonzo. The results of the eleventh ballot exhibited a strong turn to Ratti, although the conservatives had rallied once more behind La Fontaine:

Pietro Gasparri	2
Pietro La Fontaine	23
Achille Ratti	24
Camillo Laurenti	4

The cardinals proceeded to vote again, and then anxiously awaited the tally to see if Ratti could gain any further support from the conservatives or whether the election would founder now on a Ratti-La Fontaine crisis as it had done on the Gasparri-La Fontaine bloc. The results were:

Pietro Gasparri	1
Pietro La Fontaine	22
Achille Ratti	27
Camillo Laurenti	3

As the cardinals left the Sistine for their supper, most of them knew that Ratti was about to emerge as the fully acceptable alternative. If the conservatives could be won over, even vote by vote, as had been done by Della Chiesa at the war's start, then Ratti's eventual enthronement was certain. The negotiations among the cardinals that night went on at a more feverish pace than at any time since the death of Benedict. A group of integrists proposed a last-ditch rally behind one of their own, perhaps Laurenti, but their choice refused to have anything to do with the move.

In the evening, Merry del Val made one final effort to save the integrity of his bloc. He called upon Ratti in his cell and offered the whole of the integrist vote if only the latter would promise not to reäppoint Gasparri as secretary of state. Ratti, realizing that such a bargain might gain him a throne but compromise a reign, curtly refused. Merry del Val was not the only visitor to the Milanese archbishop's cell that evening, however, and many other callers were far more pleasant. They came to meet and converse with the man many of them hardly knew but for whom they would vote in the morning. Ratti's conclavist, Monsignor Carlo Confalonieri, by 1978 himself the dean of the College of Cardinals, recorded his surprise at the stream of cardinals waiting on his master.

When the electors had assembled at 9:30 on the morning of Monday, February 6, the air was filled with expectancy, awaiting the conclusion of the meditations and negotiations carried on the night before. Merry del Val made no move to release his party and his command over them was now to be challenged to the fullest. The voting on the thirteenth ballot revealed a tide for Ratti running at the full:

Pietro La Fontaine	18
Achille Ratti	30
Gaetano de Laï	1
Camillo Laurenti	4

Ratti's cause had pulled together all the progressive votes as well as two of the integrists. Were the two conservative suffrages showing the way? The electors quickly prepared and held the fourteenth scrutiny. Would Ratti be able to win over six more integrists and achieve the throne? When the tally was finished the longest conclave in a century was over:

Pietro La Fontaine	9
Achille Ratti	42
Camillo Laurenti	2

One by one, the cardinals lowered the canopies above their thrones until only that above Ratti's remained open. They gathered around the dean, Vincenzo Vannutelli, who was flanked by the archpriest and archdeacon of the College, Michael Logue and Gaetano Bisleti. Vannutelli stepped before the man who had received six more than the two-thirds majority of the votes. "Do you accept the election, canonically made, of yourself as sovereign pontiff?" asked the dean. Ratti composed himself for a moment, and replied, "It must never be said that I refused to submit unreservedly to the will of God. No one shall say that I shrank before a burden that was to be laid on my shoulders. No one shall say that I fail to appreciate the votes of my colleagues. Therefore, in spite of my unworthiness, of which I am deeply conscious, I accept." The cardinals immediately sank to their knees in the presence of the man who, but a few moments before, had been the least of them. "By what name will you be called?" continued Vannutelli. The new pope replied, "Under the pontificate of Pius IX, I was initiated into the Catholic Church and took the first steps in my ecclesiastical career. Pius X called me to Rome. Pius is a name of peace. Therefore, in the desire to devote my endeavors to the work of peace throughout the world, to which my predecessor, Benedict XV, consecrated himself, I choose the name Pius XI."

After a short pause, he continued, "I desire to add one word. I protest in the presence of the members of the Sacred College that it is my heart's desire to safeguard and defend all the rights of the Church and all the prerogatives of the Holy See, and, having said that, I wish that my first benediction should go forth as a symbol of that peace to which humanity aspires, not only to Rome and to Italy, but to all the Church and to the whole world. I will give my benediction from the outer balcony of Saint Peter's." The last of Pius's remarks stunned the cardinals of the integrist party. Not since 1870 had a pope shown himself from the exterior of the basilica, facing the capital of the Italian nation. This decision made all the little overtures of Gasparri insignificant by comparison. The new pontiff was revealing himself at once in a position far more progressive than any but the most liberal members of the College could imagine. At once, several of the conservative cardinals hastened to his side to expostulate and protest, almost violently. To Gaetano de Laï, with an air quite characteristic of the Trojan whose name he had chosen, he said sharply, "Remember, I am no longer a cardinal. I am the Supreme Pontiff now." The stalwart integrists were stunned into silence.

Pius then left his throne to enter the sacristy and don the best fitting of the three sets of papal robes that were held in readiness there. While awaiting the pope's return, Gasparri remarked to those near him, "It took fourteen rotations, like the stations of the cross, to set the pope firmly upon Calvary." When Pius returned, he received the first obedience from the members of the College, after which he prepared to appear on the exterior loggia.

A procession had been formed a few minutes earlier, and attendants had gone forward to open the windows onto Saint Peter's Square and unfold a large tapestry with the papal arms over the railing. The crowd outside, having seen the white smoke from the burning ballots at 11:35, pressed forward. There was a sudden crush as several thousand people tried to enter the basilica. They were certain that the first blessing of the new pope would come from the interior loggia, just as it had for the past three reigns.

A long delay now ensued. Several persons heard shouts from within the conclave's precincts of a name with two syllables ending in "i." Some were sure that it was Giovanni Tacci who had been elected, others thought Maffi to have been the choice. One newspaper had rushed a hastily printed extra into the streets with a picture of Tacci clad in pontifical vestments on the front page. An elderly priest in the throng seeing this exclaimed, "Giovanni Tacci. Madonna," before vanishing in the swirl. Then Gaetano Bisleti, the archdeacon, appeared on the interior balcony and announced the election of Pius XI in the age-old formula. When he was done, a prelate of the pontifical household stepped forward and made the surprise announcement of the location from which the pope would deliver his blessing. At once, there was another convulsive shift in the mass of people, as those inside the basilica tried to regain the favored vantage points they had lost. Then the bells of the basilica began to peal in honor of the new pontiff. Their sound was soon being echoed by the bells of every church in the city. Then, to tumultuous cheers, the new pope appeared on the exterior loggia of the great basilica. With the peals of bells framing his voice, he delivered the first pontifical blessing, the *Urbi et Orbi*, to tens of thousands of jubilant Romans.

At that moment a private train, provided by the Italian government, was just coming to rest in the Rome station. As Cardinal O'Connell alighted, he asked one of the prelates who had come to meet him the reason for the peals. He was told that the ringing was a celebration for the election of the new pope, Ratti. "Who?" roared "Number One in Boston," "Spell it." As the surname of the new pope was spelled carefully for the American cardinal's benefit he fumed down the platform and into a waiting car for the short drive to the palace—he was just one hour too late. When he arrived, Pius received him at once. The purple face of one of the College's most vigorous members told the whole story, and within a few days Pius issued a papal rescript putting forward the time that was to elapse from the death of a pope to the opening of a conclave from ten to fifteen days. No cardinal from a distant shore would ever again miss a conclave.

Pius's appearance for his first blessing signalled not only the opening of a new reign but also signalled a policy which would lead to an accommodation with the Italian government—finally accomplished seven years later in the Lateran Treaties. Inside the Vatican, the shock of rapid changes was not done yet. Pius proclaimed at once the reäppointment of Gasparri as secretary of state, without waiting the customary day or two. Gasparri thus became the first secretary of state to retain his office for a substantial period in two reigns; Merry del Val's work was completely undone.

The pope now returned to the Sistine for the second obedience of the College, at 3:30, and, after this, he went around the chapel speaking a word or two to each cardinal. The pontiff now retired to his new apartments, and the members of the College gathered their things together to leave the conclave. It was 5:00 P.M.; they had been in the Vatican just four days. Today, the reign of Pius XI—seventeen years, almost to the day—seems a little lost, a moment of rest after one global war and before the outbreak of the next. But his liberal reign did advance the progressive policies that had begun with Benedict XV, and he carried their spirit forward with others of his own. The retirement of Gasparri in 1930, after the Lateran Treaties had settled the "Roman question" and capped his career, opened the way for the rise of his most trusted lieutenant, Eugenio Pacelli, who served as cardinal-secretary of state during the last nine years of Pius XI's pontificate. The effect that Pacelli had, however, is best judged through his own story, in another place.

VI

EPILOGUE

Pius XII (1939–1958) was the first pope since at least the time of Innocent XI (1676–1689) whose position in world affairs was regarded as one of considerable importance. As an informal source of information for the Allies during World War II, he proved invaluable at several major points of the war effort; and the general diplomatic position of the Vatican was so great that every great power was eager to be heard by the pope and at the papal court.

Woodrow Wilson certainly did not regard Benedict XV as a major figure in his political thinking about World War I, and did not make any effort at all to connect the government of the United States with the pope and the curia. Franklin Roosevelt, by contrast, realized that, although he could not secure senatorial approval for a full recognition of the Vatican, he needed an avenue of communication to Rome and an ear at the papal court. These reasons underlay his appointment of Myron Charles Taylor (1874–1959) as his personal representative to Pius XII. The value of this American presence in Rome also was realized by Harry S Truman, who kept Taylor in his quasi-diplomatic position until 1950. Later, Presidents Nixon, Ford, Carter, and Reagan also appointed officials to act in much the same capacity. On January 10, 1984, the United States and the Vatican finally established formal diplomatic relations, and, on the following March 7, William A. Wilson was confirmed by the Senate as the first American ambassador to the State of the City of the Vatican.

The apostolic delegation in Washington had been established by Leo XIII as a device to have a papal representative in the United States to act as a direct link to the American Catholic hierarchy. Especially during the 1940's and 1950's, in the term of Amleto Giovanni Cicognani, later Pope John XXIII's cardinal-secretary of state, the importance of the apostolic delegation grew until it functioned no less as an embassy, however informal, than it did as the papal observer and, in some real sense, supervisor of the American

Catholic Church. In 1984, with the arrival of mutual diplomatic recognition, the apostolic delegate in office then, Pio Laghi, later cardinal, was raised to the status of pro-nuncio.

This evolution of the formal relationships between the United States and the Vatican has its parallel in the modern history of most other nations. When Leo XIII celebrated the silver anniversary of his election in 1903, the entire diplomatic corps then accredited to the Vatican came to offer its congratulations at a formal reception. Only a handful of Catholic men were present. At the end of the twentieth century, the diplomatic representatives of other nations at the Vatican are as numerous as the diplomatic corps in any other major European capital, and the diplomatic activity which takes place daily in the *camere* of the secretariat of state is as vigorous as that in Washington, London, or Paris.

In the Catholic world, Pius XII presented the *persona* of an austere and aristocratic, yet almost saintly, man. His distance and reserve were tempered by the impression of his compassion for humanity in general and the suffering in particular. In fact, he was a consummate and wily diplomat, carefully groomed for a decade for the papal throne by Pius XI, who weighed every consequence of every action in the political and military world in terms of its effect on the Church and the papacy. The results of his skill as an administrator and diplomat were to raise the Church and the papacy to levels of prestige not generally seen since at least the sixteenth century. In the developed world, after World War II, the number of conversions to Catholicism rose from thousands, to tens of thousands, to hundreds of thousands each year as his reign went on.

His successor, John XXIII (1958–1963), added to the papal *persona* a deep, genuine love for people combined with a simplicity and directness of thought and expression unseen in the popes of recent centuries. Although he, too, was a master of diplomacy—a mastery that had been honed and improved during years of service in the diplomatically-troubled capitals of Sofia and Paris, and further refined during five years as patriarch of Venice—his deep and authentic faith in the message of the Gospels combined with his joy in participating in the richness of humanity prevented him from succumbing to the cynicism and hardness which traps men of power in the Church no less than it does similar figures in secular life. The vast number of favorable stories and myths about him which began to accrete from the beginning of his short reign of little more than four and a half years is one measure of the devotion to the Church, to the papacy, and to himself that he inspired in millions of people of every social and ethnic background and degree.

To illustrate his simple faith and his lack of pretension, the story was told of how his secretary, Monsignor Loris Capovilla, who slept on a cot outside John's door, heard him thrashing about in his sleep one night, and then a voice which said in a steady tone, "It does not matter. I will ask the pope about it in the morning." Then, after a few moments of silence, Capovilla heard another, softer expression, "Oh, dear, I *am* the pope." To illustrate his love for others and his approachability came the story of how the Catholic wife of the president of the United States came to the Vatican for a papal audience while she was touring Rome. She was instructed on the formal, traditional structure of the proceedings, including sinking to her knees for a blessing when she was shown into John's presence. When the event transpired, and she was shown into the pope's study, she had no chance to follow her instructions, because John leapt to his feet, rushed from behind his desk, open his arms wide before her, and elatedly cried out, "Jacqueline." To her delight, the audience soon became an animated conversation in French, a language in which both were natively fluent.

When John XXIII died on June 3, 1963, following the first session of the Second Vatican Council, the papacy was at a zenith of prestige, if not of power, that it probably had not enjoyed since the later thirteenth century. His two major encyclicals, *Pacem in Terris* and *Mater et Magistra*, already were regarded by Catholics and non-Catholics, by Christians and non-Christians, as among the leading significant moral teachings of the twentieth century.

Paul VI (1963–1978), whom John XXIII had once presciently described as being "a little like Hamlet," lost something of what Pius XII and John XXIII had gained. He did not steer the barque of Peter to a safe port in the years following the close of the Council. He, too, however, presented the *persona* of a man desperately concerned for the spiritual well-being of all mankind. With the brief reign of the next pope, John Paul I (August 26–September 29, 1978), came a resurgence of popular affection for the pope and respect for the papal office. "The Smiling Pope" seemed to be about to restore the strong link between pope and common man that had been forged by John XXIII and weakened by Paul VI. His large public audiences were covered favorably, regularly, and extensively by the news media throughout Europe and the Americas. His reign proved too short, however, for any firm judgment of his place in the history of the modern papacy.

John Paul II, his successor, though a conservative reactionary in many ways, was the heir to, and was formed by, the Church recreated by Pius XII and his successors. As the first Slavic pope, he played a major, if not pivotal, rôle in the collapse of the Soviet Union's empire in Eastern Europe, which itself hastened the end of the Soviet Union itself. If this was not the zenith of modern papal prestige, it was that of modern papal power.

John XXIII revived the habit of papal traveling, first in Rome itself and then farther afield in Italy, notably in his journey to the shrine of Loreto. Paul VI expanded the possibilities by becoming an infrequent traveler to major sites of importance in the Catholic world. John Paul II has made frequent journeys and has reached almost every corner of the globe. These air voyages have increased and strengthened the ties between pope and common humanity, ties first made by Leo XIII in his publication of the encyclical *Rerum Novarum* and elaborated by Pius XI in his encyclical *Quadragesimo Anno*.

All these, and many other, accomplishments and impressions of recent popes seem to many to spring unheralded from the brilliance of spirit and intellect that some believe to be characteristic of popes in the later twentieth century. In fact, they were made possible by the work of the four earlier popes of the Age of Transition, especially Leo XIII, who took the papacy from the edge of collapse, from a moment in which the pope seemed merely a spectator of the affairs of the world, to a time when the pope bestrides it as a major spiritual figure and a major political and diplomatic force, and does so with sureness and confidence.

APPENDIX

Tables of Electors

The College of Cardinals at the time of the conclave of February 18–20, 1878, arranged according to rank. Sixty-one cardinals participated in the election.

Luigi Amat di San Filippo e Sorso, cardinal-bishop of Ostia e Velletri, dean of the College
Camillo di Pietro, cardinal-bishop of Porto e Santa Ruffina
Carlo Sacconi, cardinal-bishop of Palestrina; prefect, Segnatura di Giustizia
Filippo Maria Guidi, O.P., cardinal-bishop of Frascati
Luigi Bilio, cardinal-bishop of Sabina
Carlo Luigi Morichini, cardinal-bishop of Albano
Friedrich Johann Josef Celestin, Prinz von Schwarzenberg, prince-archbishop of Prague
Fabio Maria Asquini, secretary of briefs
Domenico Carafa di Traetto, archbishop of Benevento
François Auguste Ferdinand Donnet, archbishop of Bordeaux
Goiacchino Vincenzo Raffaele Luigi Pecci, bishop of Perugia
Antonio Benedetto Antonucci, archbishop-bishop of Ancona
Anton Maria Panebianco, O.F.M.Conv., penetentiary major
Antonino de Luca, prefect of the Congregation of the Index
Jean Baptiste Pitra, O.S.B., librarian and archivist of the Church
Henri Marie Gaston de Boisnormand de Bonnechose, archbishop of Rouen
Paul Cullen, archbishop of Dublin
Gustav Adolf von Hohenlohe
Lucien Louis Joseph Napoleon Bonaparte
Innocenzo Ferrieri, prefect of the Congregation of Indulgences
Giuseppe Berardi
Juan Ignacio Moreno, archbishop of Toledo
Raffaele Monaco La Valetta, secretary *dei Memoriali*
Ignacio do Nascimento Moraes Cardoso, patriarch of Lisbon
René François Régnier, archbishop of Cambrai
Flavio Chigi

Alessandro Franchi, secretary of the Congregation for the Propagation of the Faith
Joseph Hippolyte Guibert, O.M.I., archbishop of Paris
Luigi Oreglia di Santo Stefano
Johann Simor, archbishop of Esztergom
Tommaso Maria Martinelli, O.S.A.
Ruggero Luigi Emidio Antici Mattei, Latin partriarch of Constantinople
Pietro Giannelli
Mieczyslaw Halka Ledochowski, archbishop of Gneizno and Poznan
John McCloskey, archbishop of New York
Henry Edward Manning, archbishop of Westminster
Victor Auguste Isidor Deschamps, archbishop of Malines
Giovanni Simeoni, archbishop of Calcedonia *in partibus*, pro-nuncio to Spain
Domenico Bartolini
Geoffroi Brossais Saint-Marc, archbishop of Rennes
Bartolomeo D'Avanzo
Johann Baptist Franzelin, S.J.
Francisco de Paula Benavides y Navarrete, archbisop of Granada
Francesco Saverio Apuzzo, archbishop of Capua
Emmanuele García Gil, O.P., archbishop of Saragossa
Edward Henry Howard
Miguel Payá y Rico, archbishop of Santiago de Compostela
Louis Marie Joseph Eusebe Caverot, archbisop of Lyon
Luigi Di Canossa, bishop of Verona
Luigi Serafini, bishop of Viterbo
Josef Mihalovic, archbishop of Zagreb
Johann Baptist Rudolf Kutschker, archbishop of Vienna
Lucido Maria Parocchi, archbishop of Bologna
Vincenzo Moretti, archbishop of Ravenna
Antonio Pellegrini
Prospero Caterini, prefect of the Congregation of the Council
Teodolfo Mertel
Domenico Consolini, president, *Camera degli Spogli*
Edoardo Borromeo, prefect, Congregation of the Fabric of Saint Peter's
Lorenzo Ilarione Randi
Bartolomeo Pacca, *giuniore*
Lorenzo Nina
Enea Sbarretti
Fréderíc de Falloux de Coudray

Those who did not participate in the election were Geoffroi Brossais Saint-Marc, archbishop of Rennes, who was too ill to travel; and Paul Cullen, archbishop of Dublin, and John McCloskey, archbishop of New York, who were both *en route*. Both Cullen and McCloskey attended the coronation of Leo XIII.

The College of Cardinals at the time of the conclave of July 31–August 4, 1903, arranged according to rank. Sixty-two cardinals participated in the election.

Luigi Oreglia di Santo Stefano, cardinal-bishop of Ostia and Velletri, dean of the College
Serafino Vannutelli, cardinal-bishop of Porto e Santa Ruffina
Vincenzo Vannutelli, cardinal-bishop of Palestrina
Mario Mocenni, cardinal-bishop of Sabina
Francesco di Paola Satolli, cardinal-bishop of Frascati
Antonio Agliardi, cardinal-bishop of Albano
Jose Sebastião Netto, O.F.M., patriarch of Lisbon
Alfonso Capecelatro, I.O.S.F.N., archbishop of Capua
Benoit Marie Langenieux, archbishop of Reims
James Gibbons, archbishop of Baltimore
Mariano Rampolla del Tindaro, cardinal-secretary of State
François Marie Benjamin Richard, archbishop of Paris
Pierre-Lambert Goosens, archbishop of Malines, Belgium
Anton Joseph Gruscha, archbishop of Vienna
Angelo Di Pietro
Michael Logue, archbishop of Armagh, Ireland
Klaudius Vaszary, O.S.B., archbishop of Gran, Austria-Hungary
Giorg Kopp, bishop of Breslau
Adolphe Ludovic Perraud, I.O.S.F.N., bishop of Autun
Victor Lucien Sulpice Lecot, archbishop of Bordeaux
Giuseppe Melchiore Sarto, patriarch of Venice
Ciriaco María Sancha y Hervás, archbishop of Toledo, Spain
Domenico Svampa, archbishop of Bologna
Andrea Carlo Ferrari, archbishop of Milan
Girolamo Maria Gotti, O.C.D.
Salvador Casañas y Pagès, bishop of Barcelona
Achille Manara, archbishop of Ancona
Domenico Ferrata
Serafino Cretoni

Giuseppe Prisco, archbishop of Naples
José Martín Herrera y de la Iglesia, archbishop of Santiago de Compostela, Spain
Pierre Hector Coullie, archbishop of Lyon
Guillaume Marie Joseph Labourè, archbishop of Rennes
Giovanni Battista Casali del Drago
Francesco di Paola Cassetta
Gennaro Portanova, archbishop of Reggio Calabria
Giuseppe Francica Nava di Bontife, archbishop of Catania
François Désiré Matthieu
Pietro Respighi
Agostino Richelmy, archbishop of Turin
Alessandro Sanminiatelli-Zabarella
Sebastiano Martinelli, O.S.A.
Casimiro Gennari
Leo de Skerbensky Hriste, archbishop of Prague
Giulio Boschi, archbishop of Ferrara
Jan Puzyna de Kozielsko, bishop of Kraków
Bartolomeo Bacilieri, bishop of Verona
Carlo Nocella
Beniamino Cavicchioni
Andrea Aiuti
Emidio Taliani
Sebastián Herrero y Espinosa de los Monteros, archbishop of Valencia
Johannes Katschthaler, archbishop of Salzburg
Anton Hubertus Fischer, archbishop of Cologne
Luigi Macchi
Andrew Steinhuber, S.J.
Francesco Segna
Raffaele Pierotti, O.P.
Francesco Salesio della Volpe
José de Calasanz Vives y Tutó, O.F.M.Cap.
Luigi Tripepi
Felice Cavagnis

Those who did not participate in the conclave were Pietro Geremia Michelangelo Celsesia, O.S.B., archbishop of Palermo, who was seriously ill, and Patrick Francis Moran, archbishop of Sydney, who excused himself because of the great distance to Rome.

Appendix

The College of Cardinals at the time of the conclave of August 31–September 3, 1914, arranged according to rank. Fifty-seven cardinals participated in the election.

Serafino Vannutelli, cardinal-bishop of Ostia, Porto e Santa Ruffina, dean of the College
Antonio Agliardi, cardinal-bishop of Albano, Chancellor
Vincenzo Vannutelli, cardinal-bishop of Palestrina, prefect of the Apostolic Signature
Francesco de Paola Cassetta, cardinal-bishop of Frascati; prefect, Congregation of the Council
Gaetano de Laï, cardinal-bishop of Sabina, secretary of the Consistorial Congregation
Diomede Falconio, O.F.M., cardinal-bishop of Velletri
Jose Sebastião Netto, O.F.M.
Angelo Di Pietro, Datarius
Michael Logue, archbishop of Armagh
Andrea Ferrari, archbishop of Milan
Girolamo Maria Gotti, O.C.D., prefect of the Congregation for the Propagation of the Faith
Domenico Ferrata, prefect of the Congregation for the Discipline of the Sacraments
José María Martín de Herrera y de la Iglesia, archbishop of Santiago de Compostela
Giuseppe Francica Nava di Bontife, archbishop of Catania
Agostino Richelmy, archbishop of Turin
Leo de Skerbensky Hrieste, archbishop of Prague
Giulio Boschi, archbishop of Ferrara
Bartolomeo Bacilieri, bishop of Verona
Raffaele Merry del Val, cardinal-secretary of State
Joachim Arcoverde de Albuquerque Cavalcanti, archbishop of Rio de Janeiro
Aristide Cavallari, patriarch of Venice
Aristide Rinaldini
Benedetto Lorenzelli, prefect of the Congregation of Studies
Pietro Maffi, archbishop of Pisa
Alessandro Lualdi, archbishop of Palermo
Desiré Mercier, archbishop of Malines
Pietro Gasparri
Louis Henri Luçon, archbishop of Reims

Paulin Pierre Andrieu, archbishop of Bordeaux
António Mendes Bello, patriarch of Lisbon
José María Cos y Macho, archbishop of Valladolid
Antonio Vico
Gennaro Granito Pignatelli di Belmonte
John Mary Farley, archbishop of New York
Francis Bourne, archbishop of Westminster
Leon Adolphe Amette, archbishop of Paris
Enrique Almaraz y Santos, archbishop of Seville
François Marie Anatole de Rovèriè de Cabrières, bishop of Montpelier
Basilio Pompilj, Cardinal-Vicar of Rome
Károl von Hörnig, bishop of Veszprem
Victoriano Guisasola y Menènedez, archbishop of Toledo
Domenico Serafini
Giacomo Della Chiesa, archbishop of Bologna
Franz von Bettinger, archbishop of Munich and Freising
János Csernoch, archbishop of Esztergom
Hector Irene Sèvin, archbishop of Lyon
Felix von Hartmann, archbishop of Cologne
Gustav Friedrich Piffl, archbishop of Vienna
Francesco Salesio della Volpe, Camerlengo
Ottavio Caggiano de Azevedo, prefect of the Congregation of Religious
Gaetano Bisleti
Louis Billot, S.J.
Willem Marinus van Rossum, C.SS.R.
Scipione Tecchi
Filippo Giustini
Michele Lega
Francis Aidan Gasquet, O.S.B.

William Henry O'Connell, archbishop of Boston, arrived in Rome after the election had taken place. Franziskus Bauer, archbishop of Olomouc (Olmütz), excused himself because of poor health.

The College of Cardinals at the time of the conclave of February 2–6, 1922, arranged according to rank. Fifty-three cardinals participated in the election.

Vincenzo Vannutelli, cardinal-bishop of Ostia and Palestrina, dean of the College

Appendix

Gaetano de Laï, cardinal-bishop of Sabina, secretary of the Consistorial Congregation
Antonio Vico, bishop of Porto e Santa Ruffina, prefect of the Congregation of Rites
Gennaro Granito Pignatelli di Belmonte, cardinal-bishop of Albano
Basilio Pompilj, cardinal-bishop of Velletri, Cardinal-Vicar of Rome
Giovanni Cagliero, S.D.B., cardinal-bishop of Frascati
Michael Logue, archbishop of Armagh
Giuseppe Francica Nava di Bontifé, archbishop of Catania
Agostino Richelmy, archbishop of Turin
Bartolomeo Bacilieri, bishop of Verona
Raffaele Merry del Val, secretary of the Supreme Sacred Congregation of the Holy Office
Ottavio Cagiano de Azevedo
Pietro Maffi, archbishop of Pisa
Alessandro Lualdi, archbishop of Palermo
Desiré Mercier, archbishop of Malines
Pietro Gasparri, Camerlengo
Louis Henri Luçón, archbishop of Reims
Paulin Pierre Andrieu, archbishop of Bordeaux
António Mendes Bello, patriarch of Lisbon
Francis Bourne, archbishop of Westminster
Willem Marinus van Rossum, C.SS.R.; prefect, Congregation for the Propagation of the Faith
János Csernoch, archbishop of Esztergom
Gustav Friedrich Piffl, C.C.R.S.A, archbishop of Vienna
Alfonso Maria Mistrangelo, Sch.P., archbishop of Florence
Andreas Franz Frühwirth, O.P.
Raffaele Scapinelli di Leguigno
Pietro La Fontaine, patriarch of Venice
Vittorio Amedeo Ranuzzi de' Bianchi
Donato Sbarretti, prefect of the Congregation of the Council
Louis Ernest Dubois, archbishop of Paris
Tommaso Pio Boggiani, O.P.
Alessio Ascalesi, C.PP.S., archbishop of Benevento
Louis Jean Maurin, archbishop of Lyon
Adolf Bertram, archbishop of Breslau
Augusto Silj, prefect of the Supreme Tribunal of the Apostolic Signature
Juan Soldevilla y Romero, archbishop of Saragossa
Teodoro Valfré di Bonzo, prefect of the Congregation of Religious
Aleksander Kakowski, archbishop of Warsaw

Edmund Dalbor, archbishop of Gniezno and Poznan
Francesco Ragonessi
Michael von Faulhaber, archbishop of Munich and Freising
Juan Benlloch y Vivó, archbishop of Burgos
Francisco de Asís Vidal y Barraquer, archbishop of Tarragona
Karl Joseph Schulte, archbishop of Cologne
Giovanni Tacci
Achille Ratti, archbishop of Milan
Gaetano Bisleti, prefect of the Congregation of Seminaries and Universities
Louis Billot, S.J.
Michele Lega, prefect of the Congregation for the Discipline of the Sacraments
Francis Aidan Gasquet, O.S.B., Librarian and Archivist
Niccolo Marini, secretary of the Congregation of the Oriental Church
Oreste Giorgi, Penitentiary Major
Camillo Laurenti

William Henry O'Connell, archbishop of Boston; Denis Dougherty, archbishop of Philadelphia; and Louis Nazaire Begin, archbishop of Quebec, arrived in Rome after the election had taken place.

SELECT BIBLIOGRAPHY

I. General and Reference Works for the Cardinalate and Conclaves.

Battandier, Albert. "Essai de Liste Général des Cardinaux." *Annuaire Pontifical Catholique* (1922–1939). Paris: La Bonne Presse, 1898–1939.

B[erton], C[harles]. *Dictionnaire des Cardinaux: Contenant des Notions Générales sur le Cardinalat, la Nomenclature Complète, par Ordre Alphabétique, des Cardinaux de Tous les Temps et de Tous le Pays; la Même Nomenclature par ordre Chronologique; les Détails Biographiques Essentiels sur Tous les Cardinaux sans Exception; de Longues Études sur les Cardinaux Célèbres, qui, en Si Grand Nombre, ont rempli un Rôle Supérieur dans l'Église, dans la Politique ou dans les Lettres.* Tome Unique, vol. 31 of J[acques]-P[aul] Migne, ed. *Troisième et Dernière Encyclopédie Théologique: ou Troisième et Dernière Série de Dictionnaires sur Toutes les Parties de la Science Religieuse, offrant en Français, et par Ordre Alphabétique, la Plus Claire, la Plus Facile, la Plus Commode, la Plus Variée et la Plus Complète des Théologies*, 65 vols., itself vol. 133 of *Encyclopédie Théologique: ou Troisième et Dernière Série de Dictionnaires sur Toutes les Parties de la Science Religeuse*, 168 vols. in 171 [1845–1873]. Paris: s'imprime et se vend chez J.-P. Migne, Éditeur, aux Ateliers Catholiques, Rue d'Amboise, au Petit-Montrouge, Barrière d'Enfer de Paris, 1857.

Cardella, Lorenzo. *Memorie Storiche de' Cardinali*, 9 vols. Rome: Pagliacine, 1792–1797.

Cartwright, W[illiam] C[ornwallis]. *On Papal Conclaves.* Edinburgh: Edmonston and Douglas, 1868.

Ciaconius, Alphonsus [Alphonso Ciaconio]. *Vitæ et Res Gestæ Pontificum Romanorum et S[anctæ] R[omanæ] E[cclesiæ] Cardinalium ab Initio Nascentis Ecclesiæ, usque ad Urbanum VIII Pont[ifex] Max[imus] Auctoribus.* Roma: Typis Vaticanis, MDCXXX.

Cristofori, [*Conte*] Francesco. *Storia dei Cardinali di Santa Romana Chiesa dal Secolo V all'Anno del Signore MDCCCLXXXVIII.* Roma: Tipografia de Propaganda Fide, 1888.

Dizionario Biografico Degli Italiani. Alberto Maria Ghisalberti and successors, gen. eds. Roma: Instituto della Enciclopedia Italiana, 1960– .

Dizionario Enciclopedico Italiano. Domenico Bartolini, direttore generale. Roma: Instituto della Enciclopedia Italiana, 1958.

Gams, Pius Bonifacius. *Series Episcoporum Ecclesiæ Catholicæ.* Regensburg: Verlag Josef Manz, 1873; reprinted, Graz: Akademische Druck-U. Verlagsanstalt, 1957.

Hierarchia Catholica Medii [et Recentioris] Ævi: sive, Summorum Pontificum, S[anctæ] R[omanæ] E[cclesiæ] Cardinalium, Ecclesiarum Antistitum Series. E Documentis Tabularii Præsertim Vaticani Collecta, Digesta, Edita. 8 vols. Patavii [Padua]: Typis Librariæ "Il Messaggero di S[an] Antonio" apud Basilicam S[ancti] Antonii, 1952–1969. Vols. 1–2 have the title: Hierarchia Catholica Medii Ævi. Vols. 1–4 are reprints of the 2d ed., with reproductions of original title pages. That imprint reads: Monasterii [Munich] Sumptibus et typis Librariæ Regensbergianæ, 1913–35. [v. 1] *Ab anno 1198 usque ad annum 1431 perducta*, per Conradus Eubel.; [v. 2] *Ab anno 1431 usque ad annum 1503 perducta*, per Conradus Eubel.; [v. 3] *Sæculum XVI ab anno 1503 complectens: Volumen tertium sæculum XVI ab anno 1503 complectens quod cum Societatis Goerresianæ subsidio*, quod inchoavit G. [Wilhelm Heinrich Hubert] van Gulik, absolvit C[onradus] Eubel.; [v. 4] (1935, reprinted 1960) *A pontificatu Clementis Pp. VIII (1592) usque ad pontificatum Alexandri Pp. VII (1667)* per P[atritium] Gauchat.; [v. 5 (1952)] *A pontificatu Clementis Pp. IX (1667) usque ad pontificatum Benedicti Pp. XIII (1730)* per R[emigius] Ritzler et Pirminus] Sefrin.; [v. 6] (1958) *A pontificatu Clementis Pp. XII (1730) usque ad pontificatum Pii VI (1799)* per R[emigius] Ritzler et P[irminus] Sefrin; [v. 7] (1968) *A pontificatu Pii Pp. VII (1800) usque ad pontificatum Gregorii Pp. XVI (1846)* per R[emigius] Ritzler et P[irminus] Sefrin; [v. 8] (1978). *A pontificatu Pii Pp. IX (1846) usque ad pontificatum Leonis Pp. XIII (1903)* per R[emigius] Ritzler et P[irminus] Sefrin.

Isenburg, Wilhelm Karl von. *Stammtafeln der Geschichte der Europäischen Staaten (Europäischen Stammtafeln)*, band II: *Die ausserdeutchen Staaten*. Marburg: Verlag von J. A. Stargardt, 1956.

Kelly, J[ohn] N[orman] D[avidson]. *The Oxford Dictionary of the Popes*. Oxford: Oxford University Press, 1986.

Litta, [Conte] Pompeo and successors, Federico Oderici, Luigi Passerini, and Federico Stefani. *Famiglie Celebri Italiane*, 185 fascicles in various bindings and pagings. Milano: Typografia del [P. E.] Giusti, 1819–1885.

Moroni, Gaetano. *Dizionario di Erudizioni Storico-Ecclesiastici*. Roma: Tipografia Emiliana, 1847.

Panvinius, Onuphrius [Onofrio Panvinio]. *Epitome Pontificvm Romanorvm a S. Petro usque ad Paulum IIII. Gestorum (videlicet) electionisque singulorum, & conclauium compendiaria narratio. Cardinalium item nomina, dignitatum tituli, insignia legationes, patria & obitus*. Edited by Jacobus de Strada. Venetiis [Venice]: Imp[r]ensis I. Stradæ, 1557.

Pastor, Ludwig, *Freiherr* von. *History of the Popes.* 40 vols. Translated and edited by Ralph Francis Kerr, *et al.* London: Routledge & Kegan Paul Ltd., 1923–1951.

Pirie, Valerie. *The Triple Crown: an Account of Papal Conclaves from the Fifteenth Century to the Present Day.* Wilmington, North Carolina: Consortium Books, 1976.

II. Materials on the Modern College, Cardinals, and Conclaves.

Anstruther, George Elliot. *The Election of a Pope.* London: Catholic Truth Society, 1936.

Aradi, Zsolt. *The Popes: The History of How They Are Chosen, Elected and Crowned.* London: Macmillan, 1956.

Artaud de Montor, [Alexis François]. *Histoire du Pape Leon XII.* 2 vols. Paris: A. Le Clere et Cie., 1843.

———. *Histoire du Pape Pie VIII.* Paris: Librairie d'Adrien le Clere et Cie., 1844.

——— and Bartolommeo Pacca. *Histoire du pontificat de Pie VII, Extraite en grande partie de l'ouvrage de M. Artaud et des Memoires du Cardinal Pacca.* 2d ed. Lille: L. Lefort, 1846.

Aschoff, Hans-Georg. *Kirchenfürst im Kaiserreich: Georg Kardinal Kopp.* Hildesheim: Bernward, 1987.

Baart, Peter A. *The Roman Court, or, A Treatise on the Cardinals, Roman Congregations and Tribunals, Legates, Apostolic Vicars, Protonotaries, and other Prelates of the Holy Roman Church.* 4th ed. New York: F. Pustet, 1895.

Barbier, Jean. *Le Cardinal Gerlier.* Roanne/Le Coteau: Horvath, 1987.

Barbier de Montault, X[avier]. *Le Conclave et le Pape.* 2 ed. Paris: Oudin, 1878.

Baudrillart, Alfred (Cardinal). *Les Carnets du Cardinal Baudrillart (20 novembre 1935–11 avril 1939).* Paris: Editions du Cerf, 1996.

Belardo, Marius. *De Iuribus S[anctæ] R[omanæ] E[cclesiæ] Cardinalium in Titulus.* [Romæ]: Typis Polyglottis Vaticanis, 1939.

Berkeley, George Fitz-Hardinge. *Italy in the Making.* 3 vols. Cambridge: at the University Press, 1932–1940.

Berthelet, Giovanni. *Muss der Päpst ein Italiener sein? Das Italienertum der Papste, seine Ursachen und seine Wirkungen.* Leipzig: Rengersche Buchhandlung, 1894.

———. *Storia e Rivelazioni sul Conclave del 1903 Elezione di Pio X.* Roma-Torino: Casa Editrice Nazionale, Roux e Viarengo, 1904.

Berthod, Bernard. *Cardinal Gerlier (1880–1965).* Lyon: LUGD, 1995.

Bianchi, Nicomede. *Storia Documentata della Diplomazia Europea in Italia dall'anno 1814 all'anno 1861*. 8 vols. Torino: Unione Tipografico-Editrice, 1865–1872.

Bonghi, Ruggiero. *Pio IX e il Papa Futuro*. Milano: Treves, 1877.

Bowen, Desmond. *Paul Cardinal Cullen and the Shaping of Modern Irish Catholicism*. Waterloo, Ontario, Canada: Wilfrid Laurier University Press, 1983.

Bury, J[ohn] B[agnell]. *History of the Papacy in the 19th century (1864–1878)*. London: Macmillan and Co., Limited, 1930.

Il Cardinale Alfredo Ildefonso Schuster, Avvio allo Studio. Milano: Nuove Edizioni Duomo, 1979. *Archivio Ambrosiano*, no. 38.

Ceccaroni, Agostino. *Il Conclave: Storia, Costituzioni, Ceremonie*. Torino: G. Marietti, 1901.

Le Ceremonie dei Funerali del Papa, il Conclave, Cenni Biografici dei Cardinali. Roma: Desclée, Lefebvre, 1903.

Cesare, Rafféal de. *Le Conclave de Leon XIII*. Rome: Loreto Pasqualucci, 1888.

Chadwick, Owen. *The Popes and European Revolution*. Oxford: Clarendon Press, 1981.

Cochlovius, Klaus. *Die Papstwahl und das Veto der katholischen Staaten*. Greifswald: Abel, 1910.

Consalvi, Ercole. *Memoires du Cardinal Consalvi*. Nouv. ed. Paris: Maison de la Bonne Presse, 1895.

Coppa, Frank J. *The Modern Papacy since 1789*. London: Longman, 1998.

Daniel-Rops, Henri. *The Church in an Age of Revolution, 1789–1870*. London: J. M. Dent, 1965.

Duerm, Charles van. *Correspondance du Cardinal Hercule Consalvi avec le Prince Clement de Meternich, 1815–1823*. Louvain: Polleunis & Ceuterick, 1899.

_____. *Un peu plus de Lumiere sur le Conclave de Venise: et sur les Commencements du Pontificat de Pie VII, 1799–1800: documents inedits, extraits des archives de Vienne*. Louvain, Paris: C. Peeters, editeur, V. Lecoffre, libraire, 1896.

Duffy, Leonard T. "Historical Development of the Mode of Papal Elections." Unpublished thesis (M.A.), St. Bonaventure University, 1956.

Ebers, Godehard Josef, ed. *Der Papst und die Römische Kurie*. Paderborn: F. Schöningh, 1916. *Quellensammlung zur kirchlichen Rechtsgeschichte und zum Kirchenrecht*, no. 3.

Ellis, John Tracy. *Cardinal Consalvi and Anglo-Papal Relations, 1814–1824*. Washington, D. C.: The Catholic University of America Press, 1942.

Farini, Luigi Carlo. *Lo Stato Romano dall'anno 1815 al 1850*. 3d. ed., 4 vols.,

Select Bibliography

in 2. Firenze: F. Le Monnier, 1853.

Feret, Pierre. *La France et le Saint-Siege sous le Premier Empire, la Restauration et la Monarchie de Juillet, d'apres les Documents Officiels et Inedits*. 2 vols. Paris: A. Savaete, 1911.

Gaugusch, Ludwig. *Das Rechtsinstitut der Papstwahl: eine historisch-kanonistische Studie*. Wien: Manzsche k. u. k. hof-Verlags- und Universitätsbuchhandlung, 1905.

Giese, Friedrich, ed. *Die Geltenden Papstwahlgesetze*. Bonn: A. Marcus und E. Weber, 1912.

Giuliani, D. *Un mois à Rome: la Mort de Léon XIII, l'Élection de Pie X: Impressions, Souvenirs, Anecdotes*. Lyon: E. Vitte, 1982.

Goyau, Georges, and Paul Lesourd. *Comment on élit un pape*. [Paris]: Flammarion, 1935.

Grissell, Hartwell de la Garde. *Sede Vacante: being a diary written during the conclave of 1903, with additional notes on the accession and coronation of Pius X*. Oxford: J. Parker, 1903.

Hales, Edward Elton Young. *The Catholic Church in the Modern World: A Survey from the French Revolution to the Present*. London: Eyre & Spottiswoode, in association with Burns & Oates, 1958.

_____. *Revolution and Papacy, 1769–1846*. London: Eyre & Spottiswoode, 1960.

Hayward, Fernand. *Le Dernier Siecle de la Rome Pontificale*. 2 vols. Paris: Payot, 1927.

Heriot, Angus. *The French in Italy, 1796–1799*. London: Chatto & Windus, 1957.

Hynes, Harry Gerard. *The Privileges of Cardinals: Commentary with Historical Notes*. Washington D. C.: Catholic University of America Press, 1945. Catholic University of America. Canon Law Studies, no. 217.

Iannotta, Antonio M. *Lucubratio Theologica de Ecclesia et Primatu Romani Pontificis Vacante Sede Apostolica Collata etiam Codicis Juris Canonici Doctrina*. Editio altera emendata et aucta. Roma: Tipografia dell'Unione Editrice, 1919.

Kant, Bronislaw. *Sztygar Bozej kopalni obrazki z zycia ks. Kardynala Augusta Hlonda*, 2 ed. Lodz: Wydawnictwo Salezjanskie, 1983.

Keller, Joseph Edward. *The Life and Acts of Pope Leo XIII*. New York: Benziger Brothers, 1879.

Kittler, Glenn D. *The Papal Princes: a History of the Sacred College of Cardinals*. New York: Funk & Wagnalls, 1960.

Komar, Edward. *Kardynal Puzyna, Moje Wspomnienia*. Krakow: Nakl. autora, 1912.

Laicus, Philipp. *Die Papstwahl: nach authentischen Quellen dargestellt nebst einem kurzen Abriss der letzten Lebenstage Papst Pius IX*. Einsiedeln: C. und N. Benziger, 1878.

Lector, Lucius [pseud. of Joseph Guthlin]. *Le Conclave: Origines—Histoire, Organisation, Législation, ancienne et moderne*. Paris: P. Lethielleux, 1894.

Leflon, Jean. *Pie VII*. Paris: Plon, 1958.

Life of His Holiness Pope Pius X. New York: Benziger, 1904.

Lo Stato della Chiesa in Epoca Napoleonica: atti del 19. Convegno del Centro di studi avellaniti: Fonte Avellana, 24-25-26 agosto 1995. [S. l.: s. n.], 1996.

Maier, Hans. *Revolution und Kirche: zur Fruhgeschichte der christlichen Demokratie*, 5th ed. Freiburg im Breisgau: Herder, 1988. First edition translated as *Revolution and Church: the Early History of Christian Democracy, 1789–1901*. Notre Dame, Indiana: University of Notre Dame Press, 1969.

Maioli, Giovanni, ed. *Pio IX, da Vescovo a Pontefice: Lettere al Card[inale] Luigi Amat [di San Filippo e Sorso] (agosto 1839–luglio 1848)*. Modena: Società Tipografica Modenese, 1949.

Martin, Victor. *Les cardinaux et la Curie: Tribunaux et Offices, la Vacance du Siège Apostolique*. [Paris]: Bloud & Gay, 1930.

Martina, Giacomo. *Pio IX*. 3 vols. Roma: Università Gregoriana, 1974–1990.

Mathiez, Albert. *Rome et le Clerge Français sous la Constituante: La Constitution Civile du Clerge, L'affaire d'Avignon*. Paris: Armand, 1911.

Matthieu, François Désiré. *Le Concordat de 1801*. 2d ed. Paris: Perrin et cie, 1904.

Mayol de Lupe, Marie Eugene Henri. *La Captivité de Pie VII d'apres des Documents Inedits*. Paris: Emile-Paul freres, 1912.

Metternich-Winneburg, Richard Clemens Lothar, Fürst von, and Alfons, Freiherr von Klinkowstrom, eds. *Memoirs of Prince [Clemens Wenzel Lothar, Fürst von] Metternich, 1773–1835*. Translated by Gerard W. Smith. 3 vols. New York: Harper, 1881–1882.

Monti, Antonio. *Pio IX nel Risorgimento Italiano*. Bari: G. Laterza & figli, 1928.

O'Dwyer, Margaret M. *The Papacy in the age of Napoleon and the Restoration: Pius VII, 1800–1823*. Lanham, Maryland: University Press of America, 1985.

O'Neil, Robert J. *Cardinal Herbert Vaughan: Archbishop of Westminster, Bishop of Salford, Founder of the Mill Hill Missionaries*. Tunbridge Wells, Kent: Burns & Oates, 1995.

Pacca, Bartolommeo. *Memorie Storiche del Ministero de' Due Viaggi in Francia e della Prigionia nel Forte di S[an] Carlo*. 2d ed. Roma: F. Bour-

Select Bibliography

lie, 1830. Translated as *Historical Memoirs of Cardinal Pacca, Prime Minister to Pius VII*; trans. Sir George Head. 2 vols. London: Longman, Brown, Green, and Longmans, 1850.

———. *Memorie Storiche di Monsignor Bartolomeo Pacca poi Cardinale di S[anta] Chiesa sul di lui Soggiorno in Germania dall'anno MDCCLXXXVI al MDCCXCIV*. Nuova ed. Roma: Tip[ografia] Poliglotta della S [acra] C[ongregazione] di Propaganda Fide, 1891.

Pasolini, Pier Desiderio, ed. *Giuseppe Pasolini, 1815–1876: Memorie*. 3d ed. Torino: Fratelli Bocca, 1887.

Pennington, Arthur Robert. *The Papal Conclaves*. New York: E. & J. B. Young, 1897.

Peries, G[eorge]. *L'Intervention du Pape dans l'Élection de Son Successeur*. Paris: A. Roger & F. Chernoviz, 1902.

Petrocchi, Massimo. *La Restaurazione, il Cardinale Consalvi e la Riforma del 1816*. Firenze: F. Le Monnier, 1941.

Peyrefitte, Roger. *Les Secrets des Conclaves*. Paris: Flammarion, 1964.

Pichon, Charles. *Le Pape: le Conclave, l'Élection, et les Cardinaux*. Paris: A. Fayard, 1955.

Pillon, Adrien. *Biographies des Cardinaux et des Prélats Contemporains*. Paris: Librairie du Rosier de Marie, 1861.

Pistolesi, Erasmo. *Vita del Sommo Pontefice Pio VII*. 4 vols. Roma: Presso F. Bourlie, 1824–1830.

Quazza, Romolo. *Pio IX e Massimo D'Azeglio nelle Vicende Romane del 1847*. [Modena]: Società Tipografica Editrice Modenese, 1954.

Rinieri, Ilario. *Il Congresso di Vienna e la S[anta] Sede, 1813–1815*. Roma: Civilta Cattolica, 1904.

———. *La Diplomazia Pontificia nel Secolo XIX*. 6 vols. in 7. Roma: Civiltà Cattolica, 1902–1903.

———. *Napoleone e Pio VII, 1804–1813*. 2 vols. Torino: Unione Tipografico-Editrice, 1906.

Rota, Livio. *Le Nomine Vescovili e Cardinalizie in Francia*. Roma: Pontificia Università Gregoriana, 1996. *Miscellanea Historiæ Pontificiæ*, v. 62.

Sagmüller, Johannes Baptist. *Die Papstwahlbullen und das staatliche Recht der Exklusive*. Tübingen: H. Laupp, 1892.

Sala, Giuseppe Antonio. *Diario Romano degli Anni 1798–1799*. 3 vols. Roma: Presso La Societa [Romana di Storia Patria], 1980.

Salamon, Louis Sifrein Joseph Foncrose de. *Correspondance Secrete de l'Abbe de Salamon, Charge des Affaires du Saint-Siege, Pendant la Revolution avec le Cardinal de Zelada (1791–1792)*. Paris: Plon, Nourrit et cie., 1898.

Schmidlin, Joseph. *La Papauté et les Papes de la Restauration (1800–1846)*. 2

vols. Paris: E. Vitte, 1938–1940.

Serafini, Alberto. *Pio Nono: Giovanni Maria Mastai Ferretti, dalla Giovinezza alla Morte nei Suoi Scritti e Discorsi Editi e Inetiti.* [Citta del Vaticano]: [Tipografia] Poliglotta Vaticana, 1958.

Sladen, Douglas Brooks Wheelton. *The Pope at Home.* London: Hurst and Blackett, 1913.

Spellanzon, Cesare, and Ennio di Nolfo (vols. 6, 7, and 8). *Storia del Risorgimento e dell'Unita d'Italia.* 8 vols. Milano: Rizzoli, 1934.

Taschereau, (Cardinal) Elzear-Alexandre. *Mandement de Monseigneur E.-A. Taschereau, archevêque de Québec, sur l'élection de Notre Saint-Père le pape Léon XIII, 20 février 1878.* S. l.: s. n., 1878.

Thompson, J[ames] M[atthew]. *Napoleon Bonaparte.* New York: Barnes & Noble, 1996.

Vinatier, Jean. *Le Cardinal Suhard (1874–1949): l'Évêque du Renouveau Missionnaire en France.* Paris: Le Centurion, 1983.

Washburn, Henry Bradford. *The College of Cardinals and the Veto.* S.l.: s.n., 1914; reprinted from the *Papers of the American Society of Church History*, Second Series, vol. IV, 1914.

Wayman, Dorothy G[odfrey]. *Cardinal O'Connell of Boston: a Biography of William Henry O'Connell, 1859–1944.* New York: Farrar, Straus and Young, 1955.

Weiss, Richard, Edler von Starkenfels. *Pio IX e la Politica Austriaca in Italia dal 1815 al 1948 nella Relazione del Diplomatico Riccardo Weiss di Starkenfels.* Firenze: Le Monnier, 1958.

Wurm, Hermann Joseph. *Die Papstwahl: ihre Geschichte und Gebräuche.* Köln: J. P. Bachem, 1902.

III. Frequently-consulted Serials and Newspapers.

Annuario Pontificio. (Title varies: *Notizie per l'anno . . .* (1716–1858); *Annuario Pontificio* (1860–1871); *Gerarchia Cattolica* (1872–1911); *Annuario Pontificio* (1912–). Città del Vaticano: Tipografia Poliglotta Vaticana, 1716– (Imprint varies: Original imprint: Roma: G. F. Chracas).

Archivum Historiæ Pontificiæ. Editum a Facultate Historiæ Ecclesiastica in Pontificia Universitate Gregoriana. Romæ: s.n., 1963– .

Catholic Almanac. (Title varies: 1904–1910, *St. Anthony's Almanac*; 1911, *Franciscan Almanac*; 1912–1929, St Anthony's Almanac; 1931–1933, *The Franciscan: Almanac Edition*; 1936–1939, *The Franciscan Almanac*; 1940–1968, *The National Catholic Almanac*. Felician A. Foy, ed. (1969–). Huntington, Indiana: Our Sunday Vistor, Inc., annual. (Imprint varies in editions before 1968.)

The Catholic Year Book for . . . (Title varies: *Catholic Year Book, Catholic Almanac and Year Book*). London: Burns Oates & Washbourne, 1951– (annual).
The New York Times.
L'Osservatore Romano (Citta del Vaticano). Frequency has varied: weekly, 1849–1851 [Anno 1., no. 1 (5 sett. 1849)–]; three times a week, 1852–1859; daily (except Sunday) 1861– [Anno 1, num. 1 (1 luglio 1861)–].
L'Osservatore Romano. Weekly edition in English (Vatican City). 1st year, no. 1 (Apr. 4, 1968)– .
The Tablet. London: The Tablet Publishing Company, 1840– . Weekly, May 16, 1840– .
The Times (London).
The Washington Post (Washington, D.C.).

IV. Selected Electronic Resources.

Den Katolske Kirke: http://www.katolsk.no
New Advent: http://www.sni.net/advent
Aquinas Multimedia: http://www.aquinas-multimedia.com
Christus Rex: http://christusrex.org
Saint Michael's Depot: http://abbey.apana.org.au
The Holy See: http://www.vatican.va
Woodstock Theological Center: http://guweb.georgetown.edu/woodstock
The Tablet: http://www.thetablet.co.uk
Salvador Miranda's site for the College of Cardinals: http://www.fiu.edu/~mirandas/cardinal.htm

INDEX

This is an index of personal names and papal documents.

A

Agliardi, Antonio, 81–82, 86, 99–102, 104, 108–109, 111
Albani, Giovanni Francesco, 8, 10–11
Albani, Giovanni Francesco (Clement XI), 64
Albani, Giuseppe, 22, 26, 28
Alexander VII, Pope, 46, 65
Alfonso XII, king of Spain, 47
Almaraz y Santos, Enrique, 105, 112, 115, 133
Althaan, Michael Friedrich von, 84
Altieri, Vincenzo Maria, 6
Amat di San Filippo e Sorso, Luigi, 45, 51, 53, 55, 60, 62, 65, 67–68
Amette, Leon Adolphe, 104, 111
Amici, Diomede, 96
Andrassy, Julius, 46
Andrieu, Paulin Pierre, 104, 117–119, 132
Antici, Tommaso, 6
Antonelli, Giacomo, 36–37, 42, 49
Antonelli, Leonardo, 5–6, 10–11
Antonucci, Antonio, 58
Arcoverde de Albuquerque Cavalcanti, Joachim, 105, 108, 117, 132
Ascalesi, Alessio, 133
Asquini, Fabio, 55, 68
Azara, José Nicolás de, 5

B

Bacilieri, Bartolomeo, 86, 108–110, 112, 115–116, 118, 133, 140
Baciocchi, Elise Bonaparte, 16
Baciocchi, Felice, 16
Bartolini, Domenico, 41–43, 46–51, 53, 59–62, 65–66, 68–69
Battistini, Raffaele, 124–125, 127–130, 139
Bauer, Franz, 103

Beauharnais, Eugène de, 4
Begin, Louis Nazaire, 103, 132
Bellisomi, Carlo, 9–11
Benavides y Navarrete, Francisco di Paola, 50
Benedict XIV, Pope, 1, 120
Benedict XV, Pope, xiii, 120–131, 133–135, 138, 140, 144, 146, 148, 150, 152, 155
Benlloch y Vivo, Juan, 133
Benvenuti, Giovanni Antonio, 30–31
Berardi, Filippo, 46
Berardi, Giuseppe, 46–47, 60
Bernadotte, Jean-Baptiste, 5
Bernetti, Tommaso, 24, 28–30
Bernis, François Joachim Pierre de, 2
Berthier, Louis-Alexandre, 5, 9
Bertram, Adolf, 132, 136, 138
Bettinger, Franz von, 102–103, 107, 111–112
Bignami, Amico, 124–125, 131
Bilio, Luigi, 43–44, 47–50, 52–53, 58–62, 67–68, 84
Billot, Louis, 104, 115, 129, 132
Bisleti, Gaetano, 73, 97, 113–114, 133, 138, 140–146, 150–151
Bismarck, Otto von, 41
Bofondi, Giuseppe, 36
Boggiani, Tommaso Pio, 100, 129, 134–135
Boisnormand de Bonnechose, Henri Marie Gaston, 50
Bonaparte, Joseph, 4
Bonghi, Ruggiero, 54
Boniface VIII, Pope, 1
Bonomi, Ivanoe, 131, 134
Borghese, Camillo, 16–17
Borghese, Pauline Bonaparte, 16
Borromeo, Eduardo, 47–48, 52, 54, 58–59
Boschi, Giulio, 86, 115

Bourbon-Parma, Sixtus of, 76
Bourne, Francis, 105, 112, 133, 136, 138
Braschi Onesti, Luigi, 3, 5
Brossais Saint-Marc, Geoffroy, 62
Brunty, Patrick, 7

C

Caggiano de Azevedo, Ottavio, 78, 112, 117–118, 129
Cagliero, Giovanni, 129, 138
Calenzio, Generoso, 59, 62–63, 65, 68
Cambacérès, Jean Jacques Régis de, 16
Canali, Nicola, 96, 121
Capecellatro, Alfonso, 81–82, 86–88, 90
Capovilla, Loris, 157
Cappellari, Mauro (Gregory XVI), 28
Carafa, Domenico, 55
Carlo Alberto of Savoy, 34
Carter, Jimmy, 155
Casali del Drago, Giovanni Battista, 74
Cassetta, Francesco di Paola, 78, 81, 90, 104
Castiglione, Francesco Saverio (Pius VIII), 22–23, 25
Cataldi, Antonio, 69
Caterini, Prospero, 46–47, 59–61, 67–69
Cavagnis, Felice, 75, 80–81
Caverot, Louis Marie Joseph Eusebe, 51
Celesia, Pietro, 76
Celestine IV, Pope, 22
Chabrol de Volvic, Louis de, 17, 20
Charles VI, Emperor, 84
Charles X, king of France, 27
Chateaubriand, François-Renè de, 25
Chaves, Bruno, 95
Cherubini, Lorenzo, 125
Chiaramonti, Barnabà (Pius VII), 10
Chigi, Agostino, 28
Chigi, Flavio, 46, 53, 68
Chigi, Francesco, 92
Chigi, Luigi, 92
Chigi, Mario, 55, 61, 78, 92
Chigi-Albani, Ludovico, 108, 129, 139, 143
Chotek, Sophie, 95
Cicognani, Amleto Giovanni, 155
Clary, Désirée, 4–5
Clement IX, Pope, 55, 79
Clement X, Pope, 44
Clement XI, Pope, 64
Clement XIV, Pope, 1
Commissum nobis, 92
Confalonieri, Carlo, 149
Consalvi, Ercole, 8–12, 19–23, 25–26, 28
Consolini, Domenico, 49, 53, 60, 67
Consulturi, 40
Corboli-Bussi, Giovanni, 35
Cos y Macho, José Maria, 105, 117
Csernoch, Johann, 103, 133, 137–138
Cullen, Paul, 62

D

D'Avanzo, Bartolomeo, 48, 68
d'Azeglio, Giulia Manzoni, 34
d'Azeglio, Massimo Tapparelli, 34
Dalbor, Edmond, 133, 136–137
De Angelis, Filippo, 42
de Laï, Gaetano, 101, 104–105, 109, 114–115, 118–119, 129, 138, 140–145, 149–150
De Luca, Antonino, 45, 54, 59–60, 68
de Lugo, Juan, 83
Della Chiesa, Giacomo (Benedict XV), 102–103, 106–107, 109–119
Della Chiesa, Giulia, 127
Della Chiesa, Giuseppe, 127, 129
della Genga Sermattei, Annibale (Leo XII), 22
della Somaglia, Giulio Maria, 22–25
della Volpe, Francesco Salesio, 74, 91, 97–100, 108, 120
Despuig y Dameto, Antonio, 10
Di Canossa, Luigi, 58–60, 67
Di Pietro, Angelo, 81, 86–88, 99–100
Di Pietro, Camillo, 45–48, 67–68
Dickens, Charles, 8
Dominic, Saint, xii
Donnet, François Auguste Ferdinand, 50, 58
Doria Pamfili, Giuseppe, 4–5

Index

Dougherty, Denis, 132
Dubillard, François Virgile, 103
Dubois, Louis Ernest, 132, 136
Duphot, Jean-Pierre, 4, 9
Duvoisin, Jean-Baptiste, 18

F

Falconio, Diomede, 97, 104, 109, 118–119
Falloux de Coudray, Frederic de, 48–49, 52–53, 58, 61, 65
Farley, John Mary, 105, 112
Faulhaber, Michael von, 132, 136, 138
Ferdinand I, king of Naples, 7
Ferdinand VII, king of Spain, 28
Ferdinando II, king of Naples, 27
Ferrari, Andrea, 86, 89, 108–109
Ferrata, Domenico, 81, 88–89, 101–102, 106–107, 109–113, 115, 117, 121
Ferretti, Gabriele, 36
Ferretti, Pietro, 31
Ferrieri, Innocenzo, 46–47, 51, 59–60, 62, 65, 67
Fischer, Anton Hubertus, 87
Fitzgerald, Edward, 37
Flangini, Luigi, 11
Ford, Gerald Rudolph, 155
Foschi, Frederico, 63, 67
Fouché, Joseph, 17
Francesco I, king of Naples, 27
Franchi, Alessandro, 42–43, 45, 47, 50–51, 53, 59–62, 68
Francica-Nava di Bontifé, Giuseppe, 115–117, 133, 138
Francis of Assisi, Saint, xii
François I, king of France, 17
Frankenberg, Jean-Henri de, 9
Franz II, Emperor, 8–11
Franz Ferdinand, Archduke, 95
Franz Josef I, Emperor, 50, 83–85
Franzelin, Johann, 48, 51, 53, 61, 66, 68
Frühwirth, Andreas Franz, 129, 132, 137–138

G

Galli, Aurelio, 107, 138
Gallo, Muzio, 9

García-Gil, Emmanuele, 50, 58, 66
Garibaldi, Giuseppe, 35–36
Gasparri, Pietro, xiii, 103–104, 109, 111–112, 121, 124–125, 127–129, 131–135, 137–152
Gasquet, Aidan, 105, 133
Gaysruck, Carl Cajetan, 34
George (Prince Regent), later George IV, 20
George I, king of England, 7
George IV, king of England, 26
Gerdil, Giacinto Sigismondo, 10
Ghislieri, Marchese, 12–13
Giannelli, Pietro, 53, 60
Gibbons, James, 81–82, 86, 89, 99, 103
Giorgi, Oreste, 126, 130, 147
Giustini, Filippo, 115
Giustiniani, Giacomo, 24, 28
Gizzi, Tommaso Pasquale, 34–36
Gotti, Girolamo Maria, 73–74, 77, 79–80, 82, 86–88, 90–91, 105, 109, 113
Grassi-Landi, Bartolomeo, 69
Grassis, Paris de, 1, 56
Gregory I, Pope, 64
Gregory XIV, Pope, 32
Gregory XV, Pope, 29
Gregory XVI, Pope, 26, 29–34, 36, 42
Guibert, Joseph, 49–51, 68
Guidi, Filippo Maria, 45, 47, 58, 60
Guisasola y Menendez, Victoriano, 105, 115

H

Hartmann, Felix von, 102, 107, 113–114, 117
Herrera y de la Iglesia, José María Martín, 105, 133
Herrero y Espinosa de los Monteros, Sebastiano, 76–77, 80, 90, 92
Herzan von Harras, Franz, 10–11
Hindenburg, Paul von, 106
Hohenlohe, Gustav Adolf von, 46–48, 52–53, 56, 61–62
Honorius III, Pope, 55
Hornig, Karl von, 105, 107–108

Howard, Edward, 48, 53, 60

I

In hac sublimi, 39
Innocent III, Pope, xii
Innocent IX, Pope, 32
Innocent XI, Pope, 27, 155

J

Jacobini, Ludovico, 46
James II, king of England, 27
Jefferson, Thomas, 56
Jenner, Edward, 24
John XXIII, Pope, xi, 155–158
John Paul I, Pope, 158
John Paul II, Pope, xi, 158
Julius II, Pope, 56

K

Kakowski, Alexander, 133, 136–137
Kennedy, Jacqueline Bouvier, 157
Kopp, Georg, 82
Kutschker, Johann Rudolf, 46

L

La Fontaine, Pietro, 133, 140–149
Laghi, Pio, 156
Lagorse, Captain, 19
Lambruschini, Luigi, 33
Lamennais, Félicité Robert de, 31
Langenieux, Benoit Marie, 86, 90–91
Lasagni, Pietro, 55, 59, 62, 67
Laurenti, Camillo, 128, 138, 140–149
Laval Montmorency, Louis-Joseph de, 9
Lecot, Victor, 77, 81–82, 87, 90
Ledochowski, Mieczyslaw Halka, 45, 47–48, 54, 59–60
Lega, Michele, 133, 142–143
Leo I, Pope, 67
Leo XI, Pope, 23, 65
Leo XII, Pope, 23–28, 30, 32–33, 36, 62, 66–67
Leo XIII, Pope, xi–xiii, 8, 66–69, 71–73, 75, 79, 91, 93, 98, 101, 106–107, 113, 116, 120, 135, 155–156, 158
Leopold I, king of the Belgians, 27

Licet per apostolicas, 39
Livizzani, Carlo, 9
Logue, Michael, 78, 105, 117–118, 132, 148, 150
Lorenzelli, Benedetto, 108–109, 111
Louis XIV, king of France, 83
Louis XVI, king of France, 2
Louis XVIII, king of France, 13, 20, 23, 36
Lualdi, Alessandro, 109–113, 115–116, 133, 138
Luçon, Louis Henri, 104, 108, 115, 118, 132, 136, 138
Ludendorf, Erich von, 106

M

Macchi, Luigi, 74, 78, 91–92
MacMahon, Marie Edmé Patrice Maurice, 50
Maffi, Pietro, 101, 103, 109–113, 115–117, 133, 138, 140–145, 151
Mamiani, Terenzio, 31
Manara, Achille, 91
Mancini, Pietro, 46
Manning, Henry Edward, 43, 47–48, 53
Manzani, Ersilio, 128
Manzoni, Alessandro, 34
Marazzani Visconti, Francesco Maria, 25
Marcellus II, Pope, 64–65
Marchiafava, Ettore, 96, 98, 124–125
Marie Louise, Empress, 18
Marini, Niccolo, 129, 139–140
Martinelli, Sebastiano, 90, 100, 103
Martinelli, Tommaso Maria, 51, 53, 59–60, 67–68
Martiniana, Carlo Giuseppe, 13
Martinucci, Vincenzo, 48, 67, 74
Mastai-Ferretti, Giovanni Maria (Pius IX), 34
Mater et Magistra, 157
Mattei, Alessandro, 3, 10–11
Matthieu, François Desiré, 77, 85, 88, 90
Mauri, Angelo, 131
Maurin, Louis Joseph, 132
Mazzini, Giuseppe, 36

McCloskey, John, 41, 62
Mendes Bello, Antonio, 105, 133
Mendoza, Joao Francisco de, 9
Mercier, Désiré, 105, 133, 136–138, 140–141
Mercurelli, Francesco, 54
Merry del Val, Raffaele, 73–74, 84, 89, 92, 95–99, 101–102, 105–106, 108–110, 112–116, 118, 120–122, 127–128, 133–138, 140–146, 148–149, 152
Mertel, Teodolfo, 46, 49, 53, 59–61, 66–68
Metternich, Klemens von, 22, 24, 27, 31, 33, 35
Micara, Ludovico, 33–34
Migazzi de Valle a Soletturin, Cristoforo de, 2, 9
Migone, Giuseppe, 120, 124–126, 130–131
Mihalovic, Jozef, 60, 66
Miollis, Sextius Alexandre François, 14
Mirari vos, 31
Mistrangelo, Alfonso Maria, 133
Mocenni, Mario, 75
Monaco La Valetta, Raffaele, 43, 45–48, 51, 53, 59–62, 67–68
Moraes y Cardoso, Ignacio do Nascimento, 61, 66
Moran, Patrick Francis, 76
Moreno y Maisonave, Juan Ignacio, 50
Moretti, Vincenzo, 59–60, 67
Morichini, Carlo Maria, 45
Murat, Joachim, king of Naples, 14, 20–21

N

Napoleon, 2, 9, 12–15, 17–21, 30
Nasalli-Rocca di Corneliano, Giovanni Battista, 128, 130–131
Nelson, Horatio, 7
Netto, Jose Sebastião, 78, 99, 105, 108, 115
Newman, John Henry, xii
Nina, Lorenzo, 43, 48–49, 53, 59, 61
Nixon, Richard Milhous, 155

O

O'Connell, Daniel, 26
O'Connell, William, 103, 132, 152
Oppizzoni, Carlo, 32
Oreglia di Santo Stefano, Luigi, 47, 49, 51–53, 58, 61, 66, 68–69, 72–76, 78–81, 83–91, 93
Oudinot, Charles, 36
Oudinot, Nicholas Charles, 36

P

Pacca, Bartolommeo, 15–16, 19, 21, 28–29
Pacelli, Eugenio (Pius XII), xiii, 153
Pacem in Terris, 157
Pallavicini, Sforza, 65
Panebianco, Anton Maria, 42, 45, 48, 59–60, 67–68
Paolucci de' Calboli, Fabrizio, 84
Parocchi, Lucido Maria, 46, 60
Parolin, Giovanni Battista, 97, 121
Paul VI, Pope, xi, 157–158
Paya y Rico, Miguel, 50, 58
Pecci, Gioacchino (Leo XIII), 42–49, 51–55, 58–63, 65–68
Pecci, Giuseppe, 43
Peel, Sir Robert, 26
Pellegrini, Antonio, 66
Perraud, Louis Adolphe, 87, 89–90
Persico, Giovanni, 127
Philip II, king of Spain, 83
Philip IV, king of Spain, 83
Piffl, Gustav Friedrich, 101–103, 107, 115, 121, 133, 136, 138, 148
Pignatelli di Belmonte, Gennaro Granito, 133, 138, 147
Pitra, Jean Baptiste, 48, 52–53
Pius II, Pope, 81
Pius V, Pope, 12
Pius VI, Pope, 2, 4–11, 15, 20, 25, 53, 122
Pius VII, Pope, 11–23, 25, 29, 34, 53, 122
Pius VIII, Pope, 25–28
Pius IX, Pope, xi, xiii, 8, 31–32, 34–37, 39–45, 47–55, 62, 69, 72, 84, 92, 122, 135, 150

Pius X, Pope, xiii, 91–93, 95–98, 101–102, 104–106, 108, 110, 113–114, 120–122, 124–126, 135–136, 143, 150
Pius XI, Pope, xiii, 104, 150–153, 156, 158
Pius XII, Pope, xi, 155–158
Pompilj, Basilio, 98, 102, 109–110, 112–117, 129, 138, 140–147
Portanova, Gianuario, 81
Prædecessores nostri, 106, 135
Prisco, Giuseppe, 88, 103, 133
Prittwitz, Friedrich von, 106
Puzyna de Kozielsko, Jan, 83–86

Q

Quadragesimo Anno, xiii, 158

R

Radet, Etienne, 14–16
Ragonesi, Francesco, 129
Rampolla del Tindaro, Mariano, xiii, 71–75, 79–82, 84–90, 93, 99, 101–102, 113–114
Randi, Lorenzo Ilarione, 46, 51, 53–54, 60–61, 66, 68
Ranuzzi de' Bianchi, Vittorio Amadeo, 129
Ranuzzi, Vincenzo, 9
Ratti, Achille (Pius XI), 133, 137–138, 140–150, 152
Reagan, Ronald Wilson, 155
Regnier, René François, 51, 66
Rerum Novarum, xi, xiii, 158
Riario Sforza, Tommaso, 33
Riccio, Ludovico, 37
Richard, François Marie Benjamin, 91
Richelmy, Agostino, 81–82, 86, 110, 112–113, 115–119, 133
Riggi, Francesco, 76, 80–81
Rinaldini, Aristide, 115
Rochefoucauld, Domenic de la, 9
Rohan, Louis de, 9
Roosevelt, Franklin Delano, 155
Rossi, Pellegrino, 35
Roverie de Cabrieres, François Marie Anatole de, 104, 112
Ruffo, Fabrizio, 6, 22, 25

Ryan, John A., xii

S

Sacchetti, Giulio, 83
Sacconi, Carlo, 45, 47–48, 60–61, 68
Samsonov, Aleksandr, 106
Sanz de Samper, Riccardo, 129, 143
Sardi, Vincenzo, 76
Sarto Giuseppe Melchiore (Pius X), 77, 79–82, 86–91
Sarto, Anna, 97
Sarto, Maria, 97
Sarto, Rosa, 95
Satolli, Francesco di Paola, 82, 86, 89
Sbarretti, Donato, 129, 147
Sbarretti, Enea, 46, 61, 68
Scapinelli di Leguigno, Raffaele, 133, 138, 140
Schulte, Karl Josef, 132, 136, 138
Schwarzenberg, Friedrich von, 54–55, 67–68
Segna, Francesco, 81–82
Sentmanat y Cartella, Antonio de, 9
Serafini, Domenico, 101–102, 109–110, 112–119
Serafini, Luigi, 58, 60
Sercognani, Giuseppe, 30
Settembrini, Luigi, 27
Severoli, Antonio Gabriele, 22
Sevin, Hector Irene, 104
Silj, Augusto, 126
Simeoni, Giovanni, 47–48, 51–54, 59–61, 67
Simor, Johann, 50, 66
Sincero, Luigi, 134, 139
Singulari nos, 31
Skrbensky-Hriste, Leo de, 103, 105, 107, 117, 133
Soldevila y Romero, Juan, 133
Spina, Giuseppe, 7
Stuart, Henry Mary Benedict Clement, 9

T

Tacci, Giovanni, 133, 151
Taylor, Myron Charles, 155
Tecchi, Scipione, 108, 118
Thugut, Johann Amadeus Franz de

Index

Paula, 8, 11
Torlonia, Giovanni, 8
Truman, Harry S, 155

U

Umberto I, king of Italy, 43
Urban VIII, Pope, 83

V

Vacante Apostolic Sedis, 104
Valfré di Bonzo, Teodoro, 124, 129, 138, 141, 148
van Rossum, Willem, 102, 115–117, 129, 133, 137–138, 140–143
Vannutelli, Serafino, 76, 78–82, 86, 99–101, 104, 108, 119
Vannutelli, Vincenzo, 79, 81, 86, 102, 104, 108, 128, 138–140, 150
Vaszary, Klaudius, 77, 103
Vico, Antonio, 106, 129, 138
Victor Emmanuel II, king of Italy, 39, 43
Vidal y Barraquer, Francisco d'Asis, 133, 136

W

Wilhelm II, Kaiser, 82, 85
Wilson, William A., 155
Wilson, Woodrow, 121, 155
Würmser, Dagobert-Sigismond, Graf von, 2

Z

Zampini, Agostino, 126–127, 131
Zucchi, Carlo, 31
Zurlo, Giuseppe Capece, 9

ABOUT THE AUTHOR

FRANCIS A. BURKLE-YOUNG, the son of the late Ellen Louise Burkle Young, received his Ph. D. in Renaissance and Reformation history from the University of Maryland under the late Professor Hermann Everard Schuessler and Professor Clifford M. Foust. Among other places, he has taught at the University of Maryland, College Park, the George Washington University, the University of Akron, and Gettysburg College.

He is the author of *Passing the Keys: Cardinals, Conclaves, and the Election of the Next Pope*; *The Life of Cardinal Innocenzo del Monte: A Scandal in Scarlet*; *The Research Guide for the Digital Age*; and *The Art of the Footnote*. In addition, he edited three CD-ROM editions for the E-Codex Division of Insight Engineering: *Herman Melville: The Complete Works on CD-ROM*, *James Joyce: The Complete Works on CD-ROM*, and *The Works of Arthur Conan Doyle*.

Burkle-Young is the senior holder of a private research facility at the Library of Congress in Washington. Today, he is a technical documentation specialist with Delphi Technology, Inc., Chantilly, Virginia (Peyton Randolph Brown, President).